POWER AND PRIVILEGE IN THE LEARNING SCIENCES

Although power and privilege are embedded in all learning environments, the learning sciences is dominated by individual cognitive theories of learning that cannot expose the workings of power. *Power and Privilege in the Learning Sciences: Critical and Sociocultural Theories of Learning* addresses the ways in which research on human learning can acknowledge the influence of differential access to power on the organization of learning in particular settings. Written by established and emerging scholars in the learning sciences and related fields, the chapters in this volume introduce connections to critical and poststructural race theories, critical disability studies, queer theory, settler-colonial theory, and critical pedagogy as tools for analyzing dimensions of learning environments and normativity. A vital resource for students and researchers in the fields of learning sciences, curriculum studies, educational psychology, and beyond, this book introduces key literature, adapts theory for application in education, and highlights areas of research and teaching that can benefit from critical theoretical methods.

Indigo Esmonde is Associate Professor in the Department of Curriculum, Teaching, and Learning in the Ontario Institute for Studies in Education at the University of Toronto, Canada.

Angela N. Booker is Assistant Professor of Communication and faculty with the Laboratory of Comparative Human Cognition (LCHC) at University of California, San Diego, USA.

POWER AND PRIVILEGE IN THE LEARNING SCIENCES

Critical and Sociocultural Theories of Learning

Edited by Indigo Esmonde and Angela N. Booker

NEW YORK AND LONDON

First published 2017
by Routledge
711 Third Avenue, New York, NY 10017

and by Routledge
2 Park Square, Milton Park, Abingdon, Oxon, OX14 4RN

Routledge is an imprint of the Taylor & Francis Group, an informa business

© 2017 Taylor & Francis

The right of Indigo Esmonde and Angela N. Booker to be identified as the authors of the editorial material, and of the authors for their individual chapters, has been asserted in accordance with sections 77 and 78 of the Copyright, Designs and Patents Act 1988.

All rights reserved. No part of this book may be reprinted or reproduced or utilised in any form or by any electronic, mechanical, or other means, now known or hereafter invented, including photocopying and recording, or in any information storage or retrieval system, without permission in writing from the publishers.

Trademark notice: Product or corporate names may be trademarks or registered trademarks, and are used only for identification and explanation without intent to infringe.

Library of Congress Cataloging in Publication Data
Names: Esmonde, Indigo, editor.
Title: Power and privilege in the learning sciences : critical and sociocultural theories of learning / edited by Indigo Esmonde and Angela Booker.
Description: New York : Routledge, 2017. | Includes bibliographical references.
Identifiers: LCCN 2016033787 | ISBN 9781138922624 (hardback) | ISBN 9781138922631 (pbk.) | ISBN 9781315685762 (e-book)
Subjects: LCSH: Critical pedagogy. | Learning. | Educational sociology. | Power (Social sciences)
Classification: LCC LC196 .P677 2017 | DDC 370.11/5—dc23
LC record available at https://lccn.loc.gov/2016033787

ISBN: 978-1-138-92262-4 (hbk)
ISBN: 978-1-138-92263-1 (pbk)
ISBN: 978-1-315-68576-2 (ebk)

Typeset in Bembo
by Apex CoVantage, LLC

CONTENTS

Foreword: Critical Learning Opportunities for the
   Learning Sciences   vii
Acknowledgements   xiii
Contributors   xvi

1   Introduction   1
   Indigo Esmonde and Angela N. Booker

2   Power and Sociocultural Theories of Learning   6
   Indigo Esmonde

3   Interfaces between Critical Race Theory and
   Sociocultural Perspectives   28
   Eileen R. Carlton Parsons

4   Learning Discourses of Race and Mathematics in
   Classroom Interaction: A Poststructural Perspective   50
   Niral Shah and Zeus Leonardo

5   On the Complementarity of Cultural Historical
   Psychology and Contemporary Disability Studies   70
   Peter Smagorinsky, Michael Cole, and Lúcia Willadino Braga

6   Queer Theory in the Learning Sciences   93
   Jacob McWilliams and William R. Penuel

7	Towards an Ethic of Decolonial Trans-Ontologies in Sociocultural Theories of Learning and Development *Megan Bang*	115
8	Critical Pedagogy and Sociocultural Theory *Shirin Vossoughi and Kris D. Gutiérrez*	139
9	Toward Critical Sociocultural Theories of Learning *Indigo Esmonde and Angela N. Booker*	162

Index   *175*

FOREWORD

Critical Learning Opportunities for the Learning Sciences

The learning sciences began with efforts to push beyond the boundaries of traditional cognitive science's focus on individual mental functioning examined largely through experimental and quasi-experimental designs. The avowed focus, articulated in 1992 by Ann Brown, was to study fundamental theories of learning as learning unfolded in real world settings. This early focus included drawing on extant and unfolding theories of learning to design environments—largely in school, but other settings as well—that facilitated robust learning. These efforts led to the evolution of what is now called design-based research (Barab & Squire, 2004). Early work in the learning sciences also included the design of digital tools to support learning. This focus on the mediational affordances of digital tools remains a significant pillar in the breadth of research in the learning sciences.

Learning sciences evolved out of conceptions of the power of inter-disciplinarity —cognitive science, computer science, educational psychology, and linguistics. In many respects, major programs of research in the learning sciences continue to reflect integration across these disciplines. These early foci did not include attention to culture or to issues of differential power within and among communities associated with race, ethnicity, class, gender, sexual orientation, or normative conceptions of ability. The first *Handbook of the Learning Sciences* (Sawyer, 2008) reflects the integration of these disciplines. There is one chapter in the handbook on culture and learning (Nasir, Rosebery, Warren, & Lee, 2006). On the other hand, the handbook chapters clearly reflect the influence of sociocultural theories of learning in terms of learning entailing more than individual mental functioning, the role of artifacts and intra-group processes, and the idea of learning within and across settings. The chapter by Bransford and colleagues (2006) provides a synthesis of how current fundamental propositions in the learning sciences conceptualize learning in these ways. In many respects, this chapter—led by John Bransford—who also led the team that produced the National Research Council volume *How People Learn* (Bransford, Brown, & Cocking, 1999)—demonstrates how the field has expanded beyond the largely cognitive focus of the 1999 *How People Learn* volume.

At the same time, several decades before the formal institution of the learning sciences as a field of study at Northwestern University, there was developing a long line of research, certainly inspired by what we might call the Vygotskian revolution, that evolved into what has come to be called cultural psychology (Cole, 1996, 1998). These studies included the classic studies by Scribner and Cole (1981) of the Vai people in West Africa, Lave (1977) of Liberian tailors, Rogoff (1981) of the social organization of learning in a Mayan community, Greenfield (Greenfield & Childs, 1977) of weavers in Mexico, Serpell's (1980) comparative studies of situated differences in approaches to problem solving by children in Zambia compared to children in England, Saxe's (1981, 1988) studies of number systems in Papua New Guinea and children selling candy on the streets of Brazil, Hutchins' (Seifert & Hutchins, 1992) study of the distribution of cognition in how sailors on a naval boat coordinate, and others of learning unfolding in informal contexts as people were engaged in routine everyday practices where learning unfolded through the social organization of the settings and the artifacts and tools available to wrestle with complex problems of learning. Cole's (1996) conception of tools as physical (e.g. hammers) and ideational (e.g. concepts, strategies) proved a useful concept for understanding learning as distributed across people and tools. Rogoff and Chavajay (1995) provide a useful synthesis of this research. It is important to note that most of this research took place outside of the U.S. and Europe. Much of this research was explicitly pushing the boundaries of accepted Piagetian theories of stages of intellectual development as largely intra-mental functioning. In many respects these efforts to examine learning in cultural settings beyond the U.S. and Europe opened an intellective space for thinking about the centrality of culture in human learning. Without question, these foundational studies in the tradition of Cultural Psychology have become well integrated into how the learning sciences are taught in graduate programs.

This important volume introduces a complementary body of theoretical traditions that have not been widely addressed in the broad family of intellectual pillars that have evolved in the learning sciences so far. The volume raises the question of how our understandings of human learning can and should take into account how differential access to power structures the organization of learning in particular settings. Chapters in this volume introduce connections to critical race theory, critical pedagogy, and critical conceptions of normativity as tools for analyzing dimensions of learning environments and for conceptualizing the challenges learners face as they seek to engage in learning in particular settings. As such, these chapters together push the boundaries of an already inter-disciplinary field, one that has consistently evolved since its beginnings in the early 1990s. The challenge will be how to institutionalize the integration of these critical orientations into the field—within and across graduate programs; explicit attention in conferences, particularly the International Conference of the Learning Sciences; journals in the field, especially *Journal of the Learning Sciences* and *Cognition and Instruction*, as well as disseminating this expanded conception of the Learning Sciences in other journals; in handbooks; as worthy objects of scholarship for promotion and tenure in the academy; and as conceptual and methodological tools in the design and evaluation of learning environments. The design challenges are significant. Research by Megan Bang, Shirin Vossoughi, Kris D. Gutiérrez, and others reflects design principles that require viewing community constituents as partners in design and evaluation. These challenges, however, should be understood as not merely intellective. Rather, they are challenges that stand in tension with long-standing meta-beliefs and ideologies about differences across human communities (Lee, 2009). For example, conceptions of race defining presumed normative hierarchies across human communities can be traced not only to the founding of the U.S., the histories of colonialism, and slavery across European countries (Mills, 1997), but to the history of psychology and attendant fields in cognition and human development (Gould, 1981). The expression of race as deficit difference was historically quite explicit, but today continues to surface in more subtle and indirect ways, often locating deficit differences in positionings with regard to poverty. I suspect wrestling with these meta-narratives will require not only intellectual push back but political organizing as well, in the politics of our research associations, our universities, our funding agencies, and equally important, working in and with communities.

I would like to argue that underlying the challenges raised by this volume—namely understanding how issues of power operate with regard to how, what, and where people learn—is the necessity of articulating a set of core propositions and warranting those propositions as they are multiply supported by empirical and theoretical research from across disciplines (Lee, 2008; Lee, 2010):

1. Diversity within and among human communities is the strength that allows the species to survive challenge over time. The ability to adapt is central to human functioning.
2. Humans learn in different ways. There is no single normative pathway.
3. All human communities over time have constructed knowledge systems that facilitate their abilities to adapt and influence their circumstances.
4. Even in the face of the most severe challenges, humans have agency.
5. Central to human functioning are perceptions, emotions, social relationships and attachments, the need to address ego needs for a sense of safety, efficacy, health—as these are coordinated in human cognitive activity, activity that is situated, social, and dynamic.

6. Humans belong to and participate in multiple cultural communities, communities that experience both stability and change, homogeneity and heterogeneity.
7. Human functioning must be understood in the contexts of time (historical, ontogenetic, microgenetic) and as navigations within and across spaces.

These core propositions are foundational to the critiques raised in this volume.

Whether how critical pedagogies seek to examine and design education as a tool for deconstructing and resisting systemic efforts to disempower communities in the tradition of Freire, or how critical discourse analyses document the ways that language conveys positioning (e.g. the language of meta-narratives around deficit and difference, around hypothesized stable and homogenous middle-class practices as resources of power), or how queer theory resists assumptions of normativity with regard to sex and gender identity and orientations, or how a focus on indigenous knowledge systems expands our understanding of how human communities conceptualize relations between humans and the natural world, or how critical race theory articulates the centrality of race in oppressive systems in the U.S.—all challenge assumptions of normativity, of the necessity of homogeneity, all call for understanding how an array of institutions are structured to disempower because differences across human communities are not viewed as both the norm and a necessity.

While many of the chapters are addressing the affordances of sociocultural theoretical and methodological traditions, it is also important to understand the contributions of fields like Black Psychology (Boykin, 1979; Nobles, 1972; Sellers, Shelton, Cooke, Chavous, Rowley, & Smith, 1998), ecological systems theories (Spencer, 2006), and dynamic systems (Fischer & Bidell, 1998) to what we might think of as an evolving revolution in how across fields we seek to understand human learning and functioning. Across the fields addressed in this important volume—critical race theory, critical pedagogy, critical and poststructuralist discourse theories, critical disability studies, queer theory, indigenous knowledge systems—we are moving forward in understanding how humans learn to navigate and resist disempowering social systems, how humans create communities of resilience in the face of challenge, and the range of ways human communities are organized, including how they shift over time, to adapt to challenge and change. These big ideas have and continue to be explored in the other fields I have referenced.

However, moving from theory to practice, from theory to transforming historically rooted and sustained belief systems and the institutional structures that embody such belief systems are the tasks and the challenges at hand. I would argue that building institutions that embody the powerful ideas of resistance and critical sense-making put forward in this volume is one way we as researchers can think about impact and transformation. Whether the African-centred schools I and colleagues in Chicago have built over the last 48 years (Lee, 1994), or the powerful program for high school students from Migrant Families that Gutiérrez,

Vossoughi, and others built at UCLA (Espinoza, 2009), or the school–community partnerships that Moll and colleagues built with the Funds of Knowledge Program (González, Moll, & Amanti, 2004), or Ladson-Billings (2013) most recent work with communities of hip hop artists, moving beyond the walls of the academy to build institutions with long-term presence in communities is an equally compelling program of resistance, expanding the learning sciences beyond the insular walls of the academy.

Carol D. Lee

References

Barab, S., & Squire, K. (2004). Design-based research: Putting a stake in the ground. *The Journal of the Learning Sciences*, *13*(1), 1–14.

Boykin, A. W. (1979). Black psychology and the research process: Keeping the baby but throwing out the bath water. In A. W. Boykin, A. J. Anderson & J. Yates (Eds.), *Research directions of black psychologists* (pp. 85–103). New York, NY: Russell Sage Foundation.

Bransford, J., Brown, A., & Cocking, R. (1999). *How people learn: Brain, mind, experience and school*. Washington, DC: National Academy Press.

Bransford, J., Vye, N., Stevens, R., Kuhl, P., Schwartz, D., Bell, P., Meltzoff, A., Barron, B., Pea, R. D., Reeves, B., Roschelle, J., & Sabelli, N. (2006). Learning theories and education: Toward a decade of synergy. In P. A. Alexander & P. H. Winne (Eds.), *Handbook of educational psychology* (pp. 209–244). Mahwah, NJ: Lawrence Erlbaum.

Brown, A. (1992). Design experiments: Theoretical and methodological challenges in creating complex interventions in classroom settings. *The Journal of the Learning Sciences*, *2*(2), 141–178.

Cole, M. (1996). *Cultural psychology, a once and future discipline*. Cambridge, MA: The Belknap Press of Harvard University Press.

Cole, M. (1998). Can cultural psychology help us think about diversity? *Mind, Culture, and Activity*, *5*(4), 291–304.

Espinoza, M. (2009). A case study of the production of educational sanctuary in one migrant classroom. *Pedagogies: An International Journal*, *4*(1), 44–62.

Fischer, K. W., & Bidell, T. R. (1998). Dynamic development of psychological structures in action and thought. In W. Damon & R. M. Lerner (Eds.), *Handbook of child psychology: Theoretical models of human development* (5th edn., Vol. 1, pp. 467–562). New York, NY: Wiley & Sons.

González, N., Moll, L., & Amanti, C. (Eds.). (2004). *Funds of knowledge: Theorizing practices in households, communities, and classrooms*. Mahwah, NJ: Lawrence Erlbaum.

Gould, S. J. (1981). *The mismeasure of man*. New York, NY: W.W. Norton.

Greenfield, P., & Childs, C. P. (1977). Weaving, color terms and pattern representation: Cultural influences and cognitive development among the Zinancatecos of Southern Mexico. *Inter-American Journal of Psychology*, *11*, 23–48.

Ladson-Billings, G. (2013). "Stakes is high": Educating new century students. *The Journal of Negro Education*, *82*(2), 105–110.

Lave, J. (1977). Cognitive consequences of traditional apprenticeship training in West Africa. *Anthropology and Education Quarterly*, *8*(3), 177–189.

Lee, C. D. (1994). The complexities of African centered pedagogy. In M. Shujaa (Ed.), *Too much schooling, too little education: A paradox in African-American life* (pp. 295–318). Trenton, NJ: Africa World Press.

Lee, C. D. (2008). The centrality of culture to the scientific study of learning and development: How an ecological framework in educational research facilitates civic responsibility. *Educational Researcher, 37*(5), 267–279.

Lee, C. D. (2009). Historical evolution of risk and equity: Interdisciplinary issues and critiques. *Review of Research in Education, 33*, 63–100.

Lee, C. D. (2010). Soaring above the clouds, delving the ocean's depths: Understanding the ecologies of human learning and the challenge for education science. *Educational Researcher, 39*(9), 643–655.

Mills, C. W. (1997). *The racial contract*. Ithaca, NY: Cornell University Press.

Nasir, N., Rosebery, A. S., Warren, B., & Lee, C. D. (2006). Learning as a cultural process: Achieving equity through diversity. In K. Sawyer (Ed.), *Handbook of the learning sciences* (pp. 489–504). New York, NY: Cambridge University Press.

Nobles, W. (1972). African philosophy: Foundations for black psychology. In R. Jones (Ed.), *Black psychology* (pp. 18–32). New York, NY: Harper & Row.

Rogoff, B. (1981). Adults and peers as agents of socialization: A highland Guatemalan profile. *Ethos, 9*(1), 18–36.

Rogoff, B., & Chavajay, P. (1995). What's become of research on the cultural basis of cognitive development. *American Psychologist, 50*(10), 859–877.

Sawyer, K. (Ed.). (2008). *Cambridge handbook of the learning sciences*. New York, NY: Cambridge University Press.

Saxe, G. B. (1981). Body parts as numerals: A developmental analysis of numeration among the Oksapmin in Papua New Guinea. *Journal of Educational Psychology, 77*(5), 503–513.

Saxe, G. B. (1988). Candy selling and math learning. *Educational Researcher, 17*(6), 14–21.

Scribner, S., & Cole, M. (1981). *The psychology of literacy*. Cambridge, MA: Harvard University Press.

Seifert, C. M., & Hutchins, E. L. (1992). Error as opportunity: Learning in a cooperative task. *Human–Computer Interaction, 7*(4), 409–435.

Sellers, R., Shelton, N., Cooke, D., Chavous, T., Rowley, S. J., & Smith, M. (1998). A multidimensional model of racial identity: Assumptions, findings, and future directions. In R. Jones (Ed.), *African American identity development* (pp. 275–303). Hampton, VA: Cobb & Henry Publishers.

Serpell, R. (1980). Linguistic flexibility in urban Zambian schoolchildren. *Annals of the New York Academy of Sciences, 345*(1), 97–119.

Spencer, M. B. (2006). Phenomenology and ecological systems theory: Development of diverse groups. In W. Damon & R. M. Lerner (Eds.), *Handbook of child psychology* (6th edn., Vol. 1, pp. 829–893). New York, NY: Wiley.

ACKNOWLEDGEMENTS

Indigo Esmonde and Angela N. Booker would like to thank the following people:

Rebecca Novack, from Routledge, who championed this project in its earliest stages and shepherded two novice editors through the proposal process. Truly, this book wouldn't exist without your encouragement and support. We would also like to thank Daniel Schwartz and the Routledge team who took over from submission to publication.

All of our contributing authors, for joining us in this intellectual journey. We have learned so much from our conversations with you and are thrilled to share your work in this book.

Noah Kenneally, for stepping in at the last minute to help with many of the organizational details, and looking over everything with fresh eyes; the book is better because of you.

Reviewers, including Roland Sintos Coloma, Zeus Leonardo, Jacob McWilliams, Shahrzad Mojab, Niral Shah, Heather Sykes, Tanya Titchkosky, and GLITTER at University of Toronto. The Laboratory for Comparative Human Cognition (LCHC) at UC San Diego were generous with feedback on the sociocultural theory material. Special thanks to GLITTER for poring over all of the chapters and helping to conceptualize the synthesis chapter.

Our colleagues from the ICLS symposium that started it all: Joe Curnow, Paula Hooper, Dominique Riviere, and Shirin Vossoughi.

The Faculty Success Program and the folks at the National Center for Faculty Development and Diversity saved our lives and wellbeing many times, and allowed us to put this book together with a minimum of late nights and weekends.

Indigo Esmonde's acknowledgements:

First, I would like to thank Angela for joining me to edit the book. I benefited enormously from our regular conversations about the book, the theories, our lives, reading recommendations, and more. Working with you inspires, comforts, and sustains me. I am deeply grateful to have worked in partnership with you on this book, which is simultaneously an ending and a beginning for us and for the field.

GLITTER (especially years 2014–2016), you are the best research team I could have asked for. Thank you for asking tough questions and building new ideas with me. Noah, bottomless thanks for your good spirits and smarts. We make a great team!

Thank you to colleagues near and far, including my doctoral advisor Geoff Saxe and his team of graduate students, Critical Studies in Curriculum and Pedagogy at OISE, the New Collective, DiME, the LIFE Center, KSTF Research Fellows, and everyone who has helped me centre critical approaches in my work. I did not expect to edit a book, especially not this book, until you all convinced me that I could bring this work to fruition.

Finally, I'd like to thank my people (and animals), the ones who helped me live a life that made this book possible. Francisco Sapp, you have supported me in a million ways, body, mind, and spirit. My sisters, Jackie Esmonde, Jill Esmonde, Sam Reaume, and Katie Esmonde, have provided lifelong support, intellectual conversations, karaoke nights, and holiday singalongs. You inspire me. Mike Esmonde, you are always there to lend a helping hand and your house is surprisingly well-suited to solo writing retreats. Phyllis Mawson, you raised me to be a feminist and to stand up for what I believe in. Scrubber, you are missed, and Avery, thank you for getting me out of my head and onto my feet, daily. I'd also like to thank my choir and vocal teachers for bringing such joy to my daily life, and of course, all my Toronto and Bay Area friends, too many to name, who have been partners on my own critical sociocultural journey for many years.

Angela N. Booker's acknowledgements:

For me, the road to this project began at the Institute for Research on Learning with its Seven Principles of Learning. To my friends and colleagues from that time, where I took my first steps into the realm of situated learning and sociocultural theory, I offer many thanks. I am especially grateful to Shelley Goldman, Jennifer Knudsen, and Peter Henschel for giving me my first chance to contribute through community and design-based research. Thank you also to the many kids, families, professors, colleagues, and students who have helped me engage with power and responsibility.

My family is a group of people more supportive, grounding, and insightful than I can express. Susie Plettner always calls me to my best self and believes in the power of small groups to change the world. Nikhil and Taj have just the right mix of curiosity, opinions, and impatience to keep me moving at a steady clip. And when everyone else is sleeping, Kiki never fails to keep me company.

My parents, Jean and Ron Booker, were the first people to give me a sense of learning as a social, cultural, and justice-oriented activity. My brother, Brian, believes in me unfailingly and has always met my uncertainty with wisdom and good humor.

There is a group of people I had the good fortune to meet or collaborate with on my professional path who have become precious to me and who have contributed in various ways to the development of this project. Shirin Vossoughi and Paula Hooper gave me the joy of discovering what it's like to find my tribe, and helped set this work in motion. They perpetually rekindle my optimism. Shelley Goldman and Ray McDermott model how to say what needs saying and how to listen every single day. And of course, Indigo Esmonde, you are a bright, shining light. Thank you for inviting me on this journey with you. When you joined the LIFE Center as a postdoctoral scholar, my life changed in the best possible way. From the time you organized that first writing group to today, you have shown me the kind of academic life I had always hoped existed. You are so full of life, goodness, and creative energy that I can't help but be inspired. You are my cherished colleague, my dear friend, and you give me the beautiful gift of courage to live life well.

CONTRIBUTORS

Megan Bang
University of Washington

Angela N. Booker
University of California, San Diego

Lúcia Willadino Braga
SARAH Network of Neurorehabilitation Hospitals, Brazil

Michael Cole
University of California, San Diego

Indigo Esmonde
University of Toronto

Kris D. Gutiérrez
University of California, Berkeley

Zeus Leonardo
University of California, Berkeley

Jacob McWilliams
University of Colorado, Boulder

Eileen R. Carlton Parsons
University of North Carolina

William R. Penuel
University of Colorado, Boulder

Niral Shah
Michigan State University

Peter Smagorinsky
University of Georgia

Shirin Vossoughi
Northwestern University

1
INTRODUCTION

Indigo Esmonde and Angela N. Booker

The learning sciences is an interdisciplinary field, dedicated to studying learning and teaching in a wide variety of contexts. Approaches from psychology, cognitive science, neuroscience, education, anthropology, and sociology provide multiple lenses on the field's big questions: What is learning, and how does it occur? What "should" people learn, and how do we know when they have learned it? Which teaching methods, in which contexts, are most likely to bring about "good" learning?

As such, the field is concerned with relations among people, and between people and the practices in which they participate. We study the varied forms of practice and knowledge that shape and support human participation across environments and over time. When we look more closely, we discover that wherever we find social relations, variability of experience and practice, or evaluation of knowledge and learning, we also find dynamics of power. The learning sciences, therefore, must necessarily centre conceptions of equity, diverse experience, and the dynamics of power and privilege expressed in and through learning environments. Yet, the learning sciences possesses limited theoretical underpinnings that make the relationship between power and learning visible, even as the field strives to speak across both a situated, sociocultural tradition and a more individualistic psychological tradition.

Sawyer (2006a) named five "early influences" (p. 5) on the development of the learning sciences: constructivism (as rooted in Piaget's work), cognitive science, educational technology, sociocultural studies, and studies of the nature of knowledge. From this foundation, the learning sciences has developed a strong emphasis on the design of learning spaces (including, but not limited to school classrooms), and the use of technology to support learning.

Issues of power and oppression require more committed attention in the learning sciences. Consider, for example, the two flagship publications representing the "state of the art" of the learning sciences at their time of publication, *How People Learn* (Committee on Developments in the Science of Learning with additional material from the Committee on Learning Research and Educational Practice, National Research Council, 2000) and *The Cambridge Handbook of the Learning Sciences* (Sawyer, 2006b). These two volumes make very few references to issues of power and oppression. An important exception is the *Handbook* chapter *Learning as a Cultural Process: Achieving Equity through Diversity* (Nasir, Rosebery, Warren, & Lee, 2006). But even this chapter was placed in the section entitled Learning Environments, indicating that this material may not be relevant to other sections, including Foundations (of the field), Methodologies, The Nature of Knowledge, or Learning Together.

All contexts are learning contexts, and the authors in this volume take the approach that power is ever-present in learning contexts. Some people might agree with this point, but still maintain that power is not necessarily connected to broader systems of oppression (such as racism, patriarchy, colonialism). For example, in classroom settings teachers wield power over their students, and students may have access to different kinds or levels of power over one another, relating to friendship, popularity, or perceived smartness. These are not obviously related to broad social systems, and yet, if we look beneath the surface, teachers are authorized by the government to teach state-sanctioned curriculum. In the United States, the vast majority of teachers come from the dominant racial group—white people—and from a comfortable economic class (Ball & Tyson, 2011). Again, dissenters might point out that most teachers in the U.S. are women! And what about teachers who are racialized minorities, or from the working class? Do they not wield power? We would reply that this kind of complexity is why we need *theories* of power, to explain how power circulates in contexts, how it aligns with structural oppression, how it challenges oppression, how it is subtle, and explicit, pervasive, and yet often invisible. A final protest might contend that my original statement was too general: Could it really be true that power is present in *all* (learning) contexts? We ask that the reader judge for themselves after reading through the volume (and, yes, we just used "they" as a gender neutral singular pronoun).

The sociocultural tradition offers promise to integrate a critical understanding of power with an analysis of learning. We use the term sociocultural theory to describe the diverse set of theories that are rooted in Vygotsky's work in the early 20th century, including situated learning theory, cultural-historical activity theory, distributed cognition, and others. Vygotsky was committed to developing a Marxist psychology, one that could explain how the material conditions of labour shape everyday learning and cognition. Since that time, others have taken up critical approaches to studying learning. These range from projects that have demonstrated the deep cognition required for seemingly menial or blue-collar work (e.g., Sylvia Scribner's study of dairy work, 1985), to projects that codify the development of cultural and racialized identities (e.g., Lee, 2007; Nasir, 2011), to cultural-historical activity theorists who have demonstrated how an analysis of breakdowns within an activity system (often stemming from power imbalances) can support reorganization and generative learning (e.g., Engeström, 2000, studies of medical care). Each of these studies draws from different theoretical resources and applies different concepts to the study of power.

Sociocultural approaches to the study of learning have begun the difficult work of analyzing how historically constructed systems of power and oppression can be understood in the moment-to-moment unfolding of learning. The field could benefit greatly by integrating traditions of critical theory that have largely developed outside of the learning sciences (Lewis, Enciso, & Moje, 2007). While critical theories have made substantial inroads into educational studies as a whole, these theories (e.g., critical race theory, queer theory) have largely not been concerned with the study of *learning*. Increasing numbers of learning scientists are engaged in this critical work, and the time is ripe to expand the field's analyses of power and oppression. This volume advocates a shift from ad hoc approaches to a more shared and deliberate project to grapple with the ways our work is situated and mobilized with regard to power.

In this book, we bring together a variety of theories that address the circulation and operation of power in society, to use as resources for critical sociocultural theories of learning. To aid in the process of integration, Chapter 2 provides an overview of sociocultural theories—their roots, ways of conceiving power, and the different directions that have emerged over the last fifty years. Chapters 3 through 8 address, respectively: critical race theory, poststructural theories of race, critical disability studies (with some additional material on how Vygotksy and his intellectual descendants have conceptualized disabilities), queer theory, settler colonialism studies and indigenous ways of knowing, and critical pedagogy. Inspired by Nasir and Hand's (2006) integrated review of sociocultural theory with research on race and racism, the authors of these chapters were tasked with the following guiding questions:

1. What was the theory developed to explain? What is the history of this theory?
2. What are the key themes, assumptions, or conceptual frameworks of this theory?
3. What methodologies are predominantly used?
4. How does this theory interface with theories of learning? How does this theory help to grow a more critical sociocultural theory of learning, and how can sociocultural theories of learning contribute to the development of the critical theory?

We close with Chapter 9, in which we review the material throughout the book, and put forward principles and unresolved questions towards critical sociocultural theories of learning.

This volume addresses the need for a broad and integrated approach to critical studies of learning, although we make no claims to a single theory that can answer all of our research questions. The theoretical integration and synthesis required is not easy work. These theories have different histories, assumptions, and goals, and the authors in this volume will discuss where the theories fit together and where they do not, which points of tension seem productive and generative, and which tensions have to be resolved to move forward.

Why now? And why the learning sciences, and not educational psychology, or any other field? We believe the learning sciences is uniquely positioned in several ways. First, the learning sciences is already interdisciplinary, so we are already learning to make explicit the assumptions underlying our research, and to work across difference. Second, the learning sciences wields power in the domain of educational policy and practice: educators, policy-makers, granting organizations, turn to the learning sciences for cutting-edge, innovative design work to support learning in a variety of contexts. We can shift the focus away from learning as an individual cognitive endeavour, and help the broader public see that learning is always social, relational, and cultural.

Why does this volume argue that the field as a whole needs to take on this challenge, rather than isolated efforts of those who are interested in questions of power? In part, the answer lies in each of the chapters; they argue, in different ways, that power is always present in learning contexts, and so no learning design can be successful if power is not taken into account. Second, it becomes increasingly difficult for those isolated individuals to persist, when scholarship that addresses power is pushed to the fringes, rejected from flagship journals, or derided as "activism" and not scholarship (an odd way to insult someone, in a field known for its fierce advocacy about productive learning contexts).

We invite the reader to consider how these varied theoretical frameworks can be a resource for the learning sciences. It is our hope that this volume marks the beginning of renewed and vibrant debate about our theories, priorities, conceptualizations of research, and methodologies. Such conversations can only deepen the field's capacity to work across our differences and develop more powerful and inclusive contexts for learning.

References

Ball, Arnetha F., & Tyson, Cynthia A. (Eds.). (2011). *Studying diversity in teacher education*. Lanham, MD: Rowman & Littlefield Publishers, Inc.

Committee on developments in the science of learning with additional material from the committee on learning research and educational practice, National Research Council. (2000). *How people learn: Brain, mind, experience, and school: Expanded edition*. Washington, DC: National Academies Press. Retrieved from http://www.nap.edu/catalog/9853

Engeström, Y. (2000). Activity theory as a framework for analyzing and redesigning work. *Ergonomics*, *43*(7), 960–974.

Lee, C. D. (2007). *Culture, literacy and learning: Taking bloom in the midst of the whirlwind.* New York, NY: Teachers College Press.

Lewis, C., Enciso, P. E., & Moje, E. B. (Eds.). (2007). *Reframing sociocultural research on literacy: Identity, agency, and power* (1st edn.). Mahwah, NJ: Routledge.

Nasir, N. (2011). *Racialized identities: Race and achievement among African American youth.* Stanford, CA: Stanford University Press.

Nasir, N. S., & Hand, V. (2006). Exploring sociocultural perspectives on race, culture, and learning. *Review of Educational Research*, 76(4), 449–475.

Nasir, N. S., Rosebery, A. S., Warren, B., & Lee, C. D. (2006). Learning as a cultural process: Achieving equity through diversity. In R. K. Sawyer (Ed.), *Handbook of the learning sciences* (pp. 489–504). Cambridge, UK: Cambridge University Press.

Sawyer, R. K. (2006a). Introduction: The new science of learning. In R. K. Sawyer (Ed.), *Handbook of the learning sciences* (pp. 1–16). New York, NY: Cambridge University Press.

Sawyer, R. K. (Ed.). (2006b). *The Cambridge handbook of the learning sciences.* Cambridge, UK: Cambridge University Press.

Scribner, S. (1985). Knowledge at work. *Anthropology & Education Quarterly*, 16(3), 199–206.

2

POWER AND SOCIOCULTURAL THEORIES OF LEARNING

Indigo Esmonde

The purpose of this chapter is to investigate various ways that power has been taken up in the learning sciences. I begin with a brief description of the more dominant, individualist cognitive theories prevalent in the learning sciences, and explain some of the limitations of cognitive theories in regards to studying issues of power. For the remainder of the chapter, I will describe six central themes of sociocultural theory, and show how researchers have investigated the relationship between power and learning via each of these themes. I will also point out the limits of sociocultural perspectives on power up to this point. By the end of the chapter, I hope readers will have a good sense of how sociocultural perspectives conceive of learning, and will be prepared to take on the broad issues that are raised by critical theories.

The dominant perspective in learning sciences research takes what Greeno (2006) calls the "individual cognitive" perspective. Research from this perspective focuses on individual minds, "knowledge structures" inside the mind that govern how knowledge is stored and how pieces of knowledge relate to one another, or processes of learning and knowing, such as reflection, problem-solving, representation and so on (Sawyer, 2006).

One of the major differences between the individual cognitive and the sociocultural perspectives is the treatment of context. Context is not dismissed within individual cognitive approaches; on the contrary, researchers think deeply about teaching processes, and technological or other tools that can help bring about learning. For cognitivists, context matters in that some supports for learning (i.e., teaching methods) function better than others, but once knowledge is established in the mind, context recedes in importance. In contrast, sociocultural perspectives treat context as inseparable from cognition.

Individual cognitive perspectives are not well positioned to tackle power because power is fundamentally relational; it is not "in the head," it circulates among people and the objects in their environments. Cognitive approaches are also limited in the types of explanations they can offer for inequitable learning outcomes (e.g., widespread racialized, gendered and classed differences in academic attainment and achievement). When the study of the mind is the primary focus, and context is a secondary and receding support, socially situated relations of power disappear from view. For these reasons, scholars in the learning sciences who have worked to address power as an analytical category have generally built upon sociocultural perspectives, maintaining attention to context and relations among people.

Key Sociocultural Concepts

Learning theories that fall under the umbrella of "sociocultural theory"[1] have different names and terminology—such as situated learning, activity theory, distributed cognition, cultural psychology—and on the surface, they may not appear to have much in common. For example, situated learning theorizes learning as a shift in identity and participation within a community of practice (Lave & Wenger, 1991; Wenger, 1998), and explains the process by which an apprentice tailor gradually takes on the practices and identity of a master tailor. By contrast, form–function analysis (Saxe & Esmonde, 2005) looks at the way a person uses a cultural form, such as a number word, to serve a cognitive function like setting up a one-to-one correspondence when counting. The goal of analysis is to look at patterns of form–function relations within a collective practice. Both fall under the sociocultural umbrella, yet these two theories study events at different time-scales, and use different language to describe the events (learning vs. development, community of practice vs. collective practices).

Despite these differences, all sociocultural theories share some common elements (Cole, 1996; Daniels, 2008; Nasir & Hand, 2006; Wertsch, 1985). I will discuss the elements that are the most distinctive (i.e., elements that distinguish sociocultural theories from individual cognitive approaches), and those that are useful for analyses of power. Although there is substantial overlap between the following six points, separating them for the purpose of discussion makes the task more manageable.

1. Cultural artifacts (both tools and signs) mediate human activity. This means that artifacts form an inextricable part of human cognition (rather than bearing some kind of causal relationship with cognition).
2. Learning should be studied as it occurs in everyday life, not just in the laboratory.

3. As people cross boundaries between different contexts, their learning both endures and shifts. Therefore, the unit of analysis for the study of learning goes beyond the individual and must include aspects of context.
4. Multiple historical timescales are relevant for the study of learning. Learning both endures and develops across time.
5. Learning should be studied using a genetic (developmental) method that allows insight into the process of learning, not just the outcomes.
6. As they participate in joint activity, people simultaneously exercise agency and are constrained.

I will describe each of the six themes in more detail, and include illustrative examples. Examples have been selected from a number of different sociocultural approaches, so the reader may enjoy the broad variety of voices and approaches within sociocultural theories. The six themes will also be used to explain how power has been addressed in sociocultural research. The agentic-constrained aspect of sociocultural theory is perhaps the most obvious link to the study of power. After all, what are agency and constraint, if not the exercise of power? Yet, the other themes also contribute to an understanding of power. Artifacts (including language systems, discourses, and ideologies) encode systems of power, and lend power to their users. Everyday contexts are replete with negotiations of power at a micro-scale, whereas historical analyses can make power visible at a macro-scale.

Mediation

Cultural artifacts (both tools and signs) mediate human activity. This means that artifacts form an inextricable part of human cognition (rather than bearing some kind of causal relationship with cognition). The concept of mediation is perhaps Vygotsky's most fundamental contribution to theories of learning. Mediation "extend[s] natural abilities through cultural means" (Holland & Lachicotte Jr., 2007, p. 110). Mediation occurs when an artifact[2] is drawn in to a situation to alter the relationship between people and the world around them. Said another way, mediation occurs when "the individual actively modifies the . . . situation as a part of the process of responding to it" (Cole & Scribner, 1978, p. 14).

Vygotsky saw mediation as the key distinction between what he called "elementary" and "higher" psychological functions (Vygotsky, 1978). However, as Wertsch (1997) points out, "almost all human action is mediated action" (p. 25), and so today, learning scientists study primarily higher psychological functions and Vygotsky's distinction is not always germane to our research. Consider vision: while the elementary function of perception is always necessary (the eye taking in light and sending signals to the brain), even at very young ages people begin to see in concepts. Rather than seeing an assortment of colours, textures and light, we see furniture, people, text and other objects for which we have developed words. In other words, vision quickly becomes mediated by language, and is therefore a higher psychological function in school-age children and adults.

The vision example used above demonstrates that mediation through cultural tools and signs does not replace natural, unmediated action. Instead,

> . . . the incorporation of tools into the activity creates a new structural relation in which the cultural (mediated) and natural (unmediated) routes operate synergistically; through active attempts to appropriate their surroundings to their own goals, people incorporate auxiliary means (including, very significantly, other people) into their actions, giving rise to the distinctive, triadic relationship of subject–medium–object.
>
> *(Cole, 1996, p. 119)*

Mediation blurs the sharp boundaries that cognitive theories of learning have placed between individuals and their environments. Recall that for individual cognitive perspectives, context affects cognition, but is not intrinsic to it. From a sociocultural perspective, when artifacts mediate human activity, they do some of the work of seeing, remembering and problem-solving. We use mediational means to think for us. Whereas cognitive theories see the individual as separate from the environment, sociocultural theories link the individual and mediational means in a dialectical relationship. The relationship is dialectical in the sense that while people act with and on mediational means, mediational means also act on people; the person, mediational means, and the situation are all transformed through mediated action.

Power and Mediation

Mediation provides a first point of contact with sociocultural theory's conceptions of power. Vygotsky's intent was to create a Marxist psychology, "to contribute to the historical project of forging a socialist society" (Packer, 2008, p. 18). Vygotsky's theory of mediation echoes Marx's historical materialism: "According to Marx, historical changes in society and material life produce changes in 'human nature' (consciousness and behaviour)" (Cole & Scribner, 1978, p. 7). Mediation, via tools and signs, is the process by which historical change is translated into changes in human psychology.

Mediation is not neutral. In fact, "mediational means are differentially imbued with power and authority" (Wertsch, 1997, p. 66). That is, different artifacts wield power in different ways. Consider the way "authoritative" or "formal" language connotes power in a courtroom, whereas street slang does not. (As will be discussed in more detail below, context matters: there are situations in which slang is more powerful than formal talk.)

In addition, the construction and dissemination of artifacts can be an expression of power; for one example, consider the development of curriculum standards and expectations. These artifacts determine which knowledge is validated by state educational systems, and wield considerable power over teachers and students. Further, "because material resources are always limited, discourse communities produce and struggle over cultural tools, resources, and identities (both within and across communities) that provide them access to . . . material goods" (Moje & Lewis, 2007, p. 17). In other words, influence over the dissemination of particular artifacts can be linked to other forms of power (e.g., material goods or wealth).

Learning in Everyday Life

Learning should be studied as it occurs in everyday life, not just in the laboratory. I will focus on two related arguments for the importance of studying learning in everyday contexts. The first leads directly from the foregoing discussion of higher psychological functions and mediation, and the second follows from situated learning theory.

Vygotsky (1978, 2012) demonstrated that higher psychological functions have their roots in social life. For example, a young child learns the meaning of a pointing gesture because of the way caregivers respond to the child's attempts to grasp something out of reach. The pointing gesture starts as a social act, and then becomes appropriated by the child over time. Everyday life, therefore, provides a necessary social backdrop in which to understand development.

In addition, since artifacts have both material and ideal histories, they gain what Cole (1996) calls a "residue of the activity of prior generations" (p. 110). They carry history into the present. Consider a shoe. A shoe has a material history (its shape and fit are related to past examples of shoes) and an ideal history (different kinds of shoes symbolize different activities or kinds of people). Artifacts' histories never fully determine how people use them, but these histories are always at play. (This will be discussed further in the section on agency and constraints.) The only way to see the residue of its history is by examining the use of the artifact in context.

Sociocultural theorists do not dispense entirely with laboratory studies; they merely note, as have qualitative methodologists (e.g., Mishler, 1991), that the laboratory, the research interview, the questionnaire, are all contexts. There is no such thing as a decontextualized piece of learning or knowledge.

The second set of arguments for the importance of studying learning in everyday life derives from situated learning theory. According to Lave and Wenger (1991), this theory conceptualized learning as fundamentally linked to identity: learning is "increasing participation in communities of practice" (p. 49) and identities are "long-term, living relations between persons and their place and participation in communities of practice," (p. 53). By this definition, learning can only be studied in the context of communities of practice, where such relations are made visible.

The apprenticeship of Liberian tailors (Lave & Wenger, 1991) is one of the classic examples described in situated learning theory. Apprentice tailors participated in tailoring tasks from the first day of their apprenticeship, beginning with the simplest and least risky tasks. Over time, they took on more complex tasks until they became acknowledged masters. Their participation in the community of tailors changed over time in several ways, including the tasks they performed, and the rank and respect they were accorded. The community allowed some of the apprentice tailors to gradually become masters by providing opportunities to take on the skills required of masters.

In situated learning theory, learning is defined as a shift in participation; this definition implies that only those shifts in participation that are socially recognized count as learning. Knowledge, in a community of practice, is embodied and performed; it is what happens as one learns how to be recognized as a certain kind of person within a community (Daniels, 2008). One's behaviour cannot be recognized without other community members. Apprentice tailors cannot become masters, no matter what their skills or "in-the-head-knowledge," if they are not recognized as such by the other tailors. An apprentice tailor might in fact be highly competent at master-level tasks, but this learning is not relevant if it is not practiced and demonstrated within the community. According to the theory of situated learning, skills and knowledge are understood in relation to the process of becoming a kind of person, in relationship with co-participants.

The process of becoming is foregrounded in sociocultural studies that consider identity development. There are multiple different definitions of identity that circulate within sociocultural theory. For example, Nasir (2011) writes: "By identity I mean a sense of self, constructed from available social categories, taken up by individuals and ascribed by cultural groups and social settings" (p. 17). Holland and Lachicotte Jr. (2007) define identity similarly: "Identities are social and cultural products through which a person identifies the self-in-activity and learns, through the mediation of cultural resources, to manage and organize himself or herself to act in the name of an identity. Identities are personally significant, actively internalized, self-meanings" (p. 114). Others move away from definitions of identity that require an internalized sense of self, to include the ways people are identified by social others in interaction (Esmonde, Brodie, Dookie, & Takeuchi, 2009). Despite these differences, whether identity is defined primarily as an internal sense of self, or ascribed to us by others, identities are part of our social worlds and are never purely individual.

Identity is inextricably linked to context. In Lave and Wenger's original formulation, identity development is linked to a process of becoming a locally meaningful kind of person within a specific community of practice. Since people participate in multiple communities, they develop multiple identities (Wenger, 1998). Therefore, identities in sociocultural theory are "fluid and shift in relation to setting, salience, and local definitions and opportunities" (Nasir, 2011, p. 17).

Power in Everyday Learning

The social recognition that is integral to situated learning represents one way in which power circulates within learning contexts. Power can be seen in the hierarchy of master and apprentice: masters assigned tasks to apprentices, not the other way around. Masters likely had more authority to define who joined the community, and who became recognized as a master.

From its earliest incarnation, situated learning theory has insisted that understanding power is fundamental to understanding learning. Lave and Wenger (1991) acknowledged "unequal relations of power must be included more systematically in our analysis. Hegemony over resources for learning and alienation from full participation are inherent in the shaping of the legitimacy and peripherality of participation in its historical realizations" (p. 42). They argued that there is no inherent power relationship that applies generally in all communities of practice, but that "any given attempt to analyze a form of learning through legitimate peripheral participation must involve analysis of the political and social organization of that form, its historical development, and the effects of both of these on sustained possibilities for learning" (p. 64).

Almost 30 years later, power remains under-theorized in the field. In particular, overt and explicit hierarchies in learning communities are much easier to study than implicit or unspoken hierarchies. For example, it is relatively simple to check whether women are explicitly barred from participating in a community of practice, or allowed to participate but only in marginal roles. However, the field lacks specific tools to make misogyny visible in communities or practices that place a higher value on masculinity than femininity despite vocal pronouncements that people of all genders are ostensibly equal participants (Curnow & Chan, 2016).

Units of Analysis

As people cross boundaries between different contexts, their learning both endures and shifts. Therefore, the unit of analysis[3] for the study of learning goes beyond the individual and must include some aspects of context. Vygotsky (2012) believed that other researchers of his day were wrong to analyze psychological systems by breaking them down into the smallest possible elements. He argued that this approach cannot be successful:

> It may be compared to the chemical analysis of water into hydrogen and oxygen, neither of which possesses the properties of the whole and each of which possesses properties not present in the whole. The student applying this method in looking for the explanation of some property of water—why it extinguishes fire, for example—will find to his surprise that hydrogen burns and oxygen sustains fire.
>
> *(p. 4)*

Rather than breaking human psychological functioning down into elements, Vygotsky argued that the analyst must search for the smallest possible unit that still retains properties of the whole. To analyze properties of water, it would be unhelpful to break water down into atoms of hydrogen and oxygen. Instead, Vygotsky contended that it would be more useful to break water down into molecules, which are the smallest possible units that retain the properties of water.

Vygotsky made this argument in the context of his study of the relationship between thought and language (sometimes translated as thinking and speech). Whereas other researchers might analyze thought and language as two separate elements, Vygotsky knew that he had to find a unit that retained the characteristics of both thinking and speech, and could demonstrate the shifting relationship between the two. For this purpose, he selected "word meaning" as the best unit of analysis. In other words, word meaning still contains elements of both thought (meaning) and language (word), but to break words down further, perhaps into syllables or sounds, would be too far. In later work, Vygotsky argued for other possible units of analysis, depending on the goal of research. He did not argue for a single unit of analysis for all studies of cognitive development—in fact, for other studies, he adopted other units of analysis (for a broader discussion of Vygotsky's various units of analysis, see Daniels, 2008).

Post-Vygotskian researchers agreed on the importance of selecting the proper unit of analysis, and always include some form of context within the unit. Theorists have argued that the unit of analysis for learning must go beyond the individual. This is not an esoteric theoretical point; ample empirical evidence demonstrates that human cognition is distributed across the people, artifacts and social relations in a given context (e.g., Cole, 1996; Guberman, 2004; Nasir, 2005; Saxe, 2012; Scribner, 1985a; Taylor, 2009; Varenne & McDermott, 1998). For example, in one study, high school basketball players were given two sets of mathematics problems: one set of school-like problems, and one set of problems contextualized within the practice of basketball. The players used different strategies for the two sets of problems, thus showing that cognition cannot be separated from context (Nasir, Hand, & Taylor, 2008).

Sociocultural theorists have proposed a number of different units of analysis for the study of learning and development. Situated learning theorists adopted the individual within a community of practice as unit of analysis. Distributed cognition has adopted the "cognitive system," which includes minds, people, social relationships and the artifacts they use, as unit of analysis (Hutchins, 2001; Pea, 1993). Wertsch (1997) proposed mediated action, or person acting with mediational means, as the unit of analysis.

The funds of knowledge approach (González, Moll, & Amanti, 2005) looks to households and communities as the unit of analysis when considering the strengths and resources that young people can bring to bear in education. Funds of knowledge are "the strategic and cultural resources . . . that households contain" (Vélez-Ibáñez & Greenberg, 2005, p. 47), also described as the "specific strategic bodies of essential information that households need to maintain their well-being" (p. 49). This approach pushes against the individualistic view of cognitive approaches, and also contrasts with the participation focus of some sociocultural theories. Rather than thinking only about the practices in which an individual participates, funds of knowledge reminds us that people have access to networks of friends, family and neighbors, and these networks provide access to a broad set of resources.

Cultural–historical activity theory (CHAT) proposed the "activity system" as the appropriate unit of analysis (Engeström, 1999). In CHAT, an activity system is centred around an object (roughly speaking, an overarching goal), and encompasses all the people, artifacts, social norms and relationships that interact towards that object. (For a discussion of the evolution of the "three generations" of CHAT over time, and possible future directions, see Engeström, 2008; Roth & Lee, 2007.) CHAT differs from individualist cognitive psychology in that people's intentions, goals and desires, along with the overarching motive of activity, are contained within the unit of analysis. Indeed, the unit of analysis also considers the historical and contemporary organization of labour and artifacts that support and constrain human activity. As Sannino, Daniels and Gutiérrez (2009) argue:

> This methodological innovation represents a challenge to traditional thinking in human and social sciences, which rely on deep-seated individualism and on views of society as an anonymous structure. Object-oriented and artifact-mediated activity as a unit of analysis retains the importance of subjectivity, while integrating it with cultural means and constraints that inescapably characterize human practices. In doing so, this unit of analysis integrates society into activity.
>
> *(pp. xiv–xv)*

More recently, third generation cultural–historical activity theory (CHAT) has expanded the unit of analysis to include "multiple interacting activity systems focused on a partially shared object" (Engeström, 2008, p. 307). This expanded focus lends itself well to considering issues of power.

Engeström (2000) provides a CHAT analysis of multiple interacting activity systems in relation to hospital medical care. The people involved included doctors (generalists and specialists), patients and families, with the general shared object of healing ill patients. Artifacts include medical charts and tests, medical equipment (e.g., stethoscopes, x-ray machines) and specialized language. The medical field follows formal and informal routines and rules that constrain the flow and interpretation of information, interactions among people and so on. All of these must be taken into account in order to understand how the activity system operates, and how it may change over time.

This medical example illustrates five important principles of CHAT (as described in Engeström, 2001). The *first principle* is that the proper unit of analysis is a set of activity systems, with shared or overlapping objects, considered in relation to one another. For a study of patient care, the hospital activity system should be seen in relation to all the other activity systems involved in the general object of looking after the patient–specialist clinics, the family, the school. The *second principle* is multi-voicedness: activity systems comprise multiple people with different forms of participation. If one followed different actors within the hospital activity system, one would find a multitude of perspectives on the issues at hand. The *third principle* is historicity: "Activity systems take shape and get transformed over lengthy periods of time. Their problems and potentials can only be understood against their own history" (Engeström, 2001, p. 136). The hospital is the product of a long historical process of development, which can be seen in its artifacts, rules and community. The *fourth principle* is that contradictions within an activity system, or between activity systems, precipitate change. For example, contradiction arises when different medical teams (e.g., general care doctors, specialists) do not communicate adequately, thus compromising the object of effective patient care. The *fifth principle* is that activity systems change over time, in what Engeström calls "expansive transformation" (p. 137). CHAT has a history of design-oriented research, in which researchers work collaboratively with the community of an activity system to resolve contradictions and promote expansive learning—extending the boundaries of knowledge and creating something new. This is in contrast with many studies in the learning sciences, which are more concerned with reproductive learning (i.e., school pupils learning a set of discipline-specific knowledge that has been set out in advance).

Power and Units of Analysis

A unit of analysis that is capable of making power visible must extend beyond the individual to include social relations. CHAT is well positioned to consider the circulation of power within a single activity system, or across networks of activity systems. Within an activity system, power can be codified in rules that constrain activity, and hierarchical divisions of labour. Across multiple activity systems, power can be seen when there are conflicting aims with respect to a shared object; the family, for example, has limited power in relation to hospital policy. In particular, the sick or disabled patient is often quite constrained, and the values of the medical system are oriented towards narrow views of health and ability (for more, see Smagorinsky, Cole and Braga, this volume).

Still, there are limits to CHAT's analysis of power. CHAT does not have theoretical or analytic tools to allow for the study of broad systems of power. For example, racism is not an activity system. Racism may be embedded in artifacts, rules, divisions of labour, and yet it transcends a single activity system or even a network of activity systems. While CHAT holds promise as a powerful way to consider how such systems of oppression play out at the level of the activity system, to do so, I believe we must look to other theories for the necessary analytic tools to discern interactions between activity systems and ideological underpinnings of larger social systems.

History

Multiple historical timescales are relevant for the study of learning. Learning both endures and develops across time. Vygotsky's historical materialism avowed that "because socially organized activities change in history, the human nature they produce is not a fixed category that can be described once and for all; it is a changing category" (Scribner, 1985b). He was concerned with relationships between development occurring at multiple timescales. Specifically, he was concerned with four levels or timescales of development: phylogenesis (biological evolution, on a species level), cultural history (the development of tools, signs, and practices), ontogenesis (the development of an individual person over the life-span) and microgenesis (moments of development for an individual) (Scribner, 1985b; Vygotsky, 2012).

All of these levels of development are inter-related, though not always in obvious ways. The development of human biological capacities (phylogenesis) has shaped cultural history (as just one example, in the artifacts we have developed to help us thrive), and sets the stage for both ontogenesis and microgenesis (e.g., via our capacity for tool and sign use). In return, phylogenesis is shaped directly by cultural history (changes we have made in our ecological niche affect the evolution of our biological capacities), and indirectly by ontogenesis and microgenesis (individual people's development affects which genes are passed along to the next generation).

Within the learning sciences, phylogeny is not often taken up explicitly. However, the other three levels of analysis continue to be of central concern to sociocultural approaches. Studies of micro- and ontogenesis are most prominent, but cultural history is often at least implicit in sociocultural analyses. For example, artifacts are conceptualized as both carriers of cultural history and influential in shaping cultural history (Cole, 1996). The changing nature of communities or cultural activities (i.e., cultural history) is seen as tightly connected to individual development (ontogenesis). For example, Rogoff (2003) studies how "people develop as they participate in and contribute to cultural activities that themselves develop with the involvement of people in successive generations" (p. 52). Note that from this perspective, history is studied at the level of the cultural activity. There is some consensus among sociocultural theorists that history is most useful and manageable when considered at the level of the practice, community or activity system.

> Historical analyses must be focused on units of manageable size. If the unit is the individual or the individually constructed situation, history is reduced to ontogeny or biography. If the unit is the culture or the society, history becomes very general or endlessly complex. If a collective activity system is taken as the unit, history may become manageable, and yet it steps beyond the confines of individual biography.
>
> (Engeström, 1999, p. 26)

While limiting history to the level of activity system or collective practice makes the researcher's task more delimited and therefore tractable, it may prevent historical analyses of broader systems of oppression, as referenced in the critical theories addressed in the remaining chapters of the book. Limiting history to the activity system also frames historical analyses as the history of human objects (motives), and the practices that humans have developed to reach those objects. As Bang (this volume) explains, this limited frame of history automatically excludes human relations with other living beings and the natural world. Bang describes some of the negative outcomes of this human-centred history in the chapter on colonial and settler colonial studies, and indigenous ways of knowing.

Power and History

We have already discussed the ways in which artifacts carry history with them, and argued that the creation and dissemination of artifacts is linked to social relations of power. Enciso (2007) warns of the dangers of simple, linear and conflict-free versions of history: "too often in sociocultural research and practice, the language and imagery associated with meanings of history create the illusion of a unified, equitable, and accessible past" (p. 50). Enciso goes into more detail in a discussion of school curriculum as historical artifact:

> . . .without exception, the cultural artifacts, concepts, and forms of mediation circulating and brought into action for making meaning in U.S. schooling are associated with contemporary and historical forms of racism, sexism, heterosexism, and ableism. . . . troubling the meaning of history in sociocultural scholarship is vital to a more robust theory and practice of educational research.
>
> (p. 51)

To paraphrase, sociocultural scholars must consider the ways in which broad systems of power and oppression are embedded in the histories of mediational means. The same can be said for other aspects of activity systems: power can be analyzed in the histories of the rules, divisions of labour and communities, as well as in historical relations between activity systems.

Genetic Method

Learning should be studied using a genetic (developmental) method that allows insight into the process of learning, not just the outcomes. Sociocultural theories follow Vygotsky's (1978) admonition that development is a process, and therefore our research methodologies must attend to development in process, rather than simply endpoints or stages of development. In his study of the development of word meaning, Vygotsky (2012) developed an experimental technique that he called double stimulation. I will explain this method with an example from Vygotsky's study of the relationship between thought and language. Recall that Vygotsky had selected "word meaning" as the appropriate unit of analysis. He needed a research methodology that would allow him to see word meaning during the process of development. If he had tried to study word meaning using conventional or familiar words, he could not guarantee that he would see new development; at least some of his study participants would begin the study already knowing the words he chose. Instead, he used the double stimulation method to investigate how children developed a meaning for a set of nonsense words that he invented for the experiment.

The method is called "double stimulation" because he provided two sets of stimuli for participants to use.[4] The primary stimulus was a set of blocks that varied by colour, shape, height and size. He labelled each one with a nonsense word, the secondary stimulus. The nonsense words captured a new concept for which there was no existing Russian word. For example, "lag" described objects that were both tall and large. Vygotksy's idea was to observe how the children used the secondary stimulus (the new words) to make meaning of the primary stimulus (the different kinds of blocks). With this experiment, Vygotsky investigated how children at different ages developed new concepts. While he could not study ontogenesis directly by this method, he used his data to make claims about how children's meaning-making processes developed as they aged.

The Change Lab has adopted a modified version of the double-stimulation method for research and design projects coming out of the Center for Activity Theory and Developmental Work Research (Engeström, 2007). The Change Lab works with activity systems (such as health care systems, or schools) to help them identify what is not working, and to promote expansive learning in which the system reorganizes itself to function better. The primary artifacts are videos, interviews and other tools to document the functioning of the activity systems. The secondary artifact is activity theory itself, which is used to help the participants organize their thinking. The researchers work with participants to help them analyze contradictions within their activity system and propose changes.

Another methodological approach devised to consider development-in-progress is Saxe's (1991) form–function analysis. Saxe investigates the relationships between cultural forms and the cognitive functions they serve, at three distinct levels: micro-, onto- and sociogenesis. Cultural forms are tools and signs, artifacts that have historical meaning. Examples include currency (bills and coins), number words and number symbols. These forms do not inherently serve any particular function, but "in microgenetic activity, individuals turn forms . . . into numerical means in relation to their emerging goals" (Saxe & Esmonde, 2005, p. 210). For example, if a person wanted to find out the quantity of coins in front of them, they might use counting words and gestures (cultural forms) to create a numerical representation (function) of the value of the coins. Ontogenesis is the pattern of form–function relations as they shift over the lifespan. Sociogenesis is a pattern of changes in form–function relations at the community level.

It is important to note that form–function analysis always takes into account the overarching collective practice, because form–function relations do not remain static when considered across different collective practices. For example, Brazilian children who sold candy for a living used very different strategies when computing problems related to candy-selling, than when computing school-like mathematics problems (Saxe, 1991). To the researcher, the problems seemed to be mathematically identical, but the children's performance demonstrates how different these problems actually were. Same-ness is determined by the people operating within a collective practice, not by some outside objective measure.

Patterns of form–function relations at the micro-, onto- and sociogenetic levels are related, but the relationship is not static or unidirectional. After all, a person's history (ontogenesis) is made up of small moments (microgenesis), within the context of a broader community (sociogenesis). However, if a person solves a mathematical task in a particular way once, they may not do so again. Nor will the community necessarily adapt to a single person's solution method—and vice versa, a person does not necessarily do things in the accepted community way.

Power and Sociocultural Research Methodologies

The Change Lab's expansion of the double-stimulation method provides an interesting take on issues of power in research. As previously discussed, CHAT has some capacity for exposing issues of power, perhaps especially when analysis focuses on contradictions within and across activity systems. The Change Lab method is similar to participatory action research (PAR) (Cammarota & Fine, 2008; Tuck, Allen, Bacha, Morales, Quinter, Thompson, & Tuck, 2008); PAR is a methodology in which researchers work collaboratively and transparently with community members, to analyze and take action on issues of justice that are important to the community. In both PAR and Change Lab work, community members are co-researchers and expertise travels both ways: researchers share theoretical tools with the community and the community provides their deep knowledge of their shared activity system. Researchers and community members jointly study how to apply the theory to resolve problems identified by community members.

Form–function analysis can also be used to study relations of power. The framework has been adapted to consider identity development in relation to ethnic identity and broader systems of race (Nasir & Saxe, 2003). Nasir and Saxe argue for the value of a "cultural practice perspective on emerging tensions" between various kinds of identities; in the case of racialized minorities, tensions between "ethnic and school identities" (2003, p. 15). Their analysis showed ethnic and academic identities constructed at the micro-, onto- and sociogenetic levels, and pointed to tensions that developed for African American students between their ethnic identities and their school-based identities. This type of analysis is promising in that it centres a recurring problem in educational research aimed at equity: the difficulty of connecting the broad historical development of systems of oppression, and the moment-to-moment interactions in which people live. Further research in this area is needed.

Agency and Constraint

As they participate in joint activity, people simultaneously exercise agency and are constrained. Rather than taking an extreme view that individuals are completely free to act as they wish, or the opposite view that individuals exercise no agency, "a focus on mediated action and the cultural tools employed in it makes it possible to 'live in the middle' and to address the sociocultural situatedness of action, power, and authority" (Wertsch, 1997, p. 65). This middle view has already been apparent in our discussion of mediation, and of participation in communities of practice.

Mediation, by definition, demonstrates people's capacity to exercise agency by altering their situations.

> Vygotsky argued that, without semiotic mediation, people would be buffeted about by the stimuli they happened to encounter as they went about in the world. Instead, semiotic mediation provides the means for humans to control, organize, and resignify their own behavior.
>
> *(Holland & Lachicotte Jr., 2007, p. 115)*

Mediational means also constrain possibilities. Wertsch (1997) illustrated this point with an extended discussion of pole vaulting as mediated action. Undoubtedly, the pole allows the person to clear heights that would be impossible without it; however, the makeup of the pole (bamboo, aluminum, fibreglass) constrains how high the vaulter can go. And, to state the obvious, a vaulting pole is useful in only a limited set of circumstances.

Power in Agency and Constraint

Power is made visible in the ways social relations between people enable some forms of agency, and constrain others. The tension between agency and constraint comes into focus in analyses of the historical development of communities of practice. One of the tasks of a community of practice is to reproduce itself over time; as a result, communities of practice may resist change. Paradoxically, the very nature of the process of legitimate peripheral participation encourages change, or newcomers would never become old-timers (Lave & Wenger, 1991). Reproduction actually requires change. Even in practices that seem relatively stable over time, "the relatively stable characteristics of these environments are in constant tension with the emergent goals and practices participants construct, which stretch and change over time and with other constraints" (Gutiérrez & Rogoff, 2003, p. 21).

Further constraint comes from the way participation is regulated within a community. As discussed earlier, learning and identity formation are embedded in social relations with others; shifts in participation (i.e., learning) require legitimation from social others within the community. Moreover, communities commonly place constraints on who is allowed to participate, and in which ways. These constraints often reflect social systems and categories like race, gender, and language use:

> These categories [ethnicity, race, and language use] have long-standing influences on the cultural practices in which people have the opportunity to participate, often yielding shared circumstances, practices, and beliefs that play important and varied roles for group members. People do not just choose to move in and out of different practices, taking on new and equal participation in cultural communities.
>
> *(Gutiérrez & Rogoff, 2003, p. 21)*

Patterns of participation and exclusion can echo broader societal norms (i.e., uphold kyriarchical[5] views), but they can also challenge them. This unpredictability reflects the loose connection between sociogenesis, ontogenesis and microgenesis: the community norms, and one's own past, always inform moment-to-moment participation, but they do not determine it.

One inspiration for the theoretical integration that is the goal of this book comes from the practice-based theory of identity developed by Holland, Lachicotte, Skinner and Cain (2001). This sociocultural theory of the relation between power, identity and learning draws from Vygotsky, Bourdieu and Foucault. Vygotsky contributes the importance of mediation; Holland et al. emphasize that mediation involves the interconnected actions of "assigning of meaning to an object or a behaviour" (2001, p. 36) and then placing that object or behaviour in the environment so as to influence physical or mental events. The authors note that mediation takes place in, and is made meaningful in, a "locus of social activity, a place in the social world" (2001, p. 36); this point allowed them to draw similarities between activity theory and Bourdieu's (1977) concept of 'practice.' Both activity and practice represent "a third way to grasp social action, one that mediates between objectivism (environment) and subjectivism (person or group)" (Holland et al., 2001, p. 39).

Holland et al. (2001) also point out common ground between mediational means and Foucault's discourse theory, with its "cultural forms," which "affect and shape subjectivity" (p. 26). They argue:

> Discourse (or discursive) theory emphasizes many of the aspects of cultural resources that we discuss here, especially their existence as public forms and social tools. Discourses and their categories are like the artifacts that Cole describes. They originate outside their performers and are imposed upon people, through recurrent institutional treatments and within interaction, to the point that they become self-administered. Categories carry an association to those who use them and are subject to them—an association with power—as artifacts do an association with tasks and those who perform them.
>
> (p. 62)

The parallel between artifacts and discourses is used to highlight the way broad social systems and institutions get enacted in daily social interactions, through repeated encounters with material and symbolic artifacts. People always exercise agency, within the confines of participation in activity/practice, with the historically meaningful artifacts/discourses made available for use.

Figured worlds are "socially and culturally constructed realm[s] of interpretation in which particular characters and actors are recognized, significance is assigned to certain acts, and particular outcomes are valued over others" (Holland et al., 2001, p. 52). They are akin to Bourdieu's "field," which "closely parallels [the] notion of figured world" (Holland et al., 2001, p. 58). It can be useful to conceive figured worlds as setting a context in which people know what to expect and can improvise appropriate roles. For example, the figured world of "school" includes teacher and student characters, and anyone familiar with school will have a general sense of how people act there. Any given action takes meaning within its figured world; looking up a fact on the internet might be acceptable when sitting at home talking with friends, but not when taking a test in the classroom. In an abstract sense these may seem like "the same act," but in a socially meaningful sense, they are completely different.

Figured worlds, as an analytical framework, makes visible the collective construction and enactment of generalized storylines, and the actions that people take to appropriate or contest these storylines. For example, Holland and Eisenhart's (1990) ethnography of women's experiences in college demonstrates the possibilities and constraints of the college figured world. Holland and Eisenhart found that the college peer culture was organized primarily around romance, and both men and women built identities around attractiveness. In the college world of romance, it was simply not possible to opt out. A woman could completely reject the idea that she was only valuable if she could date an attractive man. However, she could not control how her actions were interpreted by others. Like it or not, she could not step off the "sexual auction block" (Holland et al., 2001, p. 144).

Critical and Sociocultural Theories

Throughout this review of treatments of power in sociocultural theories, I have focused mainly on the commonalities across the distinct theories. However, the examples have also illustrated some key differences between sociocultural theories. As we move into the rest of the book, and consider broader social theories rooted in various academic disciplines, it will be important to carefully compare each theory's underlying assumptions.

Sociocultural theories differ in what they sought to explain. Vygotsky (1978, 2012) studied higher psychological functions, and the relationship between learning and development. Other scholars have focused on participation (Lave & Wenger, 1991), cognitive development (Saxe, 1991), object-oriented activity (Engeström, 2001), identity (Holland et al., 2001; Nasir & Saxe, 2003) or mediated action (Wertsch, 1997). These concepts have a family resemblance, but differ in important ways.

Units of analysis also varied, from individuals acting with mediational means, to networks of activity systems with a shared object. On a related note, the time scales of analyses varied: from a moment of problem-solving, to years spent developing skills in a trade, to generations of historical change. Theories also differ in the degree to which they articulate the separability of person from environment, and the degree to which they focus on processes rather than objects (Sawyer, 2002).

And of course, scholars differ in their assessments of Vygotsky's original work, of the legitimacy of various sub-branches of sociocultural theory, and about whether or not these theories are commensurable. This chapter has represented my own view of the major principles of sociocultural theories, a view that has been shaped by my research interests and my engagement in the learning sciences community.

As others have pointed out before me, sociocultural theory is well positioned to consider broad issues of power and their relation to learning (e.g., John-Steiner, 1999). Yet, one of the enduring challenges of sociocultural analyses of learning has been to identify the relationship of broad systems of oppression (macro-level), with moment-to-moment interaction (micro-level) (Nasir & Hand, 2006). Sociocultural theories excel at the micro- and meso-levels of analysis, and offer fewer explanations of the macro-level (Lemke, 2001).

Many sociocultural researchers who include macro-level analyses in their research have turned to critical theories for inspiration and for conceptual tools (e.g., Lewis, Enciso, & Moje, 2007). The field is richer for it, but there are difficulties in juxtaposing theories that were developed in different disciplines and to address different kinds of research questions. Critical theory can be a more powerful tool for sociocultural researchers if we understand the history of these theories, their underlying assumptions and their compatibility or incompatibility with sociocultural theory. Our goal in the next six chapters is to lay out six critical theories and provide sociocultural researchers with sufficient detail to decide, for themselves, whether and how critical theory can expand their work. In the concluding chapter, Angela N. Booker and I will discuss the promise, and the challenge, of integrating critical theories with sociocultural theories of learning.

Notes

1. Within the fields of the learning sciences, cultural psychology, and educational psychology, terminology is contested and the term "sociocultural theory" takes on different meanings. Here, I use it to refer to all theories of learning that are rooted in Vygotsky's work. These include cultural-historical activity theory, situated/situative learning, distributed cognition, practice-based theories of identity, and more. Daniels (2008) refers to these all as social theories of mind. There is no one term that is universally used to refer to this body of theories.
2. Vygotsky distinguished between material tools, which operate on the material world, and signs, which operate on the self. Currently, many sociocultural theorists use a single term (artifacts [Cole, 1996], mediational means [Wertsch, 1997], or cultural forms [Saxe, 2012]) and argue that all artifacts contain both material and symbolic aspects.
3. Some theorists use the term "unit of analysis," and some use "unit for analysis." In both cases, the intent is to match the unit to the problem being analyzed.
4. The procedure is difficult to understand purely from a description. In 2008, Paula Towsey re-enacted and video-recorded the original double-stimulation experiment described in *Thought and Language*. The video can be viewed at https://vimeo.com/10689139.
5. Kyriarchy is a term invented by Fiorenza (2009) to refer to intersectional oppressions based on race, class, gender, ability, sexuality and other systems of dominance.

References

Bourdieu, P. (1977). *Outline of a theory of practice* (R. Nice, Trans., 1st edn.). Cambridge, UK; New York, NY: Cambridge University Press.

Cammarota, J., & Fine, M. (2008). *Revolutionizing education: Youth participatory action research in motion*. New York, NY: Routledge.

Cole, M. (1996). *Cultural psychology: A once and future discipline*. Cambridge, MA: Belknap Press of Harvard University Press.

Cole, M., & Scribner, S. (1978). Introduction. In M. Cole, V. John-Steiner, S. Scribner & E. Souberman (Eds.), *Mind in society: The development of higher psychological processes* (pp. 1–14). Cambridge, MA: Harvard University Press.

Curnow, J., & Chan, J. R. (2016). Becoming an "expert": Gendered positioning, praise, and participation in an activist community. In C. K. Looi, J. L. Polman, U. Cress & P. Reimann (Eds.), *Transforming learning, empowering learners: The International Conference of the Learning Sciences (ICLS) 2016* (Vol. 1, pp. 146–153). Singapore: International Society of the Learning Sciences.

Daniels, H. (2008). *Vygotsky and research*. New York, NY: Routledge.

Enciso, P. (2007). Reframing history in sociocultural theories: Toward an expansive vision. In C. Lewis, P. E. Enciso & E. B. Moje (Eds.), *Reframing sociocultural research on literacy: Identity, agency, and power* (1st edn., pp. 49–74). Mahwah, NJ: Routledge.

Engeström, Y. (1999). Activity theory and individual and social transformation. In Y. Engeström, R. Miettinen & R.-L. Punamaki (Eds.), *Perspectives on activity theory* (pp. 19–38). Cambridge, UK: Cambridge University Press.

Engeström, Y. (2000). Activity theory as a framework for analyzing and redesigning work. *Ergonomics, 43*(7), 960–974.

Engeström, Y. (2001). Expansive learning at work: Toward an activity theoretical reconceptualization. *Journal of Education and Work, 14*(1), 133–156.

Engeström, Y. (2007). Putting Vygotsky to work: The change laboratory as an application of double stimulation. In H. Daniels, M. Cole & J. V. Wertsch (Eds.), *The Cambridge companion to Vygotsky* (pp. 363–382). Cambridge and New York: Cambridge University Press.

Engeström, Y. (2008). *The future of activity theory: A rough draft*. Paper presented at ISCAR Conference, San Diego.

Esmonde, I., Brodie, K., Dookie, L., & Takeuchi, M. (2009). Social identities and opportunities to learn: Student perspectives on group work in an urban mathematics classroom. *Journal of Urban Mathematics Education, 2*(2), 18–45.

Fiorenza, E. S. (2009). *Democratizing biblical studies: Toward an emancipatory educational space*. Louisville, KY: Westminster John Knox Press.

González, N., Moll, L. C., & Amanti, C. (Eds.). (2005). *Funds of knowledge: Theorizing practices in households and classrooms*. Mahwah, NJ: Lawrence Erlbaum Associates.

Greeno, J. G. (2006). Learning in activity. In K. R. Sawyer (Ed.), *Handbook of the learning sciences* (pp. 79–96). Cambridge, UK: Cambridge University Press.

Guberman, S. R. (2004). A comparative study of children's out-of-school activities and arithmetical achievements. *Journal for Research in Mathematics Education, 35*(2), 117–150.

Gutiérrez, K. D., & Rogoff, B. (2003). Cultural ways of learning: Individual traits or repertoires of practice. *Educational Researcher, 32*(5), 19–25.

Holland, D., & Eisenhart, M. A. (1990). *Educated in romance: Women, achievement, and college culture*. Chicago, IL: University of Chicago Press.

Holland, D., & Lachicotte Jr., W. (2007). Vygotsky, Mead, and the new sociocultural studies of identity. In H. Daniels, M. Cole & J. V. Wertsch (Eds.), *Cambridge companion to Vygotsky* (pp. 101–135). Cambridge, UK: Cambridge University Press.

Holland, D., Lachicotte Jr, W., Skinner, D., & Cain, C. (2001). *Identity and agency in cultural worlds*. Cambridge, MA: Harvard University Press.

Hutchins, E. (2001). Distributed cognition. In N. J. Smelser & P. B. Baltes (Eds.), *International encyclopedia of the social and behavioral sciences* (pp. 2068–2072). Oxford: Pergamon.

John-Steiner, V. (1999). Sociocultural and feminist theory: Mutuality and relevance. In S. Chaiklin, M. Hedegaard & U. J. Jensen (Eds.), *Activity theory and social practice: Cultural-historical approaches* (pp. 66–78). Aarhus, DK; Oakville, CT: Aarhus University Press.

Lave, J., & Wenger, E. (1991). *Situated learning: Legitimate peripheral participation.* Cambridge, UK: Cambridge University Press.

Lemke, J. L. (2001). Across the scales of time: Artifacts, activities, and meanings in ecosocial systems. *Mind, Culture, and Activity, 7*(4), 273–290.

Lewis, C., Enciso, P. E., & Moje, E. B. (Eds.). (2007). *Reframing sociocultural research on literacy: Identity, agency, and power* (1st edn.). Mahwah, NJ: Routledge.

Mishler, E. G. (1991). *Research interviewing: Context and narrative.* Cambridge, MA: Harvard University Press.

Moje, E. B., & Lewis, C. (2007). Examining opportunities to learn literacy: The role of critical sociocultural literacy research. In C. Lewis, P. E. Enciso & E. B. Moje (Eds.), *Reframing sociocultural research on literacy: Identity, agency, and power* (1st edn., pp. 15–48). Mahwah, NJ: Routledge.

Nasir, N. (2005). Individual cognitive structuring and the sociocultural context: Strategy shifts in the game of dominoes. *The Journal of the Learning Sciences, 14*(1), 5–34.

Nasir, N. (2011). *Racialized identities: Race and achievement among African American youth.* Stanford, CA: Stanford University Press.

Nasir, N., & Hand, V. (2006). Exploring sociocultural perspectives on race, culture, and learning. *Review of Educational Research, 76*(4), 449–475.

Nasir, N., Hand, V., & Taylor, E. V. (2008). Culture and mathematics in school: Boundaries between "Cultural" and "Domain" knowledge in the mathematics classroom and beyond. *Review of Research in Education, 32*(1), 187–240. Retrieved from http://doi.org/10.3102/0091732X07308962

Nasir, N., & Saxe, G. B. (2003). Ethnic and academic identities: A cultural practice perspective on emerging tensions and their management in the lives of minority students. *Educational Researcher, 32*(5), 14–18.

Packer, M. J. (2008). Is Vygotsky relevant? Vygotsky's Marxist psychology. *Mind, Culture, and Activity, 15*(1), 8–31.

Pea, R. (1993). Practices of distributed intelligence and designs for education. In G. Salomon (Ed.), *Distributed cognitions: Psychological and educational considerations* (pp. 47–87). Cambridge, UK; New York, NY: Cambridge University Press.

Rogoff, B. (2003). *The cultural nature of human development.* New York, NY: Oxford University Press.

Roth, W.-M., & Lee, Y.-J. (2007). "Vygotsky's neglected legacy": Cultural-Historical activity theory. *Review of Educational Research, 77*(2), 186–232.

Sannino, A., Daniels, H., & Gutiérrez, K. D. (2009). *Learning and expanding with activity theory.* Cambridge, UK: Cambridge University Press.

Sawyer, R. K. (2002). Unresolved tensions in sociocultural theory: Analogies with contemporary sociological debates. *Culture & Psychology, 8*(3), 283–305.

Sawyer, R. K. (2006). Introduction: The new science of learning. In R. K. Sawyer (Ed.), *Handbook of the learning sciences* (pp. 1–16). New York, NY: Cambridge University Press.

Saxe, G. B. (1991). *Culture and cognitive development: Studies in mathematical understanding.* Hillsdale, NJ: Lawrence Erlbaum Associates.

Saxe, G. B. (2012). *Cultural development of mathematical ideas: Papua New Guinea studies.* Cambridge, UK: Cambridge University Press.

Saxe, G. B., & Esmonde, I. (2005). Studying cognition in flux: A historical treatment of Fu in the shifting structure of Oksapmin mathematics. *Mind, Culture, and Activity, 12*(3&4), 171–225.

Scribner, S. (1985a). Knowledge at work. *Anthropology & Education Quarterly, 16*(3), 199–206.

Scribner, S. (1985b). Vygotsky's uses of history. In J. V. Wertsch (Ed.), *Culture, communication, and cognition: Vygotskian perspectives* (pp. 119–143). Cambridge, UK: Cambridge University Press.

Taylor, E. V. (2009). The purchasing practice of low-income students: The relationship to mathematical development. *The Journal of the Learning Sciences, 18*(3), 370–415.

Tuck, E., Allen, J., Bacha, M., Morales, A., Quinter, S., Thompson, J., & Tuck, M. (2008). PAR Praxes for now and future change. In J. Cammarota & M. Fine (Eds.), *Revolutionizing education: Youth participatory action research in motion* (pp. 49–83). New York, NY: Routledge.

Varenne, H., & McDermott, R. (1998). *Successful failure: The school America builds*. Boulder, CO: Westview Press.

Vélez-Ibáñez, C., & Greenberg, J. (2005). Formation and transformation of funds of knowledge. In N. González, L. C. Moll & C. Amanti (Eds.), *Funds of knowledge: Theorizing practices in households and classrooms* (pp. 47–69). Mahwah, NJ: Lawrence Erlbaum Associates.

Vygotsky, L. S. (1978). *Mind in society: The development of higher psychological processes*. Cambridge, MA: Harvard University Press.

Vygotsky, L. S. (2012). *Thought and language* (Revised and expanded edition, E. Hanfmann, G. Vakar & A. Kozulin, Eds.). Cambridge, MA: MIT Press.

Wenger, E. (1998). *Communities of practice: Learning, meaning, and identity*. Cambridge, UK: Cambridge University Press.

Wertsch, J. V. (1985). *Vygotsky and the social formation of mind*. Cambridge, MA: Harvard University Press.

Wertsch, J. V. (1997). *Mind as action*. Oxford, UK: Oxford University Press.

3

INTERFACES BETWEEN CRITICAL RACE THEORY AND SOCIOCULTURAL PERSPECTIVES

Eileen R. Carlton Parsons

Critical race theory (CRT) is a framework that centralizes race, racism, and power in the examination of phenomena. The focus of the phenomena can be as localized as interactions among individuals (Chapman, 2007) or as expansive as education policy (Gillborn, 2013). As stated by Ladson-Billings (2013), who introduced CRT to education in 1995, critical race theory violates the "race, class, and gender triumvirate" that is prevalent in social science theorizing, and instead makes "race the axis of understanding inequity and injustice in the US" (p. 34). CRT considers issues addressed by ethnic studies, multiculturalism, and civil rights, but from a more comprehensive, and some argue, critical vantage point (Ladson-Billings, 2013). That is, it

> places them [issues] in a broader perspective that includes economics, history, context, group- and self-interest, and even feelings and the unconscious. Unlike traditional civil rights, which stresses incrementalism and step-by-step progress, critical race theory questions the very foundations of the liberal order, including equality theory, legal reasoning, Enlightenment rationalism, and neutral principles of constitutional law.
>
> *(Delgado & Stefancic, 2012, p. 3)*

The primary goal of the chapter is to entertain how CRT can speak to sociocultural perspectives on learning and development. For more detailed accounts of CRT, interested readers can consult published works that describe the origin of CRT (Brown & Jackson, 2013; Dalton, 1987; Delgado & Stefancic, 2012), its development over time (Crenshaw, 2011), and its introduction and re-appropriation in education (Dixson & Rousseau, 2005; Ladson-Billings & Tate, 1995). Numerous other publications discuss CRT's themes and major concepts (Bell, 1992a, 1995;

Delgado, 1989; Gotanda, 1991; Harris, 1993) and use them to examine educational phenomena (DeCuir & Dixson, 2004; Gillborn, 2013; Howard & Reynolds, 2013; Milner, 2013; Parker & Lynn, 2002).

As the employment of CRT in educational research has proliferated since its introduction to education, scholars have proposed many different interpretations. This chapter draws largely from the original scholarship in CRT and the education research that continues in that tradition. I begin with a historical perspective on the development of CRT. Oftentimes, CRT is conflated with other frameworks like multiculturalism, diversity, and ethnic studies. Ladson-Billings and Tate (1995) contended that the aforementioned, though premised upon transformative principles, resulted in practices that did not radically change the existent status quo; these "multicultural reforms are routinely 'sucked back into the system'. . ." (p. 62). For example, multicultural education, ethnic studies, and diversity education as practiced customarily include the contributions and participation of diverse groups in events but "the criteria of valuation and perspectives and themes of the American saga remain constant" (Olneck, 1993, p. 245).

In order to comprehend how CRT differs from multicultural reforms, it is important to understand how and why it developed. Sections three and four further explain the dominant themes and assumptions of CRT, and common methodologies employed in CRT work. I close by identifying the interfaces between CRT and sociocultural perspectives on learning.

The Emergence and Evolution of CRT

Different accounts of CRT's origin exist, but all accounts concur that in 1987, CRT splintered off from critical legal studies (CLS), an intellectual movement mostly comprised of legal scholars. CLS confronted societal hierarchies, challenged the traditional norms and standards in legal theory and practice, and argued that law could not be detached from society and all its ills (Crenshaw, 2011). Specifically, proponents of CLS contended that legal theory and practice were rooted in and reflected power relationships in society. Although the founders of CRT agreed with this sociocultural construction of law, they were concerned about the stand of CLS on several other issues.

Recounts of CRT's origins discuss a number of conflicts within CLS, between dominant voices and the voices of people of colour (Crenshaw, 2011; Tate, 1997). I will discuss three areas of dissension. First, I address the distance between abstract theorizing and activist praxis. Second, I discuss debates about rights discourse. Finally, I discuss the silencing of the voices of people of colour within CLS.

First, CLS seemed driven by intellectual endeavours and abstraction. People of colour within CLS considered efforts towards praxis to be inadequate, especially efforts pertaining to race, racism, power, and the legal system (Dalton, 1987). Dalton contrasted the biography of a typical CLS adherent, white and male, to the biography of people of colour in CLS. The privileges of the white male enabled him to extend his childhood fascination with books and the world of ideas into the construction of an adult community (i.e., CLS) that encouraged him to "live in his head" (p. 438). In contrast, for people of colour in CLS "no matter how smart or bookish we were . . . we could not retreat from the sights, sounds, and smells of the communities from which we came" (Dalton, p. 439). The injustices that the typical CLS adherent theorized and debated were the lived experiences of many people of colour.

The second fracture concerned rights discourse—discussion, debate, and practices around rights as defined in the U.S. constitution and other legal doctrines (Crenshaw, 2011; Crenshaw, Gotanda, Peller, & Thomas, 1995; Dalton, 1987). Generally, CLS viewed battles for legal rights, with their emphasis on rational mediation (e.g., objective examination of perceived bias-free facts), as perpetuating the myth that law could be detached from the society that constructed it. On one hand, people of colour in CLS viewed legal rights as limited in establishing substantive social change (Delgado & Stefancic, 2012). On the other hand, legal rights have had transformative value for the racially subordinate, as evidenced by the legal rights that afforded black people access to voting in the U.S. For people of colour in CLS, the potential transformative value of legal rights outweighed the CLS philosophical position of law as a social construction (Crenshaw, 2011). That is, instead of promoting the dissolution of rights on philosophical grounds, people of colour within CLS saw the value and role of rights in alleviating oppression.

The third area of discontent pertained to voice. People of colour in CLS felt silenced in several different ways (Dalton, 1987). CLS, like other academic fields, has a distinctive discourse (i.e., practices and language), one that did not include the practices and perspectives of people of colour. For example, Williams (1987) detailed his concerns with the position of CLS on rights-based theory:

> The present paper is an attempt to detail my discomfort with that part of CLS, which rejects rights-based theory. . . . There are many good reasons for abandoning a system of rights which are premised on inequality and helplessness; yet despite the acknowledged and compelling force of such reasons, most blacks have not turned away from the pursuit of rights even if what CLS scholars say about rights—that they are contradictory, indeterminate, reified, and marginally divisive in social behavior—is so. I think this has happened because the so-called 'governing narrative,' or metalanguage, about the significance of rights is quite different for whites and blacks.
>
> (p. 404)

Additionally, people of colour felt silenced by what has come to be called white fragility, a state in which a minimum amount of race-related stress engenders a myriad of defensive moves by white people (DiAngelo, 2011). Dalton (1987) described a number of defensive moves (e.g., expression of guilt) made by white people in CLS when people of colour spoke up about race. These defensive moves tended to stop conversations about race and silenced people of colour in CLS. Furthermore, people of colour in CLS were excluded from discussions around race, racism, and power in CLS. These discussions were dominated by white CLS members who talked about and spoke for people of colour (Dalton, 1987). These three areas of dissension (praxis, voice, and rights) were among the conflicts that fuelled the early beginnings of CRT.

According to Crenshaw (2011), a workshop held in Wisconsin in 1989 marked the official beginning of CRT. The workshop was titled "New Developments in CRT," even though CRT as a field did not yet exist as more than a possibility. Crenshaw described the workshop as a gathering of veterans who had survived institutional conflict around the colour-blindness that dominated U.S. law schools. Participants "wanted to move beyond the non-critical liberalism that often cabined U.S. civil rights discourses and a non-radical radicalism that was a line of debate within CLS" (Crenshaw, p. 1264). At this gathering of like-minded souls, CRT emerged: "an intellectual identity and political practice that would take the form of a left intervention into race discourse and a race intervention into left discourse" (Crenshaw, Gotanda, Peller, & Thomas, 1995, p. xix). CRT would purposefully foreground race, racism, and power in U.S. life, and work to dismantle white dominance in social institutions (Delgado & Stefancic, 2012).

Since its inception, characterized in the history of CRT as a severing from CLS, CRT has extended beyond legal studies, its discipline of origin, and the U.S., the geographical location in which it originated, and migrated to other countries and to various academic fields. As it has grown in popularity, outgrowths with core principles of CRT as their foundations have emerged to reflect experiences of specific marginalized groups—LatCrit for Latino Americans, AsianCrit for Asian Americans, TribalCrit for Native Americans, and QueerCrit for queer and trans communities, to name a few (Delgado & Stefancic, 2012).

In addition to the gradual inclusion of multiple voices and experiences in CRT, scholars have identified two distinct generations of the theory (Morfin, Perez, Parker, Lynn, & Arona, 2006). Delgado (2003) situated the first generation of CRT in a realist school of thought. The materiality of racism was the focal point for realists, who contend, "racism is a means by which our system allocates privilege, status, and wealth" (Delgado, 2003, pp. 123–124). This inequitable allocation results in and reifies racial hierarchies with white people at the top. The shift from structures and institutions to representations and ideations marked the second generation of CRT. Delgado (2003) criticized this shift for working "almost entirely in the realm of discourse" and ignoring material realities (p. 124). Proponents of the shift towards discourse argue that the second generation of CRT has found "a way to think about race and other areas of difference as a set of shifting bottoms and rotating centers, in which not one category (e.g., race, social class, sexual orientation) dominates but multiple ways" (Morfin et al., 2006, p. 266).

Despite the internal debates and differences within CRT, it is still possible to identify a set of common themes that unites scholarship under the CRT umbrella. In the following section, I summarize five themes of CRT that are particularly relevant to sociocultural approaches.

Themes of CRT

Ladson-Billings and Tate (1995) are credited with the formal introduction of CRT to education. Since 1995, the employment of CRT in education has flourished as evinced in the emergence of different groups, and has advanced an understanding of educational inequities (Ladson-Billings, 2013). Despite variance in manifestations and prominence among the CRT groups, five themes unite critical race theorists (Matsuda, Lawrence, Delgado, & Crenshaw, 1993).

1. Racism is endemic in the U.S.
2. Core notions of liberalism facilitate racism. Neutrality, objectivity, colourblindness, and meritocracy are unattainable ideals that perpetuate and reify existing racial hierarchies. These ideals dominate a national script on race and racism, and camouflage power.
3. Phenomena in social life should be subjected to critical historical and contextual analyses.
4. The experiential knowledge of people of colour and their communities of origin are valuable and central to the analysis of social life. This experiential knowledge, commonly conveyed through stories, often counters the dominant narrative.
5. The elimination of racism is part of a broader goal to end all oppressions.

I discuss each of these five themes in turn.

Theme 1: Racism as Ordinary

Racism is endemic to U.S. life, yet in the dominant discourse, racism is portrayed as aberrant, isolated and irrational acts intentionally committed by extremists. According to CRT, racism is the normal way in which the U.S. does business; it is permanent and part of the machinery that enables the U.S. to function (Bell, 1992a, b). Ladson-Billings (2013), quoting Hochschild (1984), argued that the existence of U.S. society is due to its foundation in racial slavery, and the U.S.'s contemporary global prominence is due to the continuation of racial discrimination.

A diverse corpus of literature exists on racism, apart from CRT, with racism conceptualized and cast in various ways. The multiple levels of racism identified in this literature are useful in understanding the breadth of racism indicted in the first CRT theme. Two levels of racism are applicable here: institutional and personally mediated (Bonilla-Silva, 1997; Jones, 2000).

Institutional racism is defined as differential access by race to society's commodities. These commodities include but are not limited to goods (symbolic and material), opportunities, material conditions, and services (Jones, 2000). U.S. public schooling is one example in which institutional racism is rampant. Many decades of research and federal government reports document the inequitable distribution of material resources (e.g., facilities, equipment), human resources (e.g., highly qualified administrators and teachers), and symbolic resources (e.g., networking for future opportunities) by racial composition of U.S. schools (U.S. Department of Education Office of Civil Rights, 2014a, b, c). It is likely that a school serving a predominantly white student population will be better resourced than a school serving predominantly black, Mexican, and Filipino populations in the same geographical area, for example (U.S. Department of Education Office of Civil Rights, 2014a, b). Because institutional racism is often embedded in formal and informal codes, policies, and practices, it assumes a life of its own and there is no one culprit for its existence. For example, the current racial inequalities and racial inequities that exist in U.S. public schools could be attributed to formal codes regarding local taxation to support public schools; informal codes of what constitutes the local tax base affected by residential and commercial real estate patterns; policies with respect to state-mandated funding formulae; and practices like academic tracking that determine which students get what. In the absence of identifiable perpetrators, the system of inequities, as noted in the previous discussion of U.S. public schools, continues from one generation to the next.

Personally mediated racism, also referred to as individual racism, includes racial prejudice (assumptions about racialized groups) and racial discrimination (taking action based on prejudice) (Jones, 2000). This is the type of racism that is most commonly referenced in public discourse. Personally mediated racism can include action and inaction (i.e., complicity). It can be intentional as well as unintentional and conscious as well as unconscious (e.g., implicit bias).

The ordinariness of racism, acting at the pinnacle of society via systems and institutions and at the nadir of individual subconscious, makes it difficult to alleviate (Bell, 1995). Its persistence is evident throughout U.S. history and in contemporary times, through periods of racial progress followed by racial retrenchment.

Theme 2: Critique of Liberalism

CRT critiqued the civil rights movement and related discourses for advocating incremental social change (Crenshaw et al., 1995). This incremental social change, replete with progress and retrenchment, was largely tied to individual freedom, the cornerstone of liberalism, rather than equality and equity (Lawrence, 2001). This incrementalism aligned with an implicit social compact around race during the civil rights era. "This compact held that racial power and racial justice would be understood in very particular ways. Racial justice was embraced in the American mainstream in terms that excluded radical or fundamental challenges to status quo institutional practices in American society. . ." (Crenshaw et al., 1995, p. xiv). This incremental approach has been sustained by a number of liberal notions: 1) claims that institutions (e.g., education systems) are, or should be neutral, a reliance upon impartiality without a recognition of pre-existing biases embedded within institutions and society; 2) claims that it is possible to locate objective truths; 3) colour-blindness, the ignoring and dismissal of race; and 4) the belief that the U.S. is a meritocracy in which success depends only on hard work and ability. In fact, CRT argues that these notions have insulated racism from scrutiny and remedy.

The myths of neutrality, objectivity, colour-blindness, and meritocracy are founded on a rationalism that strips away, to varying degrees, context[1] (Delgado & Stefancic, 2012). In neglecting context, the liberal notions of neutrality and objectivity reify and normalize the racial hierarchy (e.g., school funding mechanisms and distribution of resources previously described for U.S. public schools). These liberal notions validate the racial hierarchy (e.g. white students prioritized over non-white students) as the just, expected, and naturally occurring state by obscuring the embedded view of the white majority perspective in defining and operationalizing standards (Brown & Jackson, 2013). This racial hierarchy is further perpetuated by colour-blindness, a form of colour consciousness that accepts the dominant as the default (Crenshaw et al., 1995). Colour-blindness is deemed a psychological implausibility due to the centrality of race and racism in the historical and contemporary cultural milieu and construction of the U.S (Aleinikoff, 1991; Gotanda, 2000), an assertion supported by neuroscience research investigating brain activity in racial interactions (Ito & Bartholow, 2009; Richeson, Baird, Gordon, Heatherton, Wyland, Trawalter, & Shelton, 2003). Lastly, the racial hierarchy is seemingly justified by meritocracy (Sundquist, 2002). According to meritocracy, advantaged groups excel because they work hard and have the necessary abilities; disadvantaged groups fail because they do not (McNamee & Miller, 2009). The myth of meritocracy does not acknowledge structural facilitators like social networks and generational wealth. For instance, an individual might secure a top-level job because a parent discussed the situation with the company's CEO at a social gathering. Or, the attainment of a college degree and related benefits have become generational norms because the first-generation attendees were supported by GI Bills that excluded non-white candidates.

CRT provides counterarguments to the liberal notions of neutrality, objectivity, colour-blindness, and meritocracy in the next two themes.

Theme 3: Historical and Contextual Analyses

Presentism, a view that exclusively positions phenomena within the here and now (Noblit, 2013; Parsons, 2008), is a scaffold for liberal notions of neutrality, objectivity, colour-blindness, and meritocracy. CRT challenges presentism through its advocacy and promotion of critical historical and contextual analyses that expose how these liberal notions function in the allocation and safeguarding of rights and privileges. Additionally, because race, racism, and power are human constructions in CRT, historical and contextual analyses afford the reflection of place (e.g., different geographies), space (e.g., different communities), and time (e.g., era and a specific moment) in how race, racism, and power are conceptualized and enacted.

At first glance, the dominance of the white racial group in U.S. public life implies a natural order. When white dominance is historically deconstructed, this natural order is revealed to rest upon a legacy of conquest and oppression (López, 1996; Winant, 2001). A plethora of legislations, policies, and social mores have favoured whiteness; have defined who is property and who is human; who is a citizen and who is not; and who can access commodities and legal rights and who cannot (Banks, 1995; Bonnet, 1998; Fenton, 2010; Harris, 1993). This system of advantage is controlled by white people and therefore is somewhat protected from radical change that lessens advantages for its primary beneficiaries (Donnor, 2013). The system experiences ephemeral changes, only when the interests of non-dominant groups align with the dominant group (this concept is known as "interest convergence") (Bell, 1980). When the interests of white people and people of colour diverge once again, changes that benefited people of colour are abrogated (Bell, 1980; Thompson Dorsey & Venzant Chambers, 2014). One example of the principle of interest convergence is the Bracero Program. From 1942–1964 a bi-lateral agreement between the U.S. and Mexico enabled over 4.5 million Mexican nationals to be legally contracted for highly demanding and in high demand agricultural work (National Museum of American History, 2015). At the time of this writing, such labour is in low demand, and therefore unsurprising from a CRT perspective that current immigration reforms seek to restrict Mexican immigration into the U.S.

Theme 4: Counter-storytelling and Counter-narratives

As opposed to liberal notions that mask the foregrounding of voices and perspectives of whites, CRT explicitly and intentionally centres the voices and perspectives of people of colour. The common way in which these voices and perspectives are conveyed in CRT is through what is referred to as "counter-narratives" or "counter-storytelling." This emphasis on "counter" disputes positivist conceptions about what counts as legitimate (read: objective) data, and upends the typical relationship between perspectives of subjugated groups and those of dominant groups (Delgado, 1989). The terms "counter-storytelling" and "counter-narratives" are used in some of the CRT literature and refer specifically to narratives that oppose dominant scripts around race, racism, and power (Duncan, 2005).

The narratives of dominant groups often 1) explicitly or implicitly feature their superior positions, 2) perpetuate these superior positions as the natural order, and 3) omit or distort the perspectives of less dominant groups (Delgado, 1989). The counter-stories of the marginalized often challenge the premises, assertions, and myths contained within dominant narratives (Delgado & Stefancic, 2012).

Stories are useful as data and methodology because the challenge advocated by CRT is not restricted to the abstract. CRT requires praxis that concretizes and acts on new understandings of racism. When people of colour are othered in dominant institutions, counterstories are one way of "overcoming otherness" (Delgado, 1989, p. 2438) and building solidarity.

Theme 5: Elimination of Racism

As indicated in the first CRT theme, racism in the U.S. is permanent; it cannot be completely obliterated. It is a part of the U.S. unconscious and is ingrained in its fabric. Though some have characterized the previously stated as cynical, pessimistic, and fatalistic, Bell (1987, 1992b) declared that the belief in a myth, an ephemeral racism, was both disabling and dangerous.

Instead, salvation exists in the constant struggle to ameliorate racism and other forms of oppression.[2] This alleviation requires action in every domain (e.g., social, political, economic, educational) and at all levels (e.g., societal, institutional, personal). Exposing the limitations of liberalism and how it perpetuates the racial status quo (CRT theme 2); illuminating the relationship among the contemporary state of race, racism, and power in the U.S. to systems purposefully constructed and operated throughout history and presently sustained through formal and informal contexts (CRT theme 3); and elevating perspectives that challenge those systems and their corresponding dominant, unquestioned narratives (CRT theme 4) are simultaneously the foundations and the arsenal from which the battle is fought (CRT theme 5).

Research Methodologies in CRT

Research paradigms can be examined along four dimensions: axiology (what constitutes ethical behaviour), ontology (what is the nature of reality), epistemology (what is viewed as knowledge and what is the relationship between the known and the knower), and methods (what is the systematic approach to investigations) (Mertens, 2010). CRT falls within the transformative paradigm with the use of qualitative research as the predominant mode of inquiry.

For the transformative paradigm, axiology (ethical behaviour) promotes human rights and a just society. Engagement in this ethical behaviour requires respect of cultural norms, a recognition that various versions of reality exist (ontology), and an awareness that these versions of reality are heavily influenced by one's social position (epistemology). Knowledge is historically situated, inextricably linked to power, and socially constructed by human beings. CRT is most interested in knowledge that highlights racialized power, privilege, and oppression, and draws on qualitative methods to generate such data.

In qualitative methodology, research attempts to capture what naturally occurs in settings and the data analysis is usually inductive such that knowledge is constructed from the data in lieu of imposing theory onto the data, a deductive method. This inductive approach to data analysis does not preclude the use of existing theory in analyses or other stages of the research process. For example, CRT themes do not dictate what emerges from analyses, but they may inform the questions that guide the collection and analysis of data, implications of findings, and the like. Additionally, in qualitative methodology, the subjectivities of the research participants are treated as credible sources rather than biases in need of control. Many CRT studies use narratives and stories as techniques to feature the perspectives of people of colour with respect to power, racism, and other forms of oppression. For a myriad of reasons, such studies have not had a widespread impact on policy (Covarrubias & Velez, 2013). In order to expand the impact of CRT on research, practice, and policy, scholars have called for a more concerted use of quantitative (Covarrubias & Velez, 2013) and mixed methods techniques (DeCuir-Gunby & Walker-DeVose, 2013), more widely accepted methods in education research (Bonilla-Silva & Zuberi, 2008).

Because quantitative methods and mixed methods are typically employed in positivist and post-positivist paradigms of research, their uses within a transformative paradigm would look quite different. For example, causal theories that approximate how the world operates would not be presented devoid of context (an attempt to attain neutrality and objectivity) but would be situated within the explicit articulation of the researchers' positionalities, historical and contemporary milieu, et cetera (Covarrubias & Velez, 2013). The recasting of quantitative and mixed methods within a transformative paradigm could possibly launch a third generation in CRT.

Interfaces of CRT and Sociocultural Perspectives

I now consider how the broad themes and methodology of CRT can interface with sociocultural perspectives. Since sociocultural theories are rooted in Vygotsky's scholarship, I begin with several propositions from Vygotsky's work.

Vygotskian Propositions

Vygotsky viewed Marxist thought as a valuable resource in exploring human development.

> Marx's theory of society (known as historical materialism) also played a fundamental role in Vygotsky's thinking. According to Marx, historical

changes in society and material life produces changes in 'human nature' (consciousness and behavior). Although this general proposition had been echoed by others, Vygotsky was the first to attempt to relate it to concrete psychological questions. In this effort he creatively elaborated on Engels' concept of human labor and tool use as the means by which man changes nature and, in doing so, transforms himself.

(Cole & Scribner, 1978, p. 7)

In line with Marxist thought, Vygotsky's work centralized context—past, present, and future; stressed the importance of culture[3]; and situated the relationship of the individual and society, one example of context, as a dialectic with mediation as a pivotal point. In other words, individuals not only directly relate to and are directly impacted by contexts but also engage them through mediational means that span space and time.

Vygotsky proposed a framework that integrated context, culture, and the individual-society dialectic and foregrounded their dynamism. The framework highlighted four dimensions of development that spanned across place and time: phylogenetic, cultural-historical, ontogenetic, and microgenetic (Cole, 1996). Each dimension influences, and is influenced by, the others. Accordingly, phylogenesis featured the species' history and the legacy embodied in individuals through the genetic pool that differentiates humans from other living organisms. The cultural-historical dimension referred to the legacy across generations that consists of material (e.g. cell phones) and symbolic (e.g. how to respond to flashing lights of the police) systems. Ontogenesis emphasized occurrences within the lifespan of an individual. Microgenesis, the last dimension, captured instantaneous events involving individuals within a particular context. A continuous shaping of individuals and the societies they inhabit occurs within each separate dimension and within the interactions among dimensions (Rogoff, 2003).

Tools and signs are essential in this shaping. Although discussed separately here for the purposes of clarity, tools and signs are both mediators between individuals and their environments (Vygotsky, 1978). A tool is external to the individual and is employed to reach a particular aim. The tool is the medium through which the individual exerts influence on the environment; it remains separate from the object acted upon. In contrast, a sign is internal to an individual and, in some ways, the individual is the object acted upon. Whereas the tool is wielded to achieve some physical or material outcome, signs are in the foreground when making sense of a situation is paramount. Both mediators, tools and signs, are contextually situated and context-dependent. That is, what is used as a tool (e.g., use of certain words to extort money) in one situation can function as a sign in another (e.g., use of words to signify in-group status).

CRT and Sociocultural Perspectives

In light of the fact that Marxism is considered a critical theory in western scholarship, it is not surprising that some connections on a general, conceptual level exist between Vygotsky's propositions and CRT, which is also categorized in scholarship as a critical theory. The foregrounding of context, culture, and the dialectic relationship between the individual and society is one connection between sociocultural perspectives and CRT. Context, culture, and the individual-society dialectic are explicit or implicated in all five CRT themes.

Theme 1: Racism as ordinary. Racism is embedded in the symbolic and functioning systems that constitute public and private life in the U.S. and that mediate relationships between the individual and society. It is encoded in symbols, interactions, language, and material artifacts that mediate participation in individualistic and collective practices. In addition, the multiple levels of racism (institutional and personally mediated) correspond with Vygotsky's multiple levels of development. Institutional racism aligns with cultural-historical development, whereas personally mediated racism parallels ontogenesis and microgenesis.

Theme 2: Critiques of Liberalism. The second theme, a critique of liberalism, denotes the importance of context and culture by challenging the liberal notions of neutrality, objectivity, colour-blindness, and meritocracy—ideals that diminish context and culture. Context and culture are of similar import in sociocultural perspectives and are often centralized in understanding phenomena of interest (e.g., learning specific content, performing certain skills). Context and culture are viewed at different levels and at different scales. For example, situated learning (Lave & Wenger, 1991) is a sociocultural perspective that links learning to identity construction, which is intricately linked to context at the level learning occurs (e.g., science classroom), whereas cultural historical activity theory (CHAT) (Cole, 1996) is a sociocultural approach that considers interacting systems across space and time and would likely view learning in broader contexts (e.g., a science classroom within a school located in a district in the past, present, and future).

Theme 3: Historical and Contextual Analyses. Context and culture are readily evident in the third theme, because both concepts are foregrounded in historical and contextual analyses. Sociocultural theorists and critical race theorists agree on the importance of historical analyses, although they may differ on the lens with which they view history. CRT tends to foreground history of broad societal institutions, norms, and laws, whereas sociocultural theory tends to foreground the history of an activity system, or history as embedded in mediational means.

Theme 4: Counter-storytelling and Counter-narratives. CRT validates and elevates the experiential knowledge of people and communities of colour. This experiential knowledge, prominently captured through counter-storytelling/counter-narratives, often features the individual-society dialectic. For example, in characterizing the biography of a critical race theorist and the formation of CRT, Dalton (1987) incorporated a story about his first encounter with critical legal studies when he arrived at Harvard Law School. His personal story not only chronicled the personal interactions that constituted the moment and the personal impact of the moment, but it also illuminated the racial power relations in the U.S. mirrored in CLS. This emphasis on personal stories connects with the individual-society dialectic emphasized in sociocultural approaches. However, this form of data, counter-stories, is not dominant in sociocultural analyses.

Theme 5: Elimination of Racism. CRT is an activist theory and methodology, most concerned with praxis towards the elimination of racism. Some forms of sociocultural theory also take an activist stance. Early sociocultural analyses were used to challenge mainstream cultural psychology's "deficit model of cultural variations" (Cole, 1996, p. 73). In addition, some Change Lab projects have addressed power differentials that, for example, obstructed adequate medical care (Engeström, 2007). However, the activism of sociocultural theory does not necessarily take on systems of oppression, either at the institutional or personally mediated levels.

More indirect correspondences also exist between Vygotsky's research on mediational means (tools and signs) and CRT. For example, CRT uses tools and signs in addressing race, racism, and power. First generation CRT researchers and scholars primarily emphasized materiality, specifically tools operating at the level of society and institutions (e.g., systems, legislation, regulations) whereas second generation CRT researchers and scholars mostly featured ideation, most readily evident in signs (e.g., language, images).

Even though these interfaces, by way of general Vygotskian propositions, exist between CRT and sociocultural perspectives, they are underutilized in research conducted within the sociocultural tradition. As described in relation to the five themes of CRT, context, culture, individual-society dialectic, and mediation are not often explicitly linked to race, racism, and power in the sociocultural tradition (Nasir & Hand, 2006).

According to critical race theorists, public and academic domains emphasize and value race neutrality, and do not typically discuss how the notion of race neutrality normalizes being white (Brown & Jackson, 2013). Instead, two scripts dominate public discourse: colour-blindness, which ignores, dismisses, or rationalizes away the importance of race (Gotanda, 1991; López, 1994, 1996, 2007) and post-racialism that proclaims racial atrocities no longer exist so race is irrelevant (Cho, 2009). The vast majority of sociocultural approaches do not substantively attend to race, thus lending implicit support to colour-blind and post-racial ideologies.

Setting aside race and considering the more general issue of power, sociocultural theory and empirical analyses do not often attend to power imbalance in relation to phenomena of interest (e.g., learning science content, identity development). Some of the most influential sociocultural research (e.g., Rogoff, 2003), even research that is thoroughly grounded in contextual and historical analyses, does not acknowledge or address power imbalances.

To illustrate the interplay and contradictions between sociocultural and CRT perspectives, consider the following fictitious case. The case is based on national data and research in science education. Following the case description, I view the case from a sociocultural lens and then from a CRT one.

A Contrast in Lenses

The class bell rang twenty minutes ago. An International Baccalaureate (IB) middle grades science class of 15 students (all white) is actively engaged in the day's lesson, instructed by a 14-year veteran teacher with advanced certification and a Master's degree in science. In another part of the school, the general science class of 35 students (mostly black and Mexican American students, with a few white students) has not yet started. After a few more minutes pass, their second-year teacher, who is not certified to teach science, has a Bachelor of Arts degree, and who is chronically absent, arrives.

The veteran science teacher facilitates the learning of the IB students through skillful questioning and thoughtful prodding. Very loud and seemingly chaotic, the IB class is full of activity. The IB students work in groups of three to devise questions to investigate, develop hypotheses from the research they previously conducted, design experiments utilizing multi-page lists of equipment and materials at their disposal, decide what data should be collected and how, deliberate on the most appropriate ways to analyze the data, and determine how to confirm or disconfirm findings and communicate results. After devising their plan, the groups of students enthusiastically gather the necessary materials and equipment and begin to implement experiments in order to test their hypotheses.

In contrast, the general science teacher issues orders to control student behaviour. The teacher distributes a lab worksheet with step-by-step procedures for students to follow. After reading the directions and demonstrating from the front of the room, the teacher tells the students to be judicious in their use of materials because the supplies have been exhausted, to split into groups of seven students each, and gather around the long tables that served as lab stations.

One group, consisting of two black students, two Mexican Americans, and three white students (the only three in the class), immediately engage the lab. One white student takes the lead by reading the instructions and negotiating with the white peers about what materials and equipment to employ, and how to employ them. One black student, who loves and has been very successful in science, grabs some of the materials and shares them with one of the Mexican American students while their remaining black and Mexican American peers observe. They begin to conduct a separate portion of the lab. When a dispute emerges over the use of the equipment, the teacher approaches. The teacher admonishes the black student, on the basis of limited resources, and re-establishes the order set by the white student.

An examination of this fictitious vignette, which reflects existing research in science education (e.g., Kurth, Anderson, & Palincsar, 2002; U.S. Department of Education, 2014b, 2014c), illuminates the connections and differences between critical race theory and sociocultural perspectives.

Sociocultural Considerations

There are several emphases that are likely to emerge in a sociocultural examination of the previous vignette. A sociocultural perspective might give primacy to activity and delve into the task-related meanings students construct through their participation. For example, socioculturalists might define the activity system as the science classroom, in which the main motive for the teacher is teaching (e.g., skillful questioning, dictating rules and procedures), and the students' motive is learning (e.g., solving problems through active inquiry of generating questions and experimenting to answer them, following a set of procedures to replicate what the teacher demonstrated). Such an approach would highlight students' scientific understandings and their views of science as a consequence of their participation in the activity.

In addition to centralizing activity, sociocultural theorists might examine social interactions, including student–student interactions (e.g., student groups generating research questions of interest, peers following the directions of another peer) and student–teacher interactions (e.g., thoughtful prodding, management of behaviour). Such an analysis might consider the interplay between sociogenesis (group norms for communication and meaning-making) and microgenesis (individual meaning-making). Sociocultural analysis might also consider the tools (e.g., materials and equipment, worksheet) and signs (e.g., science content and conceptualization of science conveyed by activities) available, and track how these mediational means are used.

When comparing the two classrooms, sociocultural perspectives would probably identify the IB classroom as a more productive learning space. For example, situated learning theory (Lave & Wenger, 1991) would highlight the fact that the IB classroom's norms of participation were more similar to scientific practices that are valued in school. Figured worlds, a sociocultural perspective with a focus on culturally constructed activities understood by and socially reproduced and improvised by the collective authors of the activities (Holland, Lachicotte, Skinner, & Cain, 1998), would highlight the differing storylines around what teachers and students are responsible for, and the lesser authority that is made available to students in the general classroom. An examination of the mediational means might consider the affordances and constraints of what was made available to students, and could suggest how the lack of equipment in the general classroom would constrain their learning. A CHAT analysis might consider the classrooms as part of a broader network of activity systems (Cole, 1996), perhaps including the school administration, the school district, and the state department of education. These findings are important to understanding the nature of school learning in the two cases, but the sociocultural emphases are unlikely to unearth race, racism, and power.

CRT Considerations

Race, racism, and power are the crux of a CRT perspective. In interrogating the vignette, critical race theorists might emphasize topics related to the institution of schooling, practices in the classroom, and the student experience. At the institutional level, a CRT analysis might feature the systemic and inequitable distribution of physical and human resources and the quality of those resources. For example, the examination might feature historical patterns of resource distribution and funding models for public education when considerations of race were intentionally used to segregate whites and non-whites and to advance whites as the superior race in the U.S. (Parsons & Turner, 2014). These patterns might then serve as a backdrop for discussing resource distribution in contemporary times when colour-blindness and post-racialism dominate the discourse (e.g., all white IB class with ample space, materials, and equipment; general science class of predominantly students of colour with limited space, materials, and equipment).

At the classroom level, a CRT critique might stress how the inequitable distribution of resources translates into real experiences for students and works to buttress the existent racial hierarchy. For instance, the availability of material resources and teacher quality (e.g., veteran, advanced education, skilled in pedagogical techniques) afforded students in the IB class opportunities for higher-level processing of science content whereas material resources and teacher quality (e.g., novice, lacked certification, traditional pedagogy) served as scaffolds for students in the general science class to do lower-level processing of science content.

CRT might also emphasize the messages students might internalize. The conditions in the IB class imply high expectations for the enrolled students. The activities in the IB class encourage the white students to be creative, to think, and to problem-solve, activities expected of those in the most prestigious echelons in U.S. society. Conditions in the general science class implicate low expectations for the enrolled students. Activities mandate that students follow directions and perform prescribed actions, activities typically expected of individuals who occupy low-status positions in U.S. society. A critical race theory critique might further examine the students' experiences in terms of power and privilege with respect to race and deconstruct the structures and messages that determined who had them and who did not. For example, white students exercised power and privilege within the general science group; the black student's challenge of this hierarchy was thwarted by the teacher.

A view of the fictitious research-informed vignette from a sociocultural perspective and a critical race theory perspective shows where the two frameworks intersect and diverge. Sociocultural and CRT perspectives offer different but invaluable insights to the examination of phenomena learning, and development in the fictitious vignette. Sociocultural perspectives are useful in understanding context and culture in learning and development; discerning how they shape learning and development; and comprehending mediation and the dialectic relationships among individuals, society, and education. CRT's emphasis on race, racism, and power unearths assumptions often left untouched and unexamined by sociocultural perspectives. Both traditions, if somehow joined, could possibly lead to a more comprehensive understanding of phenomena in the abstract and more robust, impactful praxis in the concrete.

Coda

The conceptual bridge between CRT and sociocultural perspectives exists. Even though sociocultural perspectives offer a valuable and often absent standpoint in academic research and scholarship that is largely positivist and post-positivist in nature, the emphases on context, culture, mediation, and individual-society dialectic are insufficient. Power imbalances, racial inequities, and racial disparities in U.S. education demand more. In other words, many forms of racial dominance and racial privilege will continue to proliferate in education even if sociocultural perspectives gain broader acceptance. As CRT asserts, substantive contestation of racism in education requires an intentional and explicit treatment of race, racism, and power, as well as an activist stance towards scholarship. The somewhat liberal foundations of sociocultural perspectives, the more prevalent approach in comparison to CRT in the U.S., are in need of an infusion: the infusion of "an intellectual identity and political practice that would take the form of . . . a race intervention into left discourse" (Crenshaw et al., 1995, p. xix). Socioculturalists must cross the conceptual bridge and more fully integrate race, racism, and power as foci. Intersections already exist; the journey is not long but likely arduous in an era when tensions mount around race and racism, when conventional power dynamics are being challenged on many fronts, and the U.S. population is becoming increasingly non-white. Will such a contentious but warranted turn in the sociocultural tradition occur? Only time will tell.

Notes

1. Context is generally defined here as that which surrounds (Bronfenbrenner, 1979). It encompasses the material (e.g., physical setting) and the symbolic (e.g., representations in a milieu) as well as what is proximal (e.g., present time and situation in which

individuals are directly involved) and distal (e.g., future time and situations that are removed from individuals but still impact them).
2. Intersectionality is one construct in CRT that foregrounds other forms of oppression (Cho, Crenshaw, & McCall, 2013; Collins, 1993; Crenshaw, 1991; Delgado, 2011).
3. Cole (1995) indicated the existence of numerous conceptualizations of culture. These views of culture are often positioned in the literature as exclusive to one another (Parsons & Carlone, 2013). The standpoint on culture employed here is an eclectic one, much akin to the iceberg analogy of culture with values aligning with parts of the iceberg invisible to the eye and practices corresponding with what can be seen of the iceberg. On one hand, culture is a change-reticent system of implicit and explicit beliefs and values that influences how the world is perceived and acted upon (Nobles, 1980; White, 1984). On the other hand, it is a dynamic repertoire of practices resulting from the prolonged engagement with and immersion in communities (Gutiérrez & Rogoff, 2003).

References

Aleinikoff, A. T. (1991). A case for race consciousness. *Columbia Law Review*, *91*(5), 1060–1123.

Banks, J. (1995). The historical reconstruction of knowledge about race: Implications for transformative teaching. *Educational Researcher*, *24*(2), 15–24.

Bell, D. (1987). *And we are not saved: The elusive quest for racial justice*. New York, New York: Basic Books.

Bell, D. (1992a). Racial realism. *Connecticut Law Review*, *24*(2), 363–380.

Bell, D. (1992b). *Faces at the bottom of the well: The permanence of racism*. New York, NY: Basic Books.

Bell, D. A., Jr. (1980). Brown v. Board of education and the interest-convergence dilemma. *Harvard Law Review*, *93*(3), 518–533.

Bell, D. Jr. (1995). Brown v. Board of education and the interest convergence dilemma. In K. Crenshaw, N. Gotanda, G. Peller & K. Thomas (Eds.), *Critical race theory: The key writings that formed the movement* (pp. 20–29). New York, NY: The New Press.

Bonilla-Silva, E. (1997). Rethinking racism: Toward a structural interpretation. *American Sociological Review*, *62*(3), 465–480.

Bonilla-Silva, E., & Zuberi, T. (2008). Toward a definition of white logic and white methods. In T. Zuberi & E. Bonilla-Silva (Eds.), *White logic, white methods: Racism and methodology* (pp. 3–27). Lanham, MD: Rowman & Littlefield.

Bonnet, A. (1998). Who was white? The disappearance of non-European white identities and formation of European racial whiteness. *Ethnic and Racial Studies*, *21*(6), 1029–1055.

Bronfenbrenner, U. (1979). *The ecology of human development: Experiments by nature and design*. Cambridge, MA: Harvard University Press.

Brown, K., & Jackson, D. D. (2013). The history and conceptual elements of critical race theory. In M. Lynn & A. D. Dixson (Eds.), *Handbook of critical race theory in education* (pp. 9–22). New York, NY: Routledge.

Chapman, T. K. (2007). Interrogating classroom relationships and events: Using portraiture and critical race theory in education research. *Educational Researcher*, *36*(3), 156–162.

Cho, S. (2009). Post-racialism. *Iowa Law Review*, *94*(5), 1589–1649.

Cho, S., Crenshaw, K. W., & McCall, L. (2013). Toward a field of intersectionality studies: Theory, applications, and praxis. *Signs*, *38*(4), 785–810.

Cole, M. (1995). Culture and cognitive development: From cross-cultural research to creating systems of cultural mediation. *Culture & Psychology*, *1*(1), 25–54.

Cole, M. (1996). *Cultural psychology: A once and future discipline*. Cambridge, MA: Belknap Press of Harvard University Press.

Cole, M., & Scribner, S. (1978). Introduction. In M. Cole, V. John-Steiner, S. Scribner & E. Souberman (Eds.), *Mind in society* (pp. 1–14). Cambridge, MA: Harvard University Press.

Collins, P. H. (1993). Toward a new vision: Race, class, and gender as categories of analysis and connection. *Race, Gender, and Class*, *1*(1), 25–45.

Covarrubias, A., & Velez, V. (2013). Critical race quantitative intersectionality: An antiracist research paradigm that refuses to "let the numbers speak for themselves". In M. Lynn & A. D. Dixson (Eds.), *Handbook of critical race theory in education* (pp. 270–285). New York, NY: Routledge.

Crenshaw, K. W. (1991). Mapping the margins: Intersectionality, identity politics, and violence against women of color. *Stanford Law Review*, *43*(6), 1241–1299.

Crenshaw, K. W. (2011). Twenty years of CRT: Looking back to move forward. *Connecticut Law Review*, *43*(5), 1253–1352.

Crenshaw, K. W., Gotanda, N., Peller, G., & Thomas, K. (1995). Introduction. In K. W. Crenshaw, N. Gotanda, G. Peller & K. Thomas (Eds.), *Critical race theory: The key writings that formed the movement* (pp. xiii–xxxii). New York, NY: The New Press.

Dalton, H. L. (1987). The clouded prism. *Harvard Civil Rights-Civil Liberties Law Review*, *22*(2), 435–447.

DeCuir, J., & Dixson, A. (2004). "So when it comes out, they aren't that surprised that it is there": Using critical race theory as a tool of analysis of race and racism in education. *Educational Researcher*, *33*(5), 26–31.

DeCuir-Gunby, J. T., & Walker-DeVose, D. C. (2013). Expanding the counterstory: The potential for critical race mixed methods studies in education. In M. Lynn & A. D. Dixson (Eds.), *Handbook of critical race theory in education* (pp. 248–259). New York, NY: Routledge.

Delgado, R. (1989). Storytelling for oppositionists and others: A plea for narrative. *Michigan Law Review*, *87*(8), 2411–2441.

Delgado, R. (2003). Crossroads and blind alleys: A critical examination of recent writing about race. *Texas Law Review*, *82*(1), 121–152.

Delgado, R. (2011). Rodrigo's reconsideration: Intersectionality and the future of critical race theory. *Iowa Law Review*, *96*(4), 1247–1288.

Delgado, R., & Stefancic, J. (2012). *Critical race theory: An introduction* (2nd edn.). New York, NY: New York University Press.

DiAngelo, R. (2011). White fragility. *International Journal of Critical Pedagogy*, *3*(3), 54–70.

Dixson, A. D., & Rousseau, C. K. (2005). And we are still not saved: Critical race theory in education ten years later. *Race, Ethnicity, and Education*, *8*(1), 7–27.

Donnor, J. (2013). Education as the property of whites: African Americans' continued quest for good schools. In M. Lynn & A. D. Dixson (Eds.), *Handbook of critical race theory in education* (pp. 195–203). New York, NY: Routledge.

Duncan, G. (2005). Critical race ethnography in education: Narrative, inequality, and the problem of epistemology. *Race, Ethnicity, and Education*, *8*(1), 93–114.

Engeström, Y. (2007). Putting Vygotsky to work: The change laboratory as an application of double stimulation. In H. Daniels, M. Cole & J. V. Wertsch (Eds.), *The Cambridge companion to Vygotsky* (pp. 363–382). Cambridge and New York: Cambridge University Press.

Fenton, S. (2010). *Ethnicity* (2nd edn.). Cambridge, UK: Polity Press.
Gillborn, D. (2013). The policy of inequity: Using CRT to unmask white supremacy in education policy. In M. Lynn & A. D. Dixson (Eds.), *Handbook of critical race theory in education* (pp. 129–139). New York, NY: Routledge.
Gotanda, N. (1991). A critique of "our constitution is color-blind". *Stanford Law Review, 44*(1), 1–68.
Gotanda, N. (2000). A critique of "our constitution is color-blind." In R. Delgado & J. Stefancic (Eds.), *Critical race theory: The cutting edge* (2nd edn.) (pp. 35–38). Philadelphia, PA: Temple University Press.
Gutiérrez, K. D., & Rogoff, B. (2003). Cultural ways of learning: Individual traits or repertoires of practice. *Educational Researcher, 32*(5), 19–25.
Harris, C. (1993). Whiteness as property. *Harvard Law Review, 106*(8), 1707–1791.
Hochschild, I. J. (1984). *The new American dilemma: Liberal democracy and school desegregation.* New Haven, CT: Yale University Press.
Holland, D., Lachicotte, W. Jr., Skinner, D., & Cain, C. (1998). *Identity and agency in cultural worlds.* Cambridge, MA: Harvard University Press.
Howard, T. C., & Reynolds, R. (2013). Examining Black male identity through a raced, classed, and gendered lens: Critical race theory and the intersectionality of the Black male experience. In M. Lynn & A. D. Dixson (Eds.), *Handbook of critical race theory in education* (pp. 232–247). New York, NY: Routledge.
Ito, T. A., & Bartholow, B. D. (2009). The neural correlates of race. *Trends in Cognitive Sciences, 13*(12), 524–531.
Jones, C. P. (2000). Levels of racism: A theoretic framework and a gardener's tale. *American Journal of Public Health, 90*(8), 1212–1215.
Kurth, L. A., Anderson, C. W., & Palincsar, A. (2002). The case of Carla: Dilemmas of helping *all* students to understand science. *Science Education, 86*(3), 287–313.
Ladson-Billings, G. (2013). Critical race theory—What it is not. In M. Lynn & A. D. Dixson (Eds.), *Handbook of critical race theory in education* (pp. 34–47). New York, NY: Routledge.
Ladson-Billings, G., & Tate, W. (1995). Toward a critical race theory of education. *Teachers College Record, 97*(1), 47–68.
Lave, J., & Wenger, E. (1991). *Situated learning: Legitimate peripheral participation.* New York, NY: Cambridge University.
Lawrence, C. R., III. (2001). Two views of the river: A critique of the liberal defense of affirmative action. *Columbia Law Review, 101*(4), 928–976.
López, I. F. H. (1994). The social construction of race: Some observations on illusion, fabrication, and choice. *Harvard Civil Rights-Civil Liberties Law Review, 29*, 1–63.
López, I. F. (1996). *White by law: The legal construction of race.* New York, NY: New York University Press.
López, I. F. H. (2007). "A nation of minorities": Race, ethnicity, and reactionary color-blindness. *Stanford Law Review, 59*(4), 985–1063.
Matsuda, M., Lawrence, C., Delgado, R., & Crenshaw, K. (1993). Introduction. In M. Matsuda, C. Lawrence, R. Delgado & K. Crenshaw (Eds.), *Words that wound: Critical race theory, assaultive speech, and the first amendment* (pp. 1–15). Boulder, CO: Westview Press.
McNamee, S. J., & Miller, R. K. (2009). *The meritocracy myth.* Lanham, MD: Rowman & Littlefield Publishers.
Mertens, D. (2010). *Research and evaluation in education and psychology: Integrating diversity with quantitative, qualitative, and mixed methods* (3rd edn.). Los Angeles, CA: Sage.

Milner, H. IV. (2013). Analyzing poverty, learning, and teaching through a critical race theory lens. *Review of Research in Education*, *37*(1), 1–53.

Morfin, O., Perez, V., Parker, L., Lynn, M., & Arona, J. (2006). Hiding the politically obvious. *Educational Policy*, *20*(1), 249–270.

Nasir, N. S., & Hand, V. M. (2006). Exploring sociocultural perspectives on race, culture, and learning. *Review of Educational Research*, *76*(4), 449–475.

National Museum of American History. (2015). *Opportunity or exploitation: The Bracero program.* Retrieved August 2015 from http://amhistory.si.edu/onthemove/themes/story_51_5.html

Nobles, W. (1980). African philosophy: Foundations for Black psychology. In R. Jones (Ed.), *Black psychology* (pp. 23–36). New York, NY: Harper & Row.

Noblit, G. (2013). Culture bound: Science, teaching, and research. *Journal of Research in Science Teaching*, *50*(2), 238–249.

Olneck, M. (1993). Terms of inclusion: Has multiculturalism redefined equality in American education? *American Journal of Education*, *101*(3), 234–260.

Parker, L., & Lynn, M. (2002). What's race got to do with it? Critical race theory's conflicts with and connections to qualitative research methodology and epistemology. *Qualitative Inquiry*, *8*(1), 7–22.

Parsons, E. C. (2008). Positionality of African Americans and a theoretical accommodation of it: Rethinking science education research. *Science Education*, *92*(6), 1127–1144.

Parsons, E. C., & Carlone, H. B. (2013). Editorial: Culture and science education in the 21st century: Extending and making the cultural box more inclusive. *Journal of Research in Science Teaching*, *50*(1), 1–11.

Parsons, E. C., & Turner, K. (2014). The importance of history in the racial inequality and racial inequity in education: New Orleans as a case example. *The Negro Educational Review*, *65*(1–4), 99–113.

Richeson, J. A., Baird, A. A., Gordon, H. L., Heatherton, T. F., Wyland, C. L., Trawalter, S., & Shelton, J. N. (2003). An fMRI investigation of the impact of interracial contact on executive function. *Nature Neuroscience*, *6*(12), 1323–1328.

Rogoff, B. (2003). *The cultural nature of human development.* New York, NY: Oxford University Press.

Sundquist, C. (2002). Equal opportunity, individual liberty, and meritocracy in education: Reinforcing structures of privilege and inequality. *Georgetown Journal on Poverty Law and Policy*, *9*(1), 227–251.

Tate, W. IV. (1997). Critical race theory and education: History, theory, and implications. *Review of Research in Education*, *22*, 195–247.

Thompson Dorsey, D. N., & Venzant Chambers, T. L. (2014). Growing C-D-R (Cedar): Working the intersections of interest convergence and whiteness as property in the affirmative action legal debate. *Race, Ethnicity and Education*, *17*(1), 56–87.

U.S. Department of Education Office of Civil Rights (2014a). *Civil rights data collection data snapshot: College and career readiness.* Issue brief no. 3. Washington, DC: U.S. Department of Education, Office of Civil Rights.

U.S. Department of Education, Office of Civil Rights (2014b). *Civil rights data collection data snapshot: Teacher equity.* Issue brief no. 4. Washington, DC: U.S. Department of Education, Office of Civil Rights.

U.S. Department of Education, Office of Civil Rights (2014c). *Civil rights data collection data snapshot: School discipline.* Issue brief no. 1. Washington, DC: U.S. Department of Education, Office of Civil Rights.

Vygotsky, L. S. (1978). *Mind in society: Development of higher psychological processes.* Cambridge, MA: Harvard University Press.
White, J. (1984). *The psychology of Blacks: An Afro-American perspective.* New York, NY: Prentice-Hall.
Williams, P. J. (1987). Alchemical notes: Reconstructing ideals from deconstructed rights. *Harvard Civil Rights-Civil Liberties Law Review, 22*(2), 401–433.
Winant, H. (2001). *The world is a ghetto: Race and democracy since World War II.* New York, NY: Basic Books.

4

LEARNING DISCOURSES OF RACE AND MATHEMATICS IN CLASSROOM INTERACTION

A Poststructural Perspective

Niral Shah and Zeus Leonardo

Research in the learning sciences has established the relationship between learning and "identity," and shown how the development of knowledge is intertwined with the process of becoming certain types of people (Lave & Wenger, 1991; Nasir & Hand, 2008; Wenger, 1998). To a more limited extent, studies have considered the learning–identity relation in terms of the power dynamics that operate at both macro- and micro-levels of social life (Esmonde & Langer-Osuna, 2013; Lewis & Moje, 2003; Wortham, 2006). Power—and how it is exercised through discourse—is of central concern in poststructural theory (Foucault, 1980). To date, though, poststructural theory has yet to gain significant traction in the learning sciences.

In this chapter, we outline core attributes of poststructural theory, as well as its overlap with—and points of departure from—sociocultural perspectives. To demonstrate its utility in conceptualizing and studying the learning process, we use poststructural theory to analyze two vignettes of racialized interactions collected as part of a study of race in high school mathematics classrooms (see Shah, 2013). In doing so, we argue that poststructural theory can deepen our understanding of the learning process in at least two ways. First, it offers new ways of analyzing the processes through which learners are positioned as having varying academic potential. And second, it problematizes a seemingly straightforward but critical question: *What*, exactly, is being learned?

Introduction to Poststructural Theory[1]

The poststructural turn in social thought and educational theory has been generative and influential. As an intellectual intervention, poststructural thought questions many aspects of accepted ways to analyze social and cultural phenomena.

The "post" in poststructuralism does not necessarily signify an "after" in relation to structuralism. Rather, it signals an interrogation of structuralism's tenets, such as the view of language as an overarching system outside of history and human context. We prefer to think of the "post" as a form of ambivalence toward the guarantees of well-accepted traditions (Leonardo, 2013), or a condition of their "slackening" hold on us (Lyotard, 1984). Poststructuralism may be distinguished from critical theory; the latter is rooted in the Frankfurt School's engagement with German idealism, Freudo-Marxism, and Nietzsche, whereas the former is organized around the work of Foucault, Derrida, and Lyotard, whose analyses privilege the role of language or discourse in the study of social life. Although critical theory began the intellectual project of both questioning the tenets and establishing the limits of the Enlightenment, poststructuralism would later take these critiques to their logical conclusion, at times showing hostility toward dearly held principles of the Enlightenment like emancipation.

With respect to methodology, poststructural discourse analysis may recruit the method of communication analysis—often called critical discourse analysis (see Wodak & Meyer, 2009)—but the two are not fully equivalent. Communication analysis focuses on various aspects of language, such as grammar and style. In contrast, poststructural discourse analysis may focus on cultural elements or the multiple meanings of social texts (Lather, 1992).

As a theory that interrogates fundamentally held ideas and beliefs, poststructuralism is rarely without a source for critique. Poststructuralism's other targets of critique include essentialism (Hall, 1996), or the idea that interactions in the world are reducible to an origin (e.g., the primacy of economic class); reductivism, or the idea that the empirical world substantiates a primary order such as the economy (Nicholson, 1987); and teleology, or the idea embedded in metanarratives such as Marxism, that history is a set of events leading to a determined end point (Lyotard, 1984). Even common-sense notions like "reality" and "truth" become suspect because they imply the existence of presocial facts to be discovered, rather than constructions that are effects of power relations (Baudrillard, 1994; Foucault, 1980). Indeed, poststructural analysts ". . . do not ask 'Is *x* true?', but rather 'What makes *x* possible?' and 'What are its effects?'" (Mendick, Moreau, & Epstein, 2009, p. 72). In all, poststructuralism interrogates the foundations of modern thought, making it all but impossible to continue social research in the same vein.

A defining feature of poststructural theory is its focus on discourse as a conduit for the exercise of power, which occurs through everyday processes of meaning making (Foucault, 1980). Certainly, communication through talk and writing are examples of discourse; however, the term "discourse" also goes beyond spoken and written words (Gee, 2011). For our purposes here, discourse refers to webs of mutually constituting statements that represent and position people and social phenomena in particular ways. These statements come in a variety of forms: they can be oral and textual, but they also can be visual, spatial, and kinetic. A photograph of a refugee, the physical layout of a city, and an athlete in the act of dunking a basketball all can be understood as elements of discourse, insofar as they can be interpreted or "read" as statements about who people are and what they value. From a poststructural perspective, then, the social world functions in a "language-like" way.

Poststructuralists argue that while meaning is constructed through discourse, this process is never neutral. Rather, language exists in a social context organized by power relations (Foucault, 1980; Lewis & Moje, 2003). The use of language across multiple arenas—from mundane interactions at the water cooler to advertisements during a presidential campaign—always involves processes of positioning that can result in domination and marginalization (cf. Davies & Harré, 1990). In that sense, discourse cannot be dismissed as nothing more than "hot air." Discourse is linked to people's lived experiences and can have a tangible impact on how material resources are distributed in society (Gee, 2011). Rather than something that is imposed from above, power circulates at the micro-level through everyday discursive practices (Foucault, 1980).

A key point in poststructural thought is that individuals are constituted as subjects through discourse (Lewis & Moje, 2003). In other words, language and language-like representations make available various subject positions (i.e., possible ways of being), but not all subject positions are equally available to all people. Discourses regulate access to subject positions through representations, based on how those representations are configured and deployed. As representations are deployed in the process of meaning making, people become "intelligible" and knowledges are constructed and perpetuated about groups of people: who they are and what they can do. These knowledges get taken up as "truth" and become part of the collective "common sense" (Foucault, 1980). In this process, some truths are centred as "normal" while others are marginalized. Poststructural theory is concerned with explaining how these processes occur and their implications.

Poststructural Theory and Sociocultural Perspectives

Historically, poststructural theory and sociocultural perspectives have been applied to study different types of problems. And yet, both theoretical paradigms overlap in ways that suggest their compatibility. Like poststructural theory, sociocultural approaches highlight the importance of context, or the idea that individual thought and behaviour are always situated in and organized by local resources and circumstances (Engeström, Miettinen, & Punamäki, 1999; Vygotsky, 1986). From Vygotsky's original insights to more recent research in the area of activity theory, sociocultural approaches have sought to account for context in increasingly sophisticated ways.

Another point of overlap is an interest in processes of change, and how transformation happens through social interaction. Much research in the sociocultural tradition has focused on matters of individual development, such as how a person's conceptual understanding of a topic evolves through the mediation of various cultural tools and signs (Vygotsky, 1986). Development is conceptualized as a process of mutual transformation, where change for a particular person can also effect changes in the immediate environment. Similarly, poststructuralists contend that not only do discourses shape local phenomena, but local changes can also lead to broader transformations in societal discourses.

There is also a shared interest in the psychological and sociological status of the individual. Both theoretical orientations reject humanist notions of individuals as unified, stable entities that move intact from situation to situation. However, a key difference between them lies in how they conceptualize the individual. Sociocultural research has shown that in addition to the acquisition and development of knowledge, learning involves the development of identity (Nasir & Hand, 2008; Wenger, 1998). In the terminology of situated theory, as people learn they move towards full participation in communities of practice (Lave & Wenger, 1991). Further, learners negotiate multiple identities as they participate in the learning process, which may hold material implications for their access to opportunities to learn.

In contrast to sociocultural approaches that focus on identity, poststructural analyses seek to understand how individuals come to be constituted as subjects of discourses (Goldberg, 1990; Lewis & Moje, 2003). This is not only a matter of terminology. As was discussed earlier, conceptualizing people as discursively constituted reflects the poststructural commitment to understanding the world in terms of power relations. Relatedly, from a poststructural perspective, the process of moving towards full participation in a learning environment is far from smooth or monotonic. Instead, "identity formation" is understood as a tension-laden process rife with conflicting goals and agendas (Lewis & Moje, 2003). Sociocultural approaches do not ignore such tensions, but they have not been a primary focus.

Another point of departure concerns units of analysis. As we have discussed, poststructural analyses focus on language as a primary unit of analysis. Language is also emphasized in sociocultural research, but alongside other types of material and nonmaterial signs and tools (Engeström, Miettinen, & Punamäki, 1999; Vygotsky, 1986). Research questions in the sociocultural paradigm also tend to operate at a finer grain size than those in the poststructural tradition. Of particular interest are the features and dynamics of the local settings in which social interactions take place, and how mediation by cultural tools and signs produces transformations in knowledge and in the self. Poststructural analyses also focus on social interactional processes, albeit at a coarser grain size. Poststructural theory understands the local in terms of global historical processes and forces, linking micro-level phenomena to macro-systems of power (Lewis & Moje, 2003). This does not mean that sociocultural approaches cannot account for issues of power, but power has not typically been their focus. In sum, sociocultural analyses tend to be more micro-focused and poststructural analyses tend to be more macro-focused, although both paradigms acknowledge the importance of both the micro- and macro-levels.

Poststructural Race Theory (PRT) in Education

Poststructuralism has been useful in conceptualizing race as a formidable social relation. In this chapter we use poststructural race theory (PRT) to explore the process of racial formation, which is the process whereby the racial organization of society is built, revised, or sometimes destroyed (Omi & Winant, 2015). PRT apprehends race as a discourse that constructs a social world whereby cultural understandings of physiognomy become meaningful as indicators of cognitive and intellectual worth (Leonardo, 2013, 2015). Importantly, conceptualizing race in this way subverts the false notion that race has an essential meaning.

PRT does not suggest that race is "made of language," because while race language matters, it is not made of matter. Racial discourse is an analytical assertion, such that if we are interested in how people understand themselves—and are understood by others—as racial beings, elevating the status of language becomes necessary because it is the medium through which race is communicated and made meaningful.

PRT is also distinguishable from critical race theory (CRT). Because there is a chapter dedicated to CRT in the current volume (see Parsons, this volume), we keep our comments brief. First, poststructuralism's focus on subject formation, or subjectivity, differs from CRT's emphasis on racial identity. Although some scholars may use the terms interchangeably, subjectivity differs from identity insofar as the first posits the subject as an effect of competing discourses without presuming the existence of an essence found in the second. That is, from the mystics to Aristotle and on to the Enlightenment, the law of identity goes to the heart of an individual or group's pre-existing social makeup. In contrast, the theory of subjectivity from Foucault onwards argues that subjects are effects of discourses that interpellate them, such that they are not constituted before they are made intelligible through language and other cultural practices. Second, PRT applies Foucault's ideas to race analysis (e.g., Goldberg, 1990; Hall, 1996), whereas CRT is a largely North American movement resulting from critiques of liberalism in legal scholarship and extensions of Marxist legal studies. Finally, they also differ in their methodological commitments: CRT prefers allegorical composite racial stories that run counter to majoritarian precepts, while PRT focuses on the politics of representation found in social texts ranging from everyday race talk to longstanding national myths about race.

Discourse and Racemaking in Learning Settings

Racial statements exist in paradigmatic relation with other statements. For example, when Asians are celebrated as "good at math," this usually comes at a cost to other racial groups (Shah, in press). The upshot is that discourses regulate the learning conditions that educators and students enter into with each other. They can affect students' participation in learning environments through interactions with teachers who position them as capable or incapable of performing cognitive tasks expected of them. For example, "smartness" is a statement about difference, and assumes the existence of its complementarity (i.e., the intellectually incapable or cognitively challenged) (Leonardo & Broderick, 2011). Similarly, racial statements exist in relation to a host of other possible statements that could have been made, or existing statements that provide its environment for difference and intelligibility (Derrida, 1985).

Poststructural theory makes sense of racial interactions as contingent on situations that expose the active nature of racemaking in local spaces (e.g., classrooms), but which also speak to larger patterns of racial positioning. In the case of Asians, their perceived ability in mathematics goes hand in hand with their problematic positioning within the model minority discourse in the U.S. (Shah, 2015). There is evidence that the "Asians are good at math" narrative lacks empirical basis (Pang, Han, & Pang, 2011). That some Asian ethnicities do succeed in mathematics speaks less to the racial nature of mathematical ability, and perhaps more to a partial and imperfect response to the racial structure that discriminates against them through linguistic racism. That is, as Sue and Okazaki (1990) have proposed, some Asians may favour educational mobility through mathematics and the sciences as a way to ameliorate the specific forms of racism they face in school and society.

PRT goes further than rejecting the notion of race as a predetermined or biological essence. It also aims to explain how a racial predicament like the U.S. recruits biological discourse to organize cultural understandings about racial difference for purposes of stratification (Goldberg, 1990). In saying this, we affirm the educative function of race, for it teaches critical lessons about "human kinds" (Hacking, 1995). As such, racemaking is the imaginary whereby humans are transformed into racialized beings, a process often legitimized with the help of science. And yet, it is not enough to reject the myth that racial difference is natural. PRT does not merely substitute a constructed world for a natural one. The interest lies in explaining the political effects that accompany discourses under the regime of a constructed world. In other words, a constructed world shaped through racial discourses produces real consequences that are registered by the body. For example, when racial discourses regulate Black boys and men as dangerous or endangered (Ferguson, 2001), it should come as no surprise that a social life that sanctions these distorted images facilitates violence against them, as in the case of police violence against Black males.

Of particular relevance here is the role of the racialized nation state (Bonilla-Silva, 2005; Omi & Winant, 2015). Poststructuralism and racial formation theory meet at the point where Omi and Winant (2015) give race representations their due weight in helping to build institutions. Or as far as Bonilla-Silva (2005) is concerned, race meaning does the work of White supremacy. Understanding the state as racial means that the state partakes in racial contestation, promotes a racial organization of society, and produces uneven consequences for its populace along racial lines. As part of this racial structure, representations become the cultural cognate of material life, the discursive logic responsible for constructing the meaning of race. By saying this, we acknowledge that poststructuralism does not reject a robust theory of "structures" but promotes a particular understanding of them that accounts for the extra-material dimensions that played a secondary role in modernist theories. It is as impossible to be anti-structure as it is to be anti-language. Within this conceptual apparatus, race discourse is built into race institutions, like schools, because the first makes the second intelligible, and therefore produces the way we conduct and administer them. Our concern is for how such a process is racially encoded in classrooms, which comprise one of the central places where young people learn about race.

Race, Regulation, and the Politics of Representation

Race exerts power through its function as a system that regulates representations. Although not celebrated as an example of poststructuralism, Patricia Hill Collins' (2000) influential book, *Black Feminist Thought*, provides clear directions on how to study representations of Blackness through controlling images. From Mammies to militants, Black representations harm Blacks by simplifying their history and identity. Because people of colour generally do not control the means of their own representation, they are subject to forces outside their immediate influence, which exert enormous power in how the social field renders them intelligible. When people of colour manage to exercise enough power to generate their own images, they face the pressure of being representative (Julien & Mercer, 1996) because they do not control the politics of representation (i.e., its general politics of truth). By contrast, Whites enjoy a vast range of representations, from heroes and love interests to villains and buffoons. Because these are representations, White images do not capture "the truth" about Whiteness, especially when generated by Whites (see Dyer, 1997), but they are more varied and allow for more complexity despite their elisions.

Representations distort how we understand the social world, and thus produce uneven repercussions for different groups. For example, it is telling when Denzel Washington and Halle Berry were awarded U.S. Academy Awards for leading actor and actress in 2002: the first for playing a corrupt, thuggish cop, and the second for playing a Black jezebel (Collins, 2004). Washington was also recognized for Best Supporting Actor in the 1989 film, *Glory*, for his role as an insubordinate soldier in the American Civil War who was publicly whipped for his infractions. Although both Washington and Berry are talented and deserve their recognition, the point is that their roles conveniently do not disrupt controlling images of Blacks. On this note, it is worth mentioning that Washington played Malcolm X a decade earlier in director Spike Lee's film on the Black revolutionary's life, a threatening role that goes against the grain of dominant Black representation in the U.S. Recognizing Washington's role in that film would have not only validated a Black counter-representation, but also Spike Lee's career trajectory and alternative voice as well. We mention these films because, as race scholars, we consider them evidence of racial trends that beg critical analysis. Poststructuralism's focus on discourse and representation are powerful tools for accomplishing this task.

In education, racial discourses circulate as a method of stratifying social groups according to perceived academic skills and abilities. In a word, students are judged on their *educability*. That is, students from different racial groups may or may not be deemed worthy of schooling in general, as well as in specific subject areas like mathematics, science, and language arts. Indeed, entire groups may be positioned either as "problems" (see Du Bois, 1989) or as "solutions" (Prashad, 2000). Racial discourses also construct norms that regulate students' participation in academic subjects. That is, specific statements circulate in schools, and these statements constrain students' choices, despite the fact that students are able to deploy power on their own behalf. As we will show, racialization in mathematics education is organized around particular discursive practices, such as statements about the supposed relationship between mathematics and race, like "Asians are good at math" (Shah, 2009, in press).

In education a distinct pattern bears out. Students of colour are represented as either lacking (as in cognition or family culture) or overabundant (as in uncontrolled energy or language use) (Gay, 2000). In the case of Black and Latin@ students, their family structure is considered blameworthy, or their choices are seen as not reflecting education as a priority (see Ladson-Billings, 2006; Valenzuela, 1999). Meanwhile, less attention is paid to the systematic and systemic racism that these students face (King, 2004).

With respect to controlling images of Blacks in educational contexts, in their study of 19 textbooks ranging from fifth, eighth, and eleventh grades, Brown and Brown (2010) found that social studies material underrepresented White violence toward Blacks by framing this type of violence as exceptional, rather than as a pervasive set of relations from everyday interactions to official laws, like slavery. Resonant with Fanon's (1963) theory of violence, Brown and Brown suggest that violence saturated the master–slave culture all the way down, including representations. Further, they argue that the persistence of problematic representations of Blacks perpetuates the violence against them: enslavement of another sort. Understanding this predicament means appreciating the power of representations to render people of colour intelligible as one-dimensional subjects. Often, they are positioned as objects rather than subjects. Likewise, sanitized representations of Whiteness by White textbook authors obscure their investment in White domination. In textbooks Whites are often portrayed as innocent purveyors of racial knowledge and beneficent leaders of the nation.

Interpellation and Creation of Racialized Subjects of Education

So far our explication of the power of discourse, specifically forms of representation found within the circuits of language, describes how previously *human* subjects are transformed into *racial* subjects. As such, the shift toward a racialized worldview has been one of the most radical events in the last several centuries, on par with the advent of other world changes like global capitalism (Mills, 1997). It represents the racialization of reality and the reality of racialization. In order for race discourse to permeate every aspect of social life, human beings must be interpellated as racial subjects (cf. Althusser, 1971). That is, racial hailing becomes a near irresistible process that rarely fails to record a response (Leonardo, 2005). By "response," we mean the ability of dominant forms of self-understanding to permeate subjective life, from daily self-identification with racial labels to common-sense understandings of social phenomena as racial in nature.

This process of racial subject making requires our participation at a fundamentally deep level, often unbeknownst to us. It is like answering to one's name when hailed on the street—taking one's name as a substitute for essence, as opposed to a representation of self. Ideological interpellation happens at the level of the unconscious (Althusser, 1971). This does not mean that racial subjects are completely unaware, but instead speaks to the racial remainder set aside and accepted as common sense.

To the extent that this racial induction is complete, it reaches a point where race has no "outside." For example, within a U.S. context, it would be stranger to be raceless than to be raced. To be raceless in a thoroughly racialized society is a failed or unintelligible identity. For as much as race is a source of injury for people of colour, it is also a fount of meaning that they rely on, a grounding that they depend on. From which kids attend school, to who we consider as partners for life: race is there, never irrelevant.

That race interpellation dominates U.S. social formation may be an overstatement in light of the existence of competing systems such as capitalism and patriarchy. But it goes without saying that class and gender relations are articulated with race (Collins, 2000; Crenshaw, 1991; hooks, 1984). Together, they create a super-system of subordination. Still, race is always in play, and at present there is no self-understanding without race in the U.S. context. The key to understanding the dynamics of race in education is to unpack social/linguistic practices for their capacity to expose or further obscure the process of racialization.

Vignette Analysis

In this section, we apply core ideas from poststructural theory to analyze two racialized interactions that took place in a high school mathematics classroom. Our purpose is to highlight the affordances of a poststructural approach, as well as to discuss some of its limitations. We begin by providing background information on the school and the mathematics classroom that comprised the research setting. Next, we present and analyze each classroom interaction. Finally, we discuss the larger theoretical issues that cut across both interactions.

Background

The data presented here were collected as part of a study on racial discourse in mathematics education conducted by the first author (see Shah, 2013). Classroom observations and student interviews were conducted at Eastwood High (pseudonym), a racially diverse high school located in Northern California. The racial demographics of the school at the time of the study were as follows: 8% Asian, 25% Black, 48% Latin@, 3% Polynesian, 14% White, and 2% Mixed or Other.

Both focal interactions occurred in a Precalculus class, which was considered an advanced course at Eastwood High. There were 27 students enrolled in the class, with the following racial demographics based on school records: five Asian students, four Black students, 11 Latin@ students, four Polynesian students, three White students, and two students identified as Mixed or Other. Relative to the school population, Asians and Polynesians in this class were slightly overrepresented, and Blacks were slightly underrepresented. Most students in the class were eleventh and twelfth graders, along with three tenth graders. Two of these tenth-grade students identified as Indian (South Asian), and the third student identified as half-Arab, half-Mexican. We provide these details because they are relevant to the forthcoming analysis.

The first classroom interaction centres on a series of events that unfolded while students were taking a Precalculus test. The second classroom interaction centres on a brief exchange between two students in the class that occurred during the first days of school. As we will show, neither interaction involved explicitly racial language. And yet, students perceived them to be racially significant. Our goal here is to understand why race became salient to participants, and how students were constituted as racial subjects in mathematics.

Vignette #1

Every month students in this Precalculus class took a unit test. For most students, these tests took nearly all of the hour-long class period to complete. As is typical in many U.S. mathematics classrooms, when students completed their tests they would stand up, walk to the front of the room, and hand the test to the teacher. The following sequence of events was documented midway through the school year in February, as students began to stand up and turn in their tests. The vignette focuses on Akshay, Vishal, and Sanjay: the three South Asian male students in the class.

> It is 8:45 am, and students have been working on today's unit test on logarithms for the past thirty minutes. Suddenly, Akshay gets up from his seat, walks to the front of the room, and hands his test to Ms. Patterson; he is the first student to turn in his test. Several students look up momentarily and then continue working. Five minutes later, Vishal stands up and turns in his test, followed a minute later by Sanjay. There are still twenty minutes to go before the bell rings. Another seven minutes pass until other students turn in their tests.
>
> (Field Notes, 2/25/11)

An interview had previously been scheduled for that day after school with Akshay, who was the first South Asian student to turn in his test. During that interview, Akshay noted that he had heard people say that Indians are good at math and technology, echoing the broader narrative in the U.S. context that "Asians are good at math." When asked for specific instances where he had seen these narratives come up in his classes, Akshay reported the following interaction:

> I just thought of something: three Indian dudes come up [to the front of the room to turn in their tests]. That was just my opinion, and I pointed it out and everyone was like, "Oh my god, they're Indian—they have to be geniuses in math!" And I was like, "Yeah, you're an idiot cause you were struggling [incomprehensible]." I find it to be that they were paying attention. Like I told my friend Rico [a Latin@ classmate], "Did you realize that the first three people in class that were done with the test were Indians?" He's like, "I know, huh?" And he's just babbling on about how Indians are smart, and I was like, "Whatever dude."

Analysis of Vignette #1

During this interaction, particular students and entire groups of people became positioned as racial subjects with varying levels of mathematical ability. To understand how this positioning occurred, consider the practices in which students were engaged. The practice of doing school mathematics in the U.S. context is associated with a particular set of meanings. Mathematics is typically viewed as the most difficult of all subjects; only the elite few are thought to possess the innate capacity to understand mathematics (Schoenfeld, 2002). Perhaps as a result, mathematical ability and intellectual capacity are believed to go hand in hand (Ernest, 1991). And because mathematical ability is viewed as innate, it tends not to be seen as something that can develop through concerted effort over time.

Another important point is that in many U.S. mathematics classrooms, students learn that speed is a signifier of mathematical ability. That is, the goal is not only to get problems right, but to get them right *as quickly as possible*. For many children, completing timed worksheets full of problems defines what it means to "do mathematics." This is relevant in the current vignette where students are taking a test. Testing is a practice in which speed and competence also tend to become conflated. Test days in school are already stressful times where students are being compared to their peers. In addition, students learn that how quickly they finish their test can affect how their competence is perceived by their peers.

Overall, then, before Akshay and his classmates even enter the classroom that morning, discourses of mathematics and schooling regulate the types of subject positions available to students. There are "fast kids" who will demonstrate their innate mathematical ability by finishing tests before their classmates, and there are "slow kids" who will prove their lack of ability by being the last to turn in their tests (cf. Horn, 2007). These discourses prefigure the learning environment, specifically in terms of how students can interpret what they observe independent of students' actual performance on the test. But this is only part of the story: Why does race emerge as significant to students in this interaction?

Mathematics classrooms in the U.S. are also situated within a racial discursive context that positions Asians as inherently superior in mathematics than other racial groups. This discourse regulates the possibilities for both Asians and non-Asians: Asian students will be *expected* to finish their tests before their non-Asian peers. However, there is no guarantee that these expectations will be fulfilled. Let us now consider the specifics of this classroom interaction to understand why it became racialized for Akshay and some of his classmates.

The interaction begins with Akshay standing up and walking to the front of the room to turn in his test, followed several minutes later by Vishal and Sanjay. Based on the earlier discussion of how discourses of mathematics, schooling, and race interact, we argue that these students' physical actions constituted a statement about mathematical competence and racial subjectivity. The data suggest that at least several classmates took notice of their actions and read them as statements about Indians being both good at mathematics and generally intelligent.

Several factors may have facilitated students' reading of this interaction. For one, the public aspect of this action is important, in that everyone can plainly see who finished the test and when they finished. Notably, they also can see who is *not* done with the test. Speed and race are made more visible and salient because of the public way in which this practice was configured in this particular classroom. Akshay's comment that "three Indian dudes come *up there*" (emphasis added) suggests that he too attended to the public aspect of their actions. Turning in tests became a legible statement that communicated lessons about race and mathematical ability. One can imagine other configurations of this practice (e.g., requiring all students to stay seated until the end of class and turn in their tests together on the way out) that might have decreased the likelihood of such a reading.

Another factor that affects how students read this interaction is time. Not only do Akshay, Vishal, and Sanjay all turn in their tests well before the bell rings, but there is also a relatively large time gap between when they and the rest of the class are finished. If this gap had been shorter, students may not have noticed. A related issue was the *number* of Asian students who turned in their tests. Students may not have racialized the interaction had Akshay been followed by two *non-Asian* students. The temporal clustering of multiple Asian students may have bolstered the salience of the "Asians are good at math" narrative for those watching the interaction.

Of course, it is unclear whether any of the three boys actually intended to position themselves as "good at math" by turning in their tests when they did. In fact, Akshay's recounting of his conversation with Rico after the test suggests that he was uncomfortable with the positioning. After he points out that, ". . . the first three people in class that were done with the test were Indians," Rico indicates that he recognized the same pattern ("I know, huh?") and then "babbles on about how Indians are smart." Other students responded in ways that suggest they were well aware of the racial–mathematical discourse about Indians ("Oh my god, they're Indian—they have to be geniuses in math"). Superficially these are compliments. And yet, Akshay rejects the interpellation ("Whatever dude"). Akshay's awareness of the racial–mathematical discourse about Indians suggests that he likely could have predicted the kinds of reactions he received—so then why did he bring it up with his classmates in the first place?

One way of interpreting this sequence of statements is that Akshay is not rejecting the fact that Indians are being positioned as good at mathematics, but that instead he is rejecting the *reason* that his classmates believe Indians are good at mathematics. This can be inferred from Akshay's response: "I find it to be that they were paying attention." The word "they" in his response refers to Vishal and Sanjay, who Akshay argues succeed because they pay attention in class and work hard. Being a hard worker was central to how Akshay viewed himself. In fact, throughout the interview he praised Indian immigrants in general for having a strong work ethic.

Thus, it could be that his classmates' "compliments" bothered him because they threatened how he positioned himself as a mathematics learner. Whereas Akshay understood his own success—as well as the success of his racial group—in mathematics as a product of sustained effort, his classmates positioned that success as a function of a racialized innate ability. This is a problem for Akshay: if he is seen as someone who was simply born with an innate talent for mathematics, then the considerable effort he puts in is unnecessary and irrelevant. It is also noteworthy that in rejecting the interpellation, Akshay attempts to subvert the dominant discourse of mathematics itself as requiring innate ability. Overall, then, both Akshay and his classmates are invoking discourses of mathematical ability, albeit conflicting ones. And ultimately, the students are (re-)learning racialized discourses of mathematics education: which racial groups are "good" at mathematics and which are not.

Vignette #2

James was a twelfth-grade student who identified as African American. He described himself as someone who had always excelled in mathematics. He spoke with pride about "knowing how to add when I was like three or four or five years old," and winning math tournaments in elementary school. In middle school he was one of only four students in his eighth-grade algebra class recommended by his teacher to be placed in geometry as a ninth grader, which meant that he was on the "advanced track" at Eastwood High. Although James failed ninth-grade geometry, he attributed his struggles to "being a freshman and not taking things seriously," as opposed to a lack of mathematical ability. Eventually, James persevered and reached Precalculus in twelfth grade.

In most U.S. high schools, Precalculus is considered an advanced mathematics course. Enrolling in Precalculus positions a high school student as having a high level of mathematical competence. In the following transcript, James recounts how classmates treated him during the first week of Precalculus class. James made these comments while reflecting on how his mathematics learning experiences would have been different had he been Asian instead of African American:

> I probably would have had a different first impression when I walked in that class, I know that. When I walked into the Precalculus class this year, like the first couple days or whatever, I was getting questions like, "Oh *you're* in this class? For real?" I think it was Troi [a Samoan friend and classmate] and like somebody else . . . I don't remember. I showed them my schedule like before we even had that class, but they were like, "*You're* in this class?" And I would say, "Yeah . . . yes I am." I mean I wouldn't really trip. I kind of looked it off like I don't even care.

Analysis of Vignette #2

Even before James's encounter with Troi and his other classmates, there is a tension between James and the Precalculus classroom itself. On the one hand, the very act of entering that elite mathematical space with a dark-skinned body constitutes a mathematical statement about who James is and what he is capable of from a mathematical standpoint. James positions himself as an African American student that belongs in an advanced mathematics class. On the other hand, the Precalculus classroom regulates the kinds of subject positions available to mathematics learners of different racial backgrounds. Metaphorically speaking, the classroom makes a racial statement about the types of people that belong in it and those that do not, and James is interpellated as someone who does not belong.

It is the tension between these racial–mathematical statements that fuels Troi's surprise when he sees James walk into the room. James is not expected to be there, so his presence violates what is considered "normal" in that context. Troi's questions ("Oh *you're* in this class? For real?") indicate that James has violated the norms of the space. From James's perspective, Troi positions him as someone who lacks mathematical ability and is incapable of handling challenging work—subject positions that conflict with how James has understood himself since he was a young boy. And Troi was not alone: James reports that he received questions of this kind from multiple students during the "first couple days or whatever."

The key word in these questions—and the one that James emphasizes with his tone—is the word "you're." There is nothing explicitly racial about this word, and it is not clear that Troi intended to make a racially disparaging remark. And yet, in that moment (and in the six months that followed it), James interpreted this word as having racial undertones. He understands the "you" as not only a hail directed at himself, but also one that is directed at all African Americans. This interpretation is made possible by James's awareness of the dominant discourse about African Americans, which incorrectly positions them as intellectually and mathematically inferior. In other situations where the discourses of race, schooling, and mathematics do not intersect so neatly, James may not have interpreted the word "you" as being racially loaded.

In response to this positioning, James is defiant. He unequivocally states that he *does* belong in Precalculus ("Yeah . . . yes, I am"), thereby rejecting his classmates' interpellation. In fact, he attempted to preempt his classmates' racial surprise by showing them his class schedule in advance, but this makes little difference. In the end, his classmates impose the racial discourse upon him, and James is left to "look it off like I don't even care." For students of certain racial backgrounds, the first day of school is a generally exciting time that involves finding out if your friends are in your classes and getting a feel for the new school year. For James, though, there is an added dimension of anxiety and tension, as he is compelled to justify his very existence in certain academic spaces. This interaction becomes a perverse opportunity to re-learn his position on the racial–mathematical order.

Cross-Cutting Theoretical Issues

In both cases, we argue that race became salient because of the discourses that prefigured the learning environment. These discourses—of schooling, mathematics, and race—converged in ways that made it possible for students to read their classmates' language and participation in social practices as racialized. In other words, the learning environment was ripe for students' racial readings. And in general, because of how they interact, the discourses regulate the types of subject positions available to mathematics learners of different racial backgrounds, thereby affecting expectations of their mathematical and academic potential.

Akshay and James are both read through racial–mathematical discourse. Akshay is *expected* to be among the first to turn in his test because Indians more broadly are expected to be among the first to turn in their tests. James is not expected to enrol in Precalculus because African Americans more broadly are not expected to enrol in Precalculus.

That is not to say that individual tendencies and histories are irrelevant. The Precalculus test was in February of that school year, and by then Akshay's classmates were well aware that Vishal, Sanjay, and Akshay were higher performing students in the class. And although the interaction between James and Troi occurred during the first week of school, both students were twelfth graders and had known each other for several years. Troi knew that James had a reputation for spotty attendance and unreliable homework completion. His challenge to James's enrolment in Precalculus could have been more related to his knowledge of James's uneven academic history. In sum, certain local discourses had formed about James and Akshay based on their individual histories, which also informed how their classmates positioned them.

And yet, the broader racial discourses about students' racial groups hold considerable weight. One way to think about this is to consider alternate scenarios that violate regulated expectations. As we discussed earlier, discourses of schooling and of mathematics suggest that completing a test quickly often signifies mathematical competence. However, imagine that rather than Akshay, *James* (or another Black student) had been first to turn in his test: Would classmates have interpreted this as a sign of competence, or would they have assumed that James did not know any of the answers and turned in his test quickly because he was apathetic and had given up? In a sense, interpreting that behaviour as signifying *in*competence is equivalent to Troi's racial surprise at James's enrolment in Precalculus. Alternatively, imagine a scenario where an Asian student had been *last* to turn in a test: Would this be understood as a sign of incompetence, or would classmates assume that this Asian student was being especially careful and took longer to complete the test because they were double-checking their work? The latter interpretation amounts to a benefit granted to Asians based on how they are perceived as racialized subjects in mathematics.

We argue that with all things being equal, the preexisting racial discourses influence students' initial interpretations of classroom activity. People are predisposed to perceive Asians in mathematics as performing competence and Blacks in mathematics as performing incompetence. However, if students from both groups behaved in ways that violated those expectations, those behaviours would tend to be re-interpreted in ways that re-synchronized with the existing discourses. In that sense, students' subjectivities are both predetermined and emergent, as course corrections are made to re-interpret social activity that may conflict with the dominant discourses. In the end, Asians will be read as Asians and

Blacks will be read as Blacks, barring recurring performances by students from those groups that can shift the discourses that interpellate them (cf. Butler, 1990). Students can and do exert agency in navigating these discourses, but the inertia the discourses exert is considerable.

Conclusion

Learning environments are not neutral spaces. As poststructural theory reveals, learning environments are sites where power is exercised through the deployment and reproduction of discourses. This chapter has sought to illuminate the processes through which students learn discourses of race and discourses of mathematics, and the processes through which those discourses can become intertwined. That is, students learn (and re-learn) what race means and how race operates, while simultaneously learning (and re-learning) what it means to do mathematics and who is perceived to have the capacity to succeed in mathematics. So *what*, exactly, is being learned? We suggest that alongside their learning of subject area content, students also learn the discourses that position them as learners. In our view, research on learning should attend to both types of learning, thereby accounting for the discursive context within which learning happens.

PRT demystifies that which over time becomes natural and normal, such as false racial narratives about differences in mathematical ability between racial groups. In doing so, PRT exposes the stratifying consequences of these narratives, as they position entire groups of students and circumscribe the kinds of academic identities to which they have access. Overall, students learn that the discourses that circulate in society and in classrooms offer them racialized subject positions that come with regulations. In that sense, poststructural theory proves useful in conceptualizing the macro-contexts of the learning process, as well as the power relations that organize it at the micro-level of everyday social interaction.

Note

1. In this chapter we recognize—but do not have the space to distinguish among—the varieties of post-theories, such as postmodernism, postcolonialism, post-pragmatism, post-foundationalism, and so on. Although they arguably emerge out of different reactions to established intellectual traditions like Enlightenment thought, post-theories share a family resemblance in their deep interrogations of generally accepted ways of explaining social and cultural phenomena. Here we use "poststructuralism" as a shorthand for this shared concern among post-theories about the limitations of what Lyotard (1984) once called "meta-narratives," or self-referential frameworks that do not appeal to explanations outside their own systems, like science. For an overview of the history behind post-theories, the shift from studies of ideology to discourse, and the linguistic turn, see Leonardo (2010).

References

Althusser, L. (1971). *Lenin and philosophy* (B. Brewster, Trans.). New York, NY: Monthly Review Press.

Baudrillard, J. (1994). *Simulacra and simulations.* Ann Arbor, MI: University of Michigan Press.

Bonilla-Silva, E. (2005). "Racism" and "new racism": The contours of racial dynamics in contemporary America. In Z. Leonardo (Ed.), *Critical pedagogy and race* (pp. 1–36). Malden, MA: Blackwell.

Brown, A., & Brown, K. (2010). Strange fruit indeed: Interrogating contemporary textbook representations of racial violence toward African Americans. *Teachers College Record, 113*(9), 2047–2079.

Butler, J. (1990). *Gender trouble: Feminism and the subversion of identity.* New York, NY; London, UK: Routledge.

Collins, P. H. (2000). *Black feminist thought: Knowledge, consciousness, and the politics of empowerment* (2nd edn.). New York, NY: Routledge. First published in 1991.

Collins, P. H. (2004). *Black sexual politics: African Americans, gender, and the new racism.* New York, NY: Routledge.

Crenshaw, K. (1991). Mapping the margins: Intersectionality, identity politics, and violence against women of color. *Stanford Law Review, 43*(6), 1241–1299.

Davies, B., & Harré, R. (1990). Positioning: The discursive production of selves. *Journal for the Theory of Social Behavior, 20*(1), 43–63.

Derrida, J. (1985). Racism's last word. *Critical Inquiry, 12*(1), 290–299.

Du Bois, W. E. B. (1989). *The souls of black folk.* New York, NY: Penguin Books. Original work published in 1903.

Dyer, R. (1997). *White.* London: Routledge.

Engeström, Y., Miettinen, R., & Punamäki, R. (1999). *Perspectives on activity theory.* Cambridge, UK: Cambridge University Press.

Ernest, P. (1991). *The philosophy of mathematics education.* London, UK: The Falmer Press.

Esmonde, I., & Langer-Osuna, J. M. (2013). Power in numbers: Student participation in mathematical discussions in heterogeneous spaces. *Journal for Research in Mathematics Education, 44*(1), 288–315.

Fanon, F. (1963). *The wretched of the earth.* (C. Farrington, Trans.). New York, NY: Grove Press.

Ferguson, A. A. (2001). *Bad boys: Public schools in the making of black masculinity.* Ann Arbor, MI: University of Michigan Press.

Foucault, M. (1980). Truth and power. In C. Gordon (Ed.), *Power/knowledge: Selected interviews & other writings 1972–1977 by Michel Foucault* (pp. 109–133). New York, NY: Pantheon Books.

Gay, G. (2000). *Culturally responsive teaching: Theory, research, and practice.* New York, NY: Teachers College Press.

Gee, J. P. (2011). *An introduction to discourse analysis: Theory and method* (3rd edn.). New York, NY: Routledge.

Goldberg, D. T. (1990). The social formation of racist discourse. In D. T. Goldberg (Ed.), *Anatomy of racism* (pp. 295–318). Minneapolis, MN: University of Minnesota Press.

Hacking, I. (1995). The looping effect of human kinds. In D. Sperber, D. Premack & A. J. Premack (Eds.), *Causal cognition: A multidisciplinary approach* (pp. 351–394). Oxford, UK: Oxford University Press.

Hall, S. (1996). What is this "black" in black popular culture? In D. Morley & K. Chen (Eds.), *Stuart Hall* (pp. 465–475). London, UK: Routledge.

hooks, b. (1984). *Feminist theory: From margin to center.* Boston, MA: South End Press.

Horn, I. S. (2007). Fast kids, slow kids, lazy kids: Framing the mismatch problem in mathematics teachers' conversations. *Journal of the Learning Sciences, 16*(1), 37–79.

Julien, I., & Mercer, K. (1996). De margin and de centre. In S. Hall (Ed.), *Representation: Cultural representations and signifying practices* (pp. 450–464). Thousand Oaks, CA: SAGE.

King, J. (2004). Dysconscious racism: Ideology, identity, and the miseducation of teachers. In G. Ladson-Billings & D. Gillborn (Eds.), *The RoutledgeFalmer reader in multicultural education* (pp. 71–83). New York, NY: RoutledgeFalmer.

Ladson-Billings, G. (2006). From the achievement gap to the education debt: Understanding achievement in U.S. schools. *Educational Researcher, 35*(7), 3–12.

Lather, P. (1992). Critical frames in educational research: Feminist and post-structural perspectives. *Theory into Practice, 31*(2), 87–99.

Lave, J., & Wenger, E. (1991). *Situated learning: Legitimate peripheral participation.* Cambridge, UK: Cambridge University Press.

Leonardo, Z. (2005). Through the multicultural glass: Althusser, ideology and race relations in post-civil rights America. *Policy Futures in Education, 3*(4), 400–412.

Leonardo, Z. (2010). Affirming ambivalence: Introduction to cultural politics and education. In Z. Leonardo (Ed.), *Handbook of cultural politics and education* (pp. 1–45). Rotterdam, The Netherlands: SensePublishers.

Leonardo, Z. (2013). The story of schooling: Critical race theory and the educational racial contract. *Discourse: Studies in the Cultural Politics of Education, 16*(4), 470–488.

Leonardo, Z. (2015). Contracting race: Writing, racism, and education. *Critical Studies in Education, 56*(1), 86–98.

Leonardo, Z., & Broderick, A. (2011). Smartness as property: A critical exploration of intersections between whiteness and disability studies. *Teachers College Record, 113*(10), 2206–2232.

Lewis, C., & Moje, E. B. (2003). Sociocultural perspectives meet critical theories. *International Journal of Learning, 10*, 1979–1995.

Lyotard, J. (1984). *The postmodern condition* (G. Bennington & B. Massumi, Trans.). Minneapolis, MN: University of Minnesota Press.

Mendick, H., Moreau, M., & Epstein, D. (2009). Special cases: Neoliberalism, choice, and mathematics. In L. Black, H. Mendick & Y. Solomon (Eds.), *Mathematical relationships in education: Identities and participation* (pp. 71–82). New York, NY: Routledge.

Mills, C. W. (1997). *The racial contract.* Ithaca, NY: Cornell University Press.

Nasir, N. S., & Hand, V. (2008). From the court to the classroom: Opportunities for engagement, learning, and identity in basketball and classroom mathematics. *Journal of the Learning Sciences, 17*(2), 143–179.

Nicholson, L. (1987). Feminism and Marx: Integrating kinship with the economic. In S. Benhabib & D. Cornell (Eds.), *Feminism as critique* (pp. 16–30). Minneapolis, MN: University of Minnesota Press.

Omi, M., & Winant, H. (2015). *Racial formation in the United States: From the 1960s to the 1990s* (3rd edn.). New York, NY: Routledge.

Pang, V. O., Han, P. P., & Pang, J. M. (2011). Asian American and Pacific Islander students: Equity and the achievement gap. *Educational Researcher, 40*(8), 378–389.

Prashad, V. (2000). *The karma of brown folk.* Minneapolis, MN: University of Minnesota Press.

Schoenfeld, A. H. (2002). Making mathematics work for all children: Issues of standards, testing, and equity. *Educational Researcher, 31*(1), 13–25.

Shah, N. (2009). A student's causal explanations of the racial achievement gap in mathematics education. In S. Swars, D. Stinson & S. Lemons-Smith (Eds.), *31st annual meeting of the North America chapter of the International Group for the Psychology of Mathematics Education* (Vol. 5, pp. 444–452). Atlanta, GA: Georgia State University.

Shah, N. (2013). *Racial discourse in mathematics and its impact on student learning, identity, and participation* (Unpublished doctoral dissertation). University of California, Berkeley, Berkeley, CA.

Shah, N. (2015, April). *The problem with a compliment: Asians as mathematical and racial subjects.* Paper presented at the American Educational Research Association, Chicago, IL.

Shah, N. (in press). Race, ideology, and academic ability: A relational analysis of racial narratives in mathematics. *Teachers College Record.*

Sue, S., & Okazaki, S. (1990). Asian-American educational achievements: A phenomenon in search of an explanation. *American Psychologist, 45*(8), 913–920.

Valenzuela, A. (1999). *Subtractive schooling: U.S.-Mexican youth and the politics of caring.* Albany, NY: State University of New York Press.

Vygotsky, L. S. (1986). *Thought and language* (A. Kozulin, Trans.). Cambridge, MA: MIT Press.

Wenger, E. (1998). *Communities of practice: Learning, meaning, and identity.* New York, NY: Cambridge University Press.

Wodak, R., & Meyer, M. (Eds.). (2009). *Methods of critical discourse analysis* (2nd edn.). London, UK: SAGE Publications.

Wortham, S. (2006). *Learning identity: The joint emergence of social identification and academic learning.* New York, NY: Cambridge University Press.

5

ON THE COMPLEMENTARITY OF CULTURAL HISTORICAL PSYCHOLOGY AND CONTEMPORARY DISABILITY STUDIES

Peter Smagorinsky, Michael Cole, and Lúcia Willadino Braga

In this chapter we juxtapose two perspectives on the study of human "disability." We place this term in quotation marks because the notion that human difference constitutes a disablement of human functioning is a social construction, not a biological necessity. In other words, biological differences don't necessarily reduce one's ability to navigate the physical and social worlds; only biological differences that are socially framed as disabilities do so.[1] Both perspectives that we feature in this chapter contest the very idea that there is a "normate," or idealized human form (Garland-Thomson, 1997).

We begin by describing an approach to cultivating the potential of people with anomalous makeups that traces its origins to L.S. Vygotsky (1929, 1934/1987, 1993), a Belarusian Soviet psychologist whose major work was carried out between 1924 and 1934, when he died at 38 years of age. We refer to this approach as cultural-historical activity theory (CHAT) (Cole, 1996). Next we compare and contrast Vygotsky's approach with recent scholarship in the contemporary fields of disability studies (DS) and critical disability studies (CDS), which have come to prominence in Western and Northern Europe, the United States, and elsewhere in the late 20th century (Goodley, 2011). For our present purposes, given that DS and CDS have considerable overlap, we combine them into a single field as DS/CDS.

Our goal in making this comparison is to better understand what different groups of scholars can contribute to providing a more humane and supportive environment for those to whom terms such as "disabled" are widely applied. Consequently, we consider both their areas of complementarity and difference. At the risk of oversimplifying, we find that DS/CDS, as a "critical" perspective focused on unpacking the power apparatus that supports hegemonic social structures, has largely emerged from the humanities and is oriented to textuality, including spoken and written constructions of "disability." Although some versions of DS/CDS are concerned with material environments, that focus is more the concern of CHAT. As a discipline grounded in the social sciences, it has a greater interest in how to investigate and understand the empirical world through studies of, and interventions in, the material world.

Vygotsky's Cultural Historical Theory

Core ideas about bodily atypicality were central to the field of cultural-historical psychology as it took shape in the early decades of the 20th century. In Vygotsky's first publication in English (1929), the second of a set of three articles presented as a series about "the cultural development of the child",[2] the opening sentences succinctly summarize key elements of the theory he and his colleagues went on to develop:

> In the process of development the child not only masters the items of cultural experience but the habits and forms of cultural behavior, the cultural methods of reasoning. We must, therefore, distinguish the main lines in the development of the child's behavior. First, there is the line of natural development of behavior which is closely bound up with the processes of general organic growth and the maturation of the child. Second, there is the line of cultural improvement of the psychological functions, the working out of new methods of reasoning, the mastering of the cultural methods of behavior.
>
> (p. 415)

"Cultural methods of behavior" were the focus of Alexander Luria's lead article in the series (Luria, 1928, p. 493). This idea rests on the assumption that human ontogeny is the emergent outcome of the interweaving of two genetic domains or scales of time. The first is phylogenesis, the natural and evolutionary history of the human species from its earliest forms preceding homo sapiens, while the second is cultural history, which dates from the appearance of homo sapiens and refers to the manner in which people mediate their collective activities as a society.

According to this view, the inclusion of tools and signs as constituents of human action in the course of human cultural history gives rise to an entirely new morphology of behaviour. Luria (1928) described it as follows: "instead of applying directly its natural function to the solution of a specific task, the child puts between that function and the task a certain auxiliary means . . . by the medium of which the child manages to perform the act" (p. 495). In somewhat different terms, in addition to acting *directly* on the object of their activity, human beings are able to act *indirectly*, by mediating their actions through tools and signs. Any cultural method of behaviour involves the coordination or merging of the two streams of history.

Working from these assumptions, Vygotsky (1929) and his colleagues argued that in the course of typical development,

> the two lines of psychological development (the natural and the cultural) merge into each other in such a way that it is difficult to distinguish them and follow the course of each of them separately. [However], in the case of sudden retardation of any one of these two lines, they become more or less obviously disconnected . . .
>
> *(p. 417)*

Two key ideas are contained in this paragraph. First, the two lines of development, the biological and the cultural, merge into each other, making it difficult to follow their development separately. Second, developmental processes can be seen especially clearly when there is a sudden disruption of either line. Disruption can upset the ordinary, integrated, merged processes of development by forcing a change in the relationship between the biological and cultural lines. For the purposes of this chapter, we consider anomalies rather than the typical rate of development. If some people do not grow according to the schedule detailed in stage theories of psychological development, or grow atypically in relation to the cultural organization of society, what is at work, and what are the consequences of those physical, cognitive, or neurological aspects of a person's makeup that produce a different developmental trajectory?

Vygotsky's Approach to the Anomalous Human

Vygotsky regarded nonconformities from typical developmental pathways as a means to understanding processes of development in general. Lengthy warfare had produced the Soviet Union in 1922, two years before he began his career in Moscow. His work in defectology (Vygotsky, 1993) was specifically oriented to providing education for the many young people who were maimed, dismembered, blinded, deafened, cognitively impaired, or otherwise affected by the starvation and violent impacts of the war. These conditions are known in Vygotsky's parlance as "primary disabilities": the specific condition that causes one to be viewed as different and often deficient. This central role of "disability" in Vygotsky's scientific program has gone relatively unnoticed, even as Vygotskian ideas became prominent in many areas of developmental psychology, including special education (Gindis, 1995; Kozulin & Gindis, 2007; Smagorinsky, 2012a, 2012b, 2016).

A number of factors help to explain the relative neglect of Vygotsky's view of anomalous children, and by extension those who grow through their teens into adulthood. As recounted by McCagg (1989), Russian academic ideas about anomalous children were heavily influenced by European, especially German, ideas at the time that the first special research and training centres were opened in the decades preceding and following the Russian Revolution of 1917. Authoritative texts of the time used the term "defective" to refer to what would now be called "special needs" children.

Although this period also corresponds to the rise of eugenics in Germany and elsewhere (including, briefly, the Soviet Union; see Graham, 1977), Vygotsky and others in the nascent Soviet Union challenged debilitating views of the physically different. They argued that if physical difference poses a problem, it is a social rather than an individual problem. In opposition to eugenics, Vygotsky's goal with the Russian concept of *defectologia*, translated as *defectology*, was to create more humane settings to help cultivate the development of atypical people, at a time when they were widely considered either to be of no social value, or more extremely, detriments to the greater good.

The Latin origins of *defectologia* invoke strong negative connotations of failure, shortcoming, and other terms associated with human deficiency. Consequently, as McCagg (1989) comments, "this term would not survive 3 minutes in a discussion of the handicapped in the Western world today because it carries too much negative connotation toward the disabled" (p. 40). With McCagg's comment now long past and with the since-launched field of DS/CDS advocating for more humane constructions of the physically different, McCagg's "3 minutes" strikes the 21st-century ear as roughly three too many.

Whatever the causes for the marginalization of Vygotsky's work under the label of defectology, such marginalization is based upon a fundamental misunderstanding (Gindis, 2003; Knox & Stevens, 1993). Vygotsky (1993) explicitly contrasts his views with those of the "old defectology," which he characterized as "Viewing a handicapped condition as a purely quantitative developmental limitation. . . . Reaction against this quantitative approach to all theoretical and practical problems is the most important characteristic of modern defectology" (p. 30). He advocated his own approach in succinct terms:

> The thesis holds that a child whose development is impeded by a defect is not simply a child less developed than his peers but is a child who has developed differently. . . . A child in each stage of his development, in each of his phases, represents a qualitative uniqueness, i.e., a specific organic and psychological structure; in precisely the same way, a handicapped child represents a qualitatively different, unique type of development. . . . Only with this idea of qualitative uniqueness (rather than the overworked quantitative variations of separate elements) in the phenomena and processes under examination, does defectology acquire for the first time, a methodological basis.
>
> (p. 154)

Vygotsky (1993) was adamantly opposed to the misguided view, predominant in both his day and ours, that "children develop 'along biological tracks' [so that] we may dismiss the laws determining the social development and formation of a normal mind. This mechanistic notion is unfounded methodologically speaking" (p. 124). Rather, he argued, the appropriate approach is to consider "the alliance of social and biological regularities in child development" (p. 124) in a dialectical fashion.

As we have noted, Vygotsky (1993) regarded the biological difference—in defectology, blindness, deafness, and brain damage—as a person's *primary disability*. The primary disability served as the sole focus of attention for established diagnosticians of Vygotsky's day, a problem that continues today. As we will detail in the next section, a primary disability is a problem to the extent that people in the environment treat the person as inferior for having these points of difference. When this belief in the inferiority of those who are bodily or cognitively different[3] is appropriated by atypical people themselves, they develop the far more damaging *secondary disability* of feelings of low self-esteem. The "problem" of disability, thus, is to Vygotsky *a social problem* that requires a re-education of the general population so that they provide avenues for wholehearted participation in cultural practices through which people of difference develop feelings of value.

Vygotsky (1993) believed that it was misguided to focus on a person's primary disability. Rather, he sought to assimilate people considered "disabled" into mainstream society by using alternative means of mediation and modes of activity to achieve cultural ends, such as the use of a cane to assist the unsighted. Vygotsky's approach to the anomalous human makeup was thus positive, optimistic, and future-oriented; "no theory," he maintained, "is possible if it proceeds from exclusively negative premises" (1993, p. 31).

The Effects of Feelings of Inadequacy

Vygotsky argued that feelings of inadequacy have two very different consequences for those whose makeup includes physical or cognitive disability. First, he asserted that the feelings of inadequacy could serve to motivate positive new ways of engaging with society. Drawing on the work of Adler (1912, 1927), Vygotsky (1993) argued that "*Via subjective feelings of inadequacy, a physical handicap dialectically transforms itself into psychological drives toward compensation*" (p. 33; emphasis in original). Compensation involves a generative response to difference, one that "represents a continually evolving adaptive process. If a blind or deaf child achieves the same level of development as a normal child, then the child with a defect achieves this *in another way, by another course, by other means*" (p. 34; emphasis in original). In this sense, a person "with a defect," as expressed through defectology's terms (at least in translation), makes adaptations through indirect, mediated means that allow for participation in social and cultural practices.

Deviation from the evolutionary norm, which Vygotsky referred to as "dys-ontogenesis," needs to be valued for its potential to motivate a personally initiated productive adaptive response, to produce a new order through cultural channels: "Cultural development is the main area for compensation of deficiency when further organic development is impossible; in this respect, the path of cultural development is unlimited" (Vygotsky, 1993, p. 169). Vygotsky's statement is true for all people, whether or not they are designated as disabled, which should not be surprising given the ways in which his work in defectology was foundational to his general approach to human development. Cultural development allows human beings to go beyond our physical capacities.

Vygotsky thus sees the necessity of mutual adaptations: one by society in providing environments that promote development toward cultural ends indirectly, via the creation of new mediational means; the other by individuals who hope to navigate their surroundings with greater fluency. A feeling of inadequacy can thus have a beneficial effect when learners are treated as productive people adapting to their environments. Within alternative developmental pathways provided by a supportive setting, "the most important and decisive condition of cultural development—precisely the ability to use psychological tools—is preserved in such children" (Vygotsky, 1993, p. 47). In contrast, the field of psychology in general took the view that people of anomalous makeup should be pitied or treated with charity. Vygotsky argued that both approaches contributed to the feelings of deficiency that comprise the secondary disability.

A reciprocal process of adaptation must be undertaken *by the people surrounding the anomalous child*, who accept these alternative mediational means nonjudgmentally and respectfully. Vygotsky (1993) argued that when a primary disability results in treatment of people as inferior, the people affected become subject to the secondary disability. To Vygotsky, in addition to adaptations undertaken by those classified as disabled, those surrounding them have an adaptive responsibility to construct alternative pathways that allow for one's positive sense of self to be affirmed. Vygotsky's approach was thus oriented to *assets* rather than *deficits*. Among his favourite examples, for instance, was his contemporary Helen Keller. Vygotsky pointed to Keller's development of ways of navigating her environment while deaf and blind, through the sensitive attention of Anne Sullivan, as illustrative of the potential of his approach.

Through the creation of future-oriented, affirmational mediational settings, alternative pathways of development are cultivated for anomalous people such that their points of difference are not foregrounded in people's construction of their potential. By asserting that problems of human difference are social rather than individual, Vygotsky (1993) shifted the terms of the debate *from re-mediation of the deficit to education of the surrounding community*.

This attention to *settings* was a critical dimension of Vygotsky's (1993) concern for children lacking normative means of engaging with the world, diverting attention from the individual and toward the social consequences of differential treatment. This context-centred approach maps neatly onto his broader interest in the necessary integration of all aspects of human development with one's affective engagement with the world (Vygotsky, 1971, 1994, 1999a, 1999b). "Full social esteem," he insisted, "is the ultimate aim of education inasmuch as all the processes of overcompensation are directed at achieving social status" (1993, p. 57).

What matters in this conception is that, through participation in activity with appropriate mediational means, children have the potential to develop higher mental functions, even in the absence of a phylogenetically typical capacity of the normate, e.g., seeing or hearing. For those who do choose to compensate for a "disability" by learning new mediational means, their unconventional ways of integrating themselves into society could lead to insights not available to those whose makeup does not require such adaptation. In Vygotsky's (1993) conception, those who develop such capabilities are encouraged and nurtured as valued productive members of society by fellow citizens whose own willingness to shift their understanding of difference helps to construct and support those alternative means of participation. His defectological work did not attend to the consequences for those who remain outside society's embrace, an indication of his belief in communism's unlimited potential for reforming whole cultures according to Marxist principles (Smagorinsky, 2012a).

Examples of Vygotskian-Inspired Work with Anomalous People

We next illustrate Vygotskian approaches to people considered disabled with examples from the Soviet Union and Brazil.

Education of Blind and Deaf[4] People in the Soviet Union

From early in his career, Vygotsky exhibited a special interest in the development of blind, deaf, and mute children. This interest was pursued through his acquaintanceship with I. A. Sokolyansky, an early Soviet pioneer in the education of blind and deaf people. Consistent with Vygotsky's views on anomalous children, Sokolyansky argued that

> The deaf-blind child possesses a normal brain and the potential for normal mental development. However, while possessing that potential he can never achieve even the most insignificant degree of mental development relying on his own efforts. Without special instruction such a child remains a complete mental cripple for the whole of his life.
>
> *(Sokolyansky, quoted in Meshcheryakov, 1974, p. 29)*

Sokolyansky's perspective came together with that of Vygotsky in the 1950s, well after Vygotsky's death from tuberculosis in 1934. In 1955, Sokolyansky and his student, Alexander Meshcheryakov, opened a special school for deaf and blind children in the cathedral town of Zagorsk, with the support of Vygotsky's surviving colleagues in the Soviet Academy of Pedagogical Sciences. In 1963 a residential home for deaf and blind children was opened in association with the school.

The cultural-historical psychologists who supported the Zagorsk program argued that the predicament of blind and deaf people was as important to modern science as it was a statement of humanitarian principles, providing an opportunity to set moral benchmarks for the state of a society. Alexander Zaporozhets (1974), a colleague of Meshcheryakov, described the special scientific importance of studies of the development of people who are blind and deaf in these terms:

> . . . blind-deafness represents a truly unique phenomenon of nature providing unparalleled opportunities for the study of the conditions necessary for the formation of human personality and the patterns to be found in that formative process. All the processes which occur at breakneck speed in the course of a normal child's development, intricately interwoven one with another and shaped by a whole host of spontaneous influences that are most difficult to assess, are easy to distinguish in the deafblind child since they unfold slowly; and what is particularly important, do not arise naturally, but are engendered with the help of special teaching methods that can easily be ascertained. It is this factor which provides unique conditions for experimental research into the dialectics of human mental development.
>
> (p. 6)

By "special teaching methods," Zaporozhets referred to those that address the biological point of difference in children considered disabled. These methods would be distinct from those employed with the general population; assigning a blind child to read a book would not be appropriate, as it would for the broader group of students. These students without disability classifications would require their own specific means of instruction, yet the two methods would depart in significant ways.

Meshcheryakov noted that when they encounter children who are blind and deaf, the first impulse of many psychologists is to focus on development of their linguistic skills, on the premise that language is the central medium through which intellectual functions can be awakened. This idea has been propagated through famous cases, such as that of Helen Keller's well-publicized "breakthrough" when she understood that the experience of water, and the sign being communicated into her hand by her teacher, were connected such that the pattern of movement "re-presented" water. This breakthrough opened up the possibility of tactile communication for Keller and other blind and deaf individuals.

Meshcheryakov (1974) explicitly rejects this emphasis on linguistic skills. While acknowledging that language acquisition is crucial to the development of blind and deaf children, he argues that "fostering speech skills in such children is not and indeed cannot be tackled as the first objective in nurturing of a human mind" (p. 84). Instead, basing his perspective on the tenets of cultural-historical psychology, he argues that the inclusion of the children in socially organized, culturally mediated, joint activity is the essential precondition for their development:

> The essence of interaction with things and people consists in the fact that in both cases this is interaction with a human factor. Expressing this idea in somewhat paradoxical terms we may say that the individual's relationships with other people are realized through things and his relationship to things through his relationship to other people.
>
> *(p. 86)*

Meshcheryakov began with the very careful creation of predictable, fundamental forms of human activity, such as those occurring in routine cultural practices involving feeding and self-care. This process was accomplished, in so far as possible, by having the caretakers insert themselves into the child's spontaneous activities to help them incorporate everyday objects into their interactions. Language learning began as an intrinsic part of actions. The details of this process are impossible to summarize in this format, but suffice it to say that its end product is a person who can read and write in dactylic or "tactile" Russian.

Meshcheryakov's process can result in a wide range of possibilities for full participation in society. This goal of constructing settings, including the intentional acceptance of those considered disabled, through which people may participate in cultural practice, is in accord with Vygotsky's (1993) goals in accommodating people of anomalous makeup. From this perspective, pedagogy and situated practice affirm inclusive civic participation, rather than relying on law or state mandates for inclusion (e.g., the laws that helped to create the field of special education in the U.S., i.e., the Education for All Handicapped Children Act in 1975, which has since been surpassed by the Individuals with Disabilities Education Act (IDEA) of 1990 and the Individuals with Disabilities Educational Improvement Act (IDEIA) of 2004 [see Wright, 2004]).

A Design Experiment in Brazil: The MetaCognitive Dimension

In the late 1990s, through a chance meeting at a memorial conference for Alexander R. Luria, co-authors Braga and Cole decided to collaborate on a project that involved Braga's work with pre-adolescent children who had experienced acquired brain injury (ABI) with Cole's development of The 5th Dimension Program (5thD), a playworld model system that was initially designed for implementation among diverse pre-adolescents of both sexes, with respect to a range of ages, ethnicities, and social classes (see Cole, 1996).[5]

Braga and Cole undertook research to determine if it would be possible to create a form of activity that brought about consequential changes in the ability of pre-adolescent children who had experienced ABI to engage in broader social participation (Braga, Rossi, & Cole, 2010, 2012). The activity they created is called the "MetaCognitive Dimension" (MCD), and illustrates many Vygotskian principles for constructing mediational settings that provide multiple avenues for entering activities, diverse ways of participating, collaboration with both peers and young adults, and a teleological goal of incorporating people of difference into valued social practices through which status differentials are flattened.

A special virtue of the 5thD playworld in this regard is that it was designed to facilitate modifiability depending upon specific populations and local circumstances. The playworld had been organized as a local idioculture (Fine, 1987), that is, a culture-within-a-culture. This idioculture was established in out-of-school, community-based settings such as youth clubs, libraries, churches, and after school programs organized at schools. For this collaboration, the setting was modified to enable participation from children with brain injuries who would typically be excluded from engaging with their normate peers.

Cole's founding 5thD playworlds in California (Cole and the Distributed Literacy Consortium, 2006) involved the participation of college undergraduates who are trained to interact with the pre-adolescents to promote joint learning using Vygotskian principles. While the students are given the opportunity for practical, hands-on experience using development theories to guide their practice, the pre-adolescents are given the chance to learn and develop in interaction with more experienced peers, who are variously known as buddies, amigos, or students, depending upon local norms. Although special needs children have participated in 5thD centres in the U.S., their inclusion was enabled by modifying the structure of the local activity to the particular child. Consistent with Vygotskian defectological principles, the people in the environment were tasked with making fundamental adaptations to the setting, to allow for the greatest participation for brain-injured children as full-fledged members of the activities.

The project we describe here took place at the SARAH Hospital in Brasilia, one of many sites within the SARAH Network of Rehabilitation Hospitals, whose mission involves the treatment of people with injuries, under the assumption that people are agents in their recovery and not objects on which techniques are applied. Its approach is consistent with Luria's (1979) method of helping to rehabilitate a man who suffered a terrible head wound from a bomb explosion, leaving his memory, vision, capacity for reading and writing, and other prior capabilities damaged or absent. Under a therapeutic regime organized by Luria encompassing many years, he was able to return to his native town where he lived independently on a disability pension.

As a co-researcher in his own recovery, Luria's patient laboriously authored, over a 25-year period, a journal initially titled "The Story of a Terrible Brain Injury" but later changed it to "I'll Fight On," designed to help others understand his experiences, including the therapeutic procedures Luria invented on the basis of cultural-historical psychological principles. The tenet of having those undergoing rehabilitative therapy participate as co-researchers of their process of recovery was adapted for the intervention at SARAH. The Brazilian MetaCognitive Dimension (MCD) was designed to enrich and stimulate the social, academic, intellectual, and neuropsychological development of pre-adolescents with ABI. Special focus was placed on the children's ability to monitor their own cognitive processes in order to promote self-regulation and other socio-cognitive functions, and doing so within highly social environments.

Although the MCD used many of the 5thD concepts, they were adapted to meet the special needs and challenges of this brain-injured population. The program was conducted twice a week for 13 weeks to coordinate with the university student schedules. Because the project took place at the SARAH Neurorehabilitation Center, located by the lake in Brasilia, instead of at the SARAH Hospital in downtown Brasilia, the hospital bussed the children and their parents to the sessions. At the beginning, the parents would arrive at the 5thD room, eager to participate in the child's activities with the undergraduates. This parental reaction is perfectly normal because they had grown accustomed to the difficulties that their child had when interacting with strangers. Strikingly, they soon noticed that the children were quickly developing relationships with the undergraduate students, and saw that they were capable of participating without parental help.

Seeing the parents' evident interest in their children's activities, the organizers arranged for the parents to meet together with the children and the undergraduates over snacks at the end of each MCD session so that the parents could get a first-hand account of what their children had been doing from the children and their undergraduate partners. In addition, the staff met on a regular basis to explore and document the parents' interpretation of the program.

During their sessions with the children, the students deployed deliberate mediational strategies to foster the pre-adolescent's neuropsychological development and metacognition. For example, if a pre-adolescent asked a student a specific question, the student would not simply answer; instead, the student would reformulate the question and pose it back to the child. At the same time, the students were careful to insure that the interactions, whether involving playing a computer game or throwing a ball through a hoop, were done together and were fun both for themselves and the children, regardless of how much assistance the child seemed to require. *With a goal of participation rather than expertise*, the emphasis was on finding ways to develop competencies through affirmational engagement, rather than seeing children as objects to be repaired, or objects of diagnosis.

A broad range of changes were seen in the children's behaviour at the end of 13 weeks. Changes in the children's behaviour were evident in the reports of the parents:

1. "My daughter was stagnated but has grown so much now. She's more independent and was even able to travel by herself during her recent vacation. She is self-confident enough to make new friends."
2. "My son has changed a lot—and so have I. Before, he was really dependent on me, and now I let him go some places by himself. Now I have more confidence in what he is able to do."
3. "[My son] was playing basketball with some normal kids. His team was losing so he called one of his teammates over. He said to him, 'Take my place, you can play better than I can.' His teacher praised him for resolving the situation without feeling diminished. I owe this change in attitude to the program."

Parents also acknowledged the importance of the undergraduates, especially with regards to the intergenerational nature of the undergraduates' relationship with their children: "The fact that there are college kids around helped my son become more centered and focused. . . . They're closer in age to the children." Finally, the parents' accounts underscore the importance of sharing experiences with other families: "When we hear another mother talking about what she is going through, we see that it's not just our kid who has problems; it's all of them. So you stop treating your kid like he's different, because you see that he's like many other children."

These observations by parents converged with the data from standard psychological tests. Tests to assess learning strategies and metacognitive abilities, and tests to evaluate the children's self-concepts both showed significant increases when compared with a control group of comparably affected children who received the normal SARAH regime of family visits and consultations with the hospital rehabilitation team.

Pre-adolescents as co-researchers, evaluated and analyzed their own recovery process across different dimensions: a) *Self-concept/self-esteem:* "I said to myself that I could be a better person and I did it. I started getting better grades. I started to like myself more in MCD"; b) *Metacognition/self-control:* "I used to hug everybody in school; I really liked hugging the girls. But I started seeing that was wrong, that I should ask first if I can give someone a hug"; c) *Plan/organize:* "I got a small pad and began writing what I had to do, and putting the reminders where I could see them, where I go often, my bedroom"; d) *Social skills:* "I realized that all I had to do was ask, like if I want to play I just have to ask a friend if he wants to, and we can do it together. It's simple."

Disability Studies and Critical Disability Studies

Taken together, the research programs carried out in Russia and Brazil demonstrate how the cultural organization of rehabilitative activity can enable radically transformed modes of social participation for children with disabilities and their caregivers and teachers. The challenge then moves into the arena of the broader society, and the willingness of people to make those new modes of social participation general in society. In this sense, there is much potential for complementarity and co-alignment between such approaches and those that fall under the rubric of the academic movement referred to as Critical Disability Studies. This is not to say that the two are parallel or mirror images of one another.

Critical Disability Studies reflects the conjoining of two movements that began from initially different intellectual roots and areas of social engagement: Critical Social Theory, on the one hand, and on the other the study of populations conventionally referred to as "disabled," Disability Studies (DS). Although the earliest Disability Studies scholarship is often linked to the emergence of disability rights activism, such as the work of blind legal scholar Jacobus tenBroek (1966), it is possible to observe critical (and not merely pathology-based) thinking about categories of difference in much earlier texts.

Virtually any contemporary academic enterprise that contains the word *critical* in its title is concerned with the role of power in human relationships and the role of political power in knowledge creation (Meekosha & Shuttleworth, 2009). Understandably then, this central critical orientating concern is a key feature distinguishing those who self-identify as critical disability theorists (Goodley, 2011).

Disability Studies (DS) has its own prior history both in academia and society at large. Disability Studies in the United States came into being as part of the broad push toward social equality represented by Disability Rights activism, which grew out of the Civil Rights, Women's, and Sexual Liberation movements characteristic of the progressive political activism in the 1960s and 1970s. During the decades when these general social movements were diffusing into the academic arena, myriad legal decisions, large-scale public events such as the Special Olympics, and Hollywood films like *Rain Man* (Levinson, 1988) made attitudes toward atypical people and how society deals with their lives a topic of broad social and academic discourse (though often failing and more often than not reproducing insidious or banal stereotypes in the process; see Longmore, 2016).

Academic interest in the concept of disability, the study of handicap, and means of rehabilitation had been long established in the medical arena, as our brief history of Russian and Soviet research makes clear. However, the "medical model" characterized difference as deficit, as a condition to be cured. When Disability Studies came into prominence among academics, a revolt against the medical model became embodied as the core definition of the field.

This point is made clear by the American Society for Disability Studies (first initiated in 1986) when it provided a widely cited definition of the field that immediately distinguishes it from its historical antecedents in medicine.

> [Disability Studies] examines the policies and practices of all societies to understand the social, rather than the physical or psychological determinants of the experience of disability. Disability Studies has been developed to disentangle impairments from the myths, ideology and stigma that influence social interaction and social policy. The scholarship challenges the idea that the economic and social statuses and the assigned roles of people with disabilities are the inevitable outcomes of their condition.
> *(quoted at www.crds.org/about/index.shtml)*

This focus on disability as a *social formation*, or as a social/environmental experience of discrimination rather than one embodied in individual pathology, became a hallmark of DS/CDS and marks a point of direct contact with CHAT. Agreement on disability as a social formation is a point where complementarity among schools of thought becomes possible, and also a point of potential conflict.

In the sections to follow, we examine key commonalities and differences between the two intellectual programs. We begin by focusing on commonalities, and then turn to examine ways in which diversity appears within the fabric of a common set of commitments.

A Focus on Commonalities

First there is a common interest in what Vygotsky referred to as the "secondary," socially formed, source of disability: the social constraints placed on the individual that interfere with the process of attaining full personhood as a member of society. Virtually everyone in both fields would agree with Vygotsky's declaration that "the social aspect formerly diagnosed as secondary and derivative, in fact, turns out to be primary and major" (Vygotsky, 1993, p. 112).

This fundamental stance finds broad acceptance in the DS/CDS literature. To Biklen (2000), critical approaches are concerned with acknowledging "disability as a social construct . . . occurring within shifting political, economic and social contexts, often highly marginalizing and discriminatory in nature" (p. 337). Davis (2010) has observed that "The problem is not the person with disabilities; the problem is the way that normalcy is constructed to create the 'problem' of the disabled person" (p. 9). This common focus on the utopian goal of inclusionary social participation, and the barriers to this goal produced by "myths, ideology, and stigma" puts both groups at odds with "ableist" views of difference that justify status quo inequalities; i.e., those that view the able-bodied person as ideal.

An important second commonality is the fact that both CHAT and DS/CDS have important roots in Marxism, albeit Marxism as interpreted from markedly different historical and geopolitical locations. Vygotsky lived during the turbulent post-Revolution period, in a society governed by Marxism/Leninism, and subsequently Stalin's directly repressive regime. His emphasis on integrating anomalous children into an egalitarian society can reasonably be understood to underpin the argument that equity would be achieved through collective human activity.

When the Frankfurt School initiated a critique of social theory in the 1930s (see Abromeit, 2011), the Soviet implementation of Marxist ideas was producing political show trials and CHAT psychologists were under heavy threat. Under duress now from Fascism, Frankfurt School theorists were highly critical of capitalism but they found the Marxism of their day insufficient on many grounds. It had failed to explain, let alone predict, the dynamics of capitalism; its road to communism had manifested in totalitarian states. The Frankfurt School sought more adequate explanations for the systematic oppression of society's least powerful citizens: those subjugated due to race, gender, socioeconomic class, and other factors.

This primary concern leads critical theorists, regardless of specific focus, to consider the manner in which social structures of control and exclusion are constructed and maintained. The terms *oppression*, *control*, and *emancipation* appear central to any *critical* theory. Meekosha and Shuttleworth (2009), for instance, include many of them in a single sentence when writing about DS/CDS: "The defining feature of *autonomy* that interweaves throughout critical theory's history is its meaning as *emancipation* from *hegemonic* and *hierarchical ideologies* that structure personal consciousness, representations, social relations and practices in everyday life" (p. 53; emphasis added).

A third commonality is the interdisciplinarity of both the CHAT and DS/CDS research programs. This possibility was not always the case with CHAT. Institutionally, Vygotsky was a psychologist. (He was also a polymath: a psychologist, a classroom teacher, medical researcher, the head of an Institute of Defektology, theorist of art and literature, husband and father.) But while he and his colleagues could and did draw upon Marx for a socio-cultural-historical theory of development, he could not engage professionally in a critical study of his own society without risking his life; political reality did not permit it (Zinchenko, 2007). Sociology, anthropology, linguistics, art, literature: the entire study of human cultural life was truncated by its highly regulated role in providing an ideological tool for Soviet power. As long as they remained within the walls of Stalin's empire, the social sciences and humanities were limited in the intellectual problems they could pursue legally. From the time, however, when cultural historical psychology began to spread beyond Russia, it was envisioned as necessarily interdisciplinary, ranging across the human sciences. (For a current assessment, see www.iscar.info/.)

As the early members of the Frankfurt School gathered adherents seeking a full-fledged critique of social theory, they did so at a time when Hitler had risen to power and began to menace all nations in the region, and communists were outlaws in capitalist societies. In seeking to maintain what they saw as useful and important in Marx, they included in their search a broad range of academic expertise that encompassed the social sciences (political science, sociology, communication, anthropology), the humanities, and the arts. Critical theory, too, was a thoroughly interdisciplinary undertaking.

Finally, a clear area of common commitment is the need for a methodology in which theory is constantly tested in the fire of practice. This commitment is clear in the examples we provided on the basis of Russian and Brazilian work with two disparate forms of physical anomaly. It plays an equally prominent role in the writing of CDS advocates. For example, Meekosha and Shuttleworth (2009) list as one of the necessary components for CDS the principle that "Critical social theory links theory with praxis in the struggle for an autonomous and participatory society" (p. 52). This declaration could easily have been made by any adherent of a CHAT perspective and bears a clear common affinity with Marx's exhortation for scholars to make the struggle to change society an integral and necessary part of their work.

Vygotsky's early formulation remains an appropriate expression of CHAT's view of the theory/practice relationships: "most complex contradictions of psychology's methodology are brought to the field of practice and can only be resolved there. Here the dispute stops being sterile, it comes to an end. . . . That is why practice transforms the whole of scientific methodology" (Vygotsky, quoted in van der Veer & Valsiner, 1991, p. 150). This agreement on an appropriate theory/practice relational methodology appears to be a key area of complementarity between CHAT and DS/CDS.

Focusing on Differences

Each of the core common foundations serves not only as a common reference point for considering the complementarity of CHAT and DS/CDS, but as a vantage point from which to re-assess the sources of differences in theory and practice that hinder greater mutual understanding.

Social Formation

While both approaches agree on the need to see disability as a social formation, a next level of specification reveals several differences.

1. From a CHAT perspective, a singular focus on the social nature of disability ignores the fact that different forms of disability require different forms of "re-mediation" to attain inclusion in the broader social world. The developmental challenges of control associated with perinatal stroke, for instance, cannot be met without taking into consideration the entire bio-cultural-social system.

2. From a DS/CDS perspective, CHAT is woefully inadequate in its ability to analyze the social forces operating to structure everyday life experience, even with its axiomatic attention to the social contexts of human development. This limitation relegates CHAT to the margins of attention for DS/CDS: physiological and psychological contributions to the study of disability were, more or less officially, declared off limits, given this field's theoretical home in the humanities and rhetorical orientation to the text, lending a discursive more than material emphasis to its formulations. DS/CDS seeks to deal with the products of social formations as social facts.
3. From a DS/CDS perspective, both CHAT and DS stop short of interrogating the notion of inclusion that is the putative goal of each approach. Where defectology aims to include and assimilate people with disabilities into streams of existing cultural practice, CDS questions this aim (Titchkosky & Michalko, 2009). Where defectology finds value in people with disabilities who have found alternative/mediated ways of engaging with nondisabled people, CDS contends that people with disabilities are valuable as they are. CDS points out that disability is, in fact, normal: virtually all human beings become temporarily or permanently disabled at some point in their lives, or in some contexts.

Marxism as a Common Source of Ideas

Seismic geopolitical changes have occurred since the 1920s in Russia and the broader Soviet Union: the years of German Fascism, the Cold War and McCarthyism, the breakup of the Soviet empire. Each shift has greatly modified the ways in which Marx's ideas have been appropriated in countries across the world. We do not presume to provide a detailed survey of the matter, which would take us radically off course. Rather, it seems safe to say that in so far as Marx's ideas prove useful in seeking to understand the phenomena of human life forms as studied in different areas of human life (as they do currently in CHAT), Marx will maintain his current influence. Marx's (1875) utopian ideal of human interaction, inscribed in the formula he adapted from Louis Blanc and Étienne-Gabriel Morelly, "From each according to his ability, to each according to his needs!" provides the moral benchmark by which a society judges itself: its ability to provide for those who need the most provision.

Interdisciplinarity

The simple fact that CHAT and DS/CDS share the characteristic of interdisciplinarity says little about the commonalities and differences that characterize them. CHAT draws upon psychology and education as its core disciplines. The enrichment it seeks is likely to come from evolutionary biology, anthropology, communication, sociology, and linguistics. DS/CDS, having discarded academic psychology and biology as irrelevant to their interests, also draws upon the social sciences but particularly in recent years, the humanities have come to play a major role in developing new theoretical concerns that go far beyond the forms of critical social theory envisioned by the Frankfurt School.

Relating Theory to Practice

Despite theoretical agreement on the necessity of adopting a theory and practice methodology in the study of disability, this crucial element in both of the research programs we have discussed remains a topic of ongoing discussion and critique. The theory/practice relationship in the two CHAT examples we provided appears straightforward. Within a circumscribed field of influence, in one case, a special school for deaf and blind children, in another case a special educational program for children with severe brain trauma, the researchers have considerable ability to organize the forms of interaction in order to realize the social changes necessary to bring about the desired forms of inclusive participation. In each case, the major challenge, assuming the success of the program, is to have it appropriated into routine social structures so that it becomes a norm and not something to remember on ritual occasions.

In the DS/CDS arena, several decades of research have demonstrated, using widely accepted norms of social science research, the enormous, inequitable, distribution of social resources to those most in need of it. The "intersectionality of race, gender, and class" with disability is depressingly evident in figures showing the desperate conditions that routinely emerge from a combination of poverty, racial, and gender exclusion in modern society (Stanford Center on Poverty and Inequality, 2014).

As McDermott and Varenne (1995) note, the model of theory–practice relationship in CDS appears to be consistent with much postmodern and poststructural thought; many in the larger DS/CDS community argue that disability is constructed discursively (e.g., Dudley-Marling & Dippo, 1995). Goodley (2013) is among those who are concerned that DS/CDS's discursive approach has at times placed them "on the veranda" and above the fray rather than in the midst of the people whose lives are affected by the discussions and writing of CDS scholars. Goodley has even argued that "while theoretical avenues have been widened, the field has lost touch with the real material problems of disabled people's lives [and a] preoccupation with theory over politics. . . . [DS/CDS] are in danger of becoming a new uncritical orthodoxy—one distanced from empirical evidence and often only internally critiqued" (p. 641).

The Case for Complementarity

Despite important ongoing debates within the CHAT and DS/CDS communities, we hope that our summary of their similarities and differences will facilitate conversation between adherents of the differing perspectives to see the value of promoting their complementarity. At a simple level, it is obvious that the CHAT perspective, with few exceptions (e.g. Smagorinsky, 2016), has focused its attention on designing theory-based activity systems that constitute existence proofs for the possibility of achieving inclusive participation. It is equally clear that each CHAT case, while successful on its own terms as a demonstration proof, has not developed a theory or a practice designed to bring about widespread social inclusion as a basic social value or realized social policy in any country.

Although it is proper to note the limits to a theory of practice that remains encapsulated in an academic discourse, it is significant that the discursive approach, too, can produce unexpected results. It should not go unnoticed that when the press sought to interview student activists in the Black Lives Matter movement, who were calling for the resignation of the University of Missouri president for a lack of action on campus racism, one of the student organizers shouted at the reporters: "We are going to control this narrative." This appropriation of the notion of a cultural narrative, and the need for productive counternarratives that fall outside dominant narratives' historical construction of events, demonstrate the manner in which discursive practices perpetuate inequity and the advantages it accords those whose privilege is so well established that it becomes invisible (Bell, 2012). The conventional narrative in which difference is equated with deficiency, and the counternarrative provided by both DS/CDS and CHAT, suggest the power of discursive construction in promoting social change. CHAT's contributions suggest, however, that new textual representations are not sufficient to effect significant change; material developments are also necessary.

The project of CHAT and DS/CDS often aligns with other human rights movements focused on race, ethnicity, class, and citizenship and their intersection with larger critiques of normativity and typicality (see, e.g., Erevelles, 2000). This coordination of discursive and material actions has often been lacking in scholarly efforts to articulate an inclusive perspective on human difference. We see the possibilities outlined in this chapter, for the benefits of continuing to critique oppressive and inequitable social structures, and for providing material alternatives via new social norms and material structures. This project is valuable in moving toward, if never quite reaching, the utopian vision of developing a society in which difference is constructed as dynamic and valuable, rather than a deficit.

Notes

1. We must emphasize that our focus on human difference refers in this chapter to differences that are constructed as disabilities. LeBron James and other anomalously outsized and gifted athletes are physically different from the majority of people, yet not considered deficient or disabled.
2. The three papers, titled "Problems in the cultural development of the child" and authored respectively by Leontiev (1932), Luria (1928), and Vygotsky (1929), constituted the first published manifesto of what would come to be called cultural historical psychology.

3. In general, our references to "difference" are concerned with those differences associated with "disability." At the same time, we should recognize that other, non-"disability" oriented points of difference, may also be treated negatively. People who are extremely short, for instance, might be subject to social ostracism. Even such a benign point of difference as hair color, while not a disablement, is at times constructed as inferior, as indicated by the phrase "red-headed stepchild" to indicate a person of low and outcast status.
4. In this chapter, we use deaf (lowercase) to refer to people who are deaf, rather than Deaf (capitalized) which refers to people who identify as part of Deaf culture and the Deaf community.
5. Although we appear to be making a great leap across time and space with our examples, they are connected by Cole's role in bringing Vygotsky to the English-speaking world as co-translator and co-editor of Vygotsky (1978) through his postdoctoral studies with Vygotsky's student/collaborator A.R. Luria in Moscow in the 1960s, and his work as editor and translator of Luria (1976, 1978), whose neurological research is indebted to Vygotsky's work in defectology.

References

Abromeit, J. (2011). *Max Horkheimer and the foundations of the Frankfurt school*. New York, NY: Cambridge University Press.

Adler, A. (1912). Ueber den nervoesen Charakter (The neurotic constitution). Wiesbaden: Bergmann.

Adler, A. (1927). Praxis und theorie der indivdiualpsychologie (The practice and theory of individual psychology). Munich, DE: Bergmann.

Bell, C. M. (Ed.). (2012). *Blackness and disability: Critical examinations and cultural interventions*. East Lansing, MI: Michigan State University Press.

Biklen, D. (2000). Constructing inclusion: Lessons from critical, disability narratives. *International Journal of Inclusive Education, 4*(4), 337–353.

Braga, L. W., Rossi, L., & Cole, M. (2010). Creating an idioculture to promote the development of children with cerebral palsy. *Educ. Pesqui, 36*, 133–143. Retrieved from http://www.scielo.br/pdf/ep/v36nspe/en_v36nspea11.pdf

Braga, L. W., Rossi, L., & Cole, M. (2012). Empowering preadolescents with ABI through metacognition: Preliminary results of a randomized clinical trial. *NeuroRehabilitation, 30*(3), 205–212.

Cole, M. (1996). *Cultural psychology: A once and future discipline*. Cambridge, MA: Harvard University Press.

Cole, M., and the Distributed Literacy Consortium. (2006). *The Fifth Dimension: An after-school program built on diversity*. New York, NY: Russell Sage Foundation.

Davis, L. (2010). Constructing normalcy. In L. Davis (Ed.), *The disability studies reader* (3rd edn., pp. 3–20). New York, NY: Routledge.

Dudley-Marling, C., & Dippo, D. (1995). What learning disability does: Sustaining the ideology of schooling. *Journal of Learning Disabilities, 28*(7), 408–414.

Erevelles, N. (2000). Educating unruly bodies: Critical pedagogy, disability studies, and the politics of schooling. *Educational Theory, 50*(1), 25–47.

Fine, G. A. (1987). *With the boys*. Chicago, IL: University of Chicago Press.

Garland-Thomson, R. (1997). *Extraordinary bodies: Figuring physical disability in American culture and literature*. New York, NY: Columbia University Press.

Gindis, B. (1995). A voice from the future. *School Psychology International, 16*(2), 99–103.

Gindis, B. (2003). Remediation through education: Socio/cultural theory and children with special needs. In A. Kozulin, B. Gindis, V. Ageyev & S. Miller (Eds.), *Vygotsky's educational theory in cultural context* (pp. 220–224). New York, NY: Cambridge University Press.

Goodley, D. (2011). *Disability studies: An interdisciplinary introduction.* Thousand Oaks, CA: Sage.

Goodley, D. (2013). Dis/entangling critical disability studies. *Disability & Society, 28*(5), 631–644.

Graham, L. R. (1977). Science and values: The eugenics movement in Germany and Russia in the 1920s. *American Historical Review, 82*(5), 1133–1164.

Knox, J., & Stevens, C. B. (1993). Vygotsky and Soviet Russian defectology: An introduction. In R. W. Rieber & A. S. Carton (Eds.); J. E. Knox & C. B. Stevens (Trans.), *The collected works of L. S. Vygotsky. Volume 2: The fundamentals of defectology (abnormal psychology and learning disabilities)* (pp. 1–25). New York, NY: Plenum.

Kozulin, A., & Gindis, B. (2007). Sociocultural theory and education of children with special needs: From defectology to remedial pedagogy. In H. Daniels, M. Cole & J. V. Wertsch (Eds.), *The Cambridge companion to Vygotsky* (pp. 332–362). New York, NY: Cambridge University Press.

Leontiev, A. N. (1932). Studies of cultural development of the child: 3. The development of voluntary attention in the child. *Journal of Genetic Psychology, 37,* 52–81.

Levinson, B. (Dir.). (1988). *Rain man.* Beverly Hills, CA: MGM.

Longmore, P. K. (2016). *Telethons: Spectacle, disability, and the business of charity.* New York, NY: Oxford University Press.

Luria, A. R. (1928). The problem of the cultural behavior of the child. *Journal of Genetic Psychology, 35,* 493–506. Retrieved from http://luria.ucsd.edu/Articles-by-Luria/PDFs/Luria_Problem.Behavior.pdf

Luria, A. R. (1976). *Cognitive development: Its cultural and social foundations* (M. Cole, Ed.; M. Lopez-Morillas & L. Solotaroff, Trans.). Cambridge, MA: Harvard University Press.

Luria, A. R. (1978). The development of writing in the child. In M. Cole (Ed.), *The selected writings of A. R. Luria* (pp. 145–194). White Plains, NY: Sharpe.

Luria, A. R. (1979). *The making of mind: A personal account of Soviet psychology* (M. Cole, Trans.). Cambridge, MA: Harvard University Press.

Marx, K. (1875). *Critique of the Gotha program.* Retrieved from https://www.marxists.org/archive/marx/works/1875/gotha/ch01.htm

McCagg, W. O. (1989). The origins of defectology. In W. O. McCagg & L. Siegelbaum (Eds.), *The disabled in the Soviet Union: Past and present, theory and practice* (pp. 39–62). Pittsburgh, PA: University of Pittsburgh Press. Retrieved from http://digital.library.pitt.edu/cgi-bin/t/text/pageviewer-idx?c=pittpress;cc=pittpress;idno=31735057895033;node=31735057895033%3A1.6.2.2;frm=frameset;rgn=full%20text;didno=31735057895033;view=image;seq=0049

McDermott, R., & Varenne, H. (1995). Culture "as" disability. *Anthropology and Education Quarterly, 26*(3), 323–348. Retrieved from http://serendip.brynmawr.edu/sci_cult/culturedisability.html

Meekosha, H., & Shuttleworth, R. (2009). What's so "critical" about critical disability studies? *Australian Journal of Human Rights, 15*(1), 47–75.

Meshcheryakov, A. (1974). *Awakening to life.* Moscow: Progress Publishers. Retrieved from https://www.marxists.org/archive/meshcheryakov/awakening/

Smagorinsky, P. (2012a). Vygotsky, "defectology," and the inclusion of people of difference in the broader cultural stream. *Journal of Language and Literacy Education* [Online], *8*(1), 1–25. Retrieved from http://jolle.coe.uga.edu/wp-content/uploads/2012/05/Vygotsky-and-Defectology.pdf

Smagorinsky, P. (2012b). "Every individual has his own insanity": Applying Vygotsky's work on defectology to the question of mental health as an issue of inclusion. *Learning, Culture and Social Interaction*, *1*(1), 67–77. Retrieved from http://www.petersmagorinsky.net/About/PDF/LCSI/LCSI_2012.pdf

Smagorinsky, P. (2016). *Creativity and community among autism-spectrum youth: Creating positive social updrafts through play and performance*. New York, NY: Palgrave Macmillan.

Stanford Center on Poverty and Inequality. (2014). *The poverty and inequality report, 2014*. Palo Alto, CA: The Stanford Center on Poverty and Inequality. Retrieved from https://web.stanford.edu/group/scspi/sotu/SOTU_2014_CPI.pdf

tenBroek, J. (1966). Right to live in the world: The disabled in the law of torts. *California Law Review*, *54*(2), 841–919.

Titchkosky, T., & Michalko, R. (2009). Introduction. In T. Titchkosky & R. Michalko (Eds.), *Rethinking normalcy: A disabilities studies reader* (pp. 1–14). Toronto, ON: Canadian Scholars Press.

van der Veer, R., & Valsiner, J. (Eds.). (1991). *Understanding Vygotsky*. Oxford, UK: Blackwell.

Vygotsky, L. S. (1925/1971). *The psychology of art* (Scripta Technica, Inc., Trans.). Cambridge, MA: MIT Press.

Vygotsky, L. S. (1929). The problem of the cultural development of the child. *Journal of Genetic Psychology*, *36*(3), 415–432. Retrieved from https://www.marxists.org/archive/vygotsky/works/1929/cultural_development.htm

Vygotsky, L. S. (1934/1987). Thinking and speech. In R. Rieber & A. Carton (Eds.); N. Minick (Trans.), *The collected works of LS Vygotsky. Vol. 1, Problems of general psychology including the volume thinking and speech* (pp. 39–285). New York, NY: Plenum.

Vygotsky, L. S. (1978). *Mind in society: The development of higher psychological processes* (M. Cole, V. John-Steiner, S. Scribner & E. Souberman, Eds.). Cambridge, MA: Harvard University Press.

Vygotsky, L. S. (1993). The fundamentals of defectology (abnormal psychology and learning disabilities). In R. W. Rieber & A. S. Carton (Eds.); J. E. Knox & C. B. Stevens (Trans.), *The collected works of L. S. Vygotsky. Volume 2: The fundamentals of defectology (abnormal psychology and learning disabilities)*. New York, NY: Plenum.

Vygotsky, L. S. (1994). The problem of the environment. In R. Van der Veer & J. Valsiner (Eds.); T. Prout (Trans.), *The Vygotsky reader* (pp. 338–354). Cambridge, MA: Blackwell.

Vygotsky, L. S. (1999a). The teaching about emotions. Historical-psychological studies. In R. Rieber (Ed.); M. J. Hall (Trans.), *The collected works of L. S. Vygotsky (Vol. 6: Scientific Legacy)* (pp. 71–235). New York, NY: Plenum.

Vygotsky, L. S. (1999b). On the problem of the psychology of the actor's creative work. In R. Rieber (Ed.); M. J. Hall (Trans.), *The collected works of L. S. Vygotsky (Vol. 6: Scientific Legacy)* (pp. 237–244). New York, NY: Plenum.

Wright, P. (2004). *The Individuals with Disabilities Educational Improvement Act of 2004: Overview, explanation, and comparison, IDEA 2004 vs. IDEA 1997*. Retrieved from http://www.wrightslaw.com/idea/idea.2004.all.pdf

Zaporozhets, A. V. (1974). The work of Alexander Meshcheryakov. In A. I. Meshcheryakov (Ed.), *Awakening to life* (pp. 5–12). Moscow: Progress Publishers.

Zinchenko, V. (2007). Thought and word: The approaches of L. S. Vygotsky and G. G. Shpet. In H. Daniels, M. Cole & J. V. Wertsch (Eds.), *The Cambridge companion to Vygotsky* (pp. 212–243). New York, NY: Cambridge University Press.

6

QUEER THEORY IN THE LEARNING SCIENCES

Jacob McWilliams and William R. Penuel

> *"Queer theory is not unique to education, of course. In this, as in other areas, we are late."*
> (Pinar, 1998)

Introduction

That queer theory has been slow to wend its way into the learning sciences is a source of frustration but not much of a surprise to those of us doing queer work in learning contexts. Queer frameworks are commonly viewed as far outside of the mainstream, the domain of literary theory and literacy scholars, gender studies faculty, and methodologists who dabble in the Foucauldian. Yet queer theory has much to offer those who take a "human sciences" approach to learning (e.g., O'Connor & Penuel, 2010; Penuel & O'Connor, 2010). Queer theorists share with this approach a commitment to investigating variations in human activity, and they delight in the gaps between "natural laws" of human nature and the everyday apparent inconsistencies and irrationalities of human action.

Queer theory offers important insights into issues of learning, identity, and methodology. It is an approach that both centralizes and extends beyond the lives and experiences of those who identify as lesbian, gay, bisexual, transgender, queer, intersex, and asexual (LGBTQIA). Queer theory aims to account for how sex, sexuality, gender, and gender identity shape and are shaped by institutional structures, including education. It invites us all to consider how gender and sexual norms are co-constructed by our lived experiences, theoretical and political commitments, and interactions with others.

The insights offered by queer theoretical perspectives can support the work of learning scientists in developing theories of human action, as well as in creating more equitable learning contexts for people across the spectrums of gender and sexual identity. In this chapter, we introduce some areas of shared interest between queer theories and key concerns within the learning sciences, and we set forth an argument for integrating queer theoretical frames into learning sciences work—particularly work that draws on design-based approaches to educational research. In the sections that follow, we present a rationale for integrating queer theory; offer a brief overview of the queer theoretical frame; and draw on two recent studies completed by the authors to illustrate principles for drawing on queer theory for learning. We end by offering a tentative way forward for learning scientists interested in integrating queer perspectives in their work and contributing to the larger projects of queer approaches to teaching, learning, and educational design.

Extending Sociocultural Theories through Queer Frameworks: An Overview and Rationale

Queer theory is at its core about a struggle for recognition: Queer theorists are working toward a world in which queer people, queer concerns, and queer narratives are both visible and legitimated (Berlant & Warner, 1995; Butler, 1999; Warner, 1993). This is an effort toward reclamation, toward challenging cultural norms that position heterosexuality and non-transgender identities as normal, good, and healthy, and non-heterosexuality and transgender identities as their binary opposites: abnormal, immoral, stunted.

This reclamation began by recovering the term "queer," historically used as a slur against those who failed to conform to sexual and gender norms (Butler, 1993). Reclamation continued during the early years of the AIDS pandemic, when activists worked to secure visibility, governmental and medical support, and public recognition that AIDS was disproportionately impacting gay men (Gould, 2009; Herek & Glunt, 1988; Shilts, 2007). Activist groups such as the AIDS Coalition To Unleash Power (ACT UP) and Queer Nation aimed to ensure that queer lives were highly visible, highly disruptive, and highly vocal (Gould, 2009; Queer Nation, 1990). An early ACT UP t-shirt slogan read "I'm out, therefore I am" (Dobber, 1995)—a cry of identity as well as of identification.

"Queer" has been taken up in a variety of ways, operating sometimes as a noun, sometimes as an adjective, and at other times as a verb. For example: One of the authors (Jacob) identifies as queer (noun); he uses this term to suggest that cultural norms surrounding sexual identity, relationship structures, and attraction fall short of accounting for his experiences and histories. Queer cinema (adjective) includes films that focus on alternatives to monogamous, heterosexual, and/or cisgender (i.e., non-transgender) experiences; queer cinema may also serve a subversive role, in challenging viewers to (re)consider their assumptions about ethics, the social order, and other aspects of human experiences. An analysis of a literary work might aim to queer (verb) interpretations of the text by considering how it reflects and resists dominant cultural norms, particularly in the configuration of romantic, sexual, family, and communal relationships.

Many have noted that queerness is itself a disruptive cultural force: Queers have historically been free, by choice or not, from traditional family arrangements, religious institutions, pro-capitalist commitments, and other social structures that maintained state interests (Berlant & Freeman, 1992; Britzman, 1998; Edelman, 1998; Halberstam, 2011). Queerness, then, became a tool for investigating assumptions about what constitutes the "normal" in society and in everyday life. The forms of inquiry and theories that emerged in this area have been clustered, more or less loosely, under the term "queer theory." Queer theory not only rejects the framing of queerness as a *lack* of something (as seen in, for example, the term "non-heterosexuality"), but it also reframes queerness as a *presence*—of desire, of subversive social or political leanings, of relationships (sexual or not) that are not recognized by, and therefore are not legible to, governmental or other institutions (Butler, 2004; Dilley, 1999; Jagose, 1996).

All of the above are examples of how this perspective aims to queer dominant assumptions, theories, and social practices: In other words, to challenge what constitutes normalcy and to offer alternative ways of thinking and acting in the world.

Queer theory shares much common ground with sociocultural theories of human action and learning. As sociocultural theories do, a queer framework takes an interest in how particular ideas, roles, and actions come to be taken as normative within valued cultural practices, as well as in how norms and practices are reproduced or resisted as people interact with cultural artifacts and each other (Berlant & Warner, 1995; Dilley, 1999; Engeström, 1987; Green, 2007; Kaptelinin & Nardi, 2006; Kozulin, 1986).

Sociocultural theories treat cognition as distributed across mind, body, activity, and context (Packer & Goicoechea, 2000) and aim to develop theories of learning that account for the historically and culturally valued practices that shape and are shaped by individuals' participation in communities of practice (Lave, 2012; Sannino, Daniels, & Gutiérrez, 2009; Stetsenko & Arievitch, 2004; Wertsch, 2005).

Queer theory, however, approaches the sociocultural dimensions of knowledge and action from a somewhat different ontological and epistemological standpoint. Queer theorists place gender and sexuality at the centre of their inquiries into human activity. A chief concern of queer theory is to expose the fiction of what Butler (1999) calls *the heterosexual matrix*—"that grid of intelligibility through which bodies, gender, and desires are naturalized" (p. 149, note 6). The heterosexual matrix positions both gender and sexual identity as a set of finite, discrete categories. There are two gender categories—male or female—and three categories for sexual identity: straight, gay, or bisexual. There are no other options. There is nothing in between. There is nothing off to one side. There is not even an "other" or "not applicable" box to mark.

The grids of gender and sexual identity are cross-referenced, resulting in a set of finite, discrete identity possibilities, as illustrated in Table 6.1:

TABLE 6.1 Representation of the Identity Categories within the Heterosexual Matrix

	Straight	*Gay*	*Bisexual*
Man	Straight man	Gay man	Bisexual man
Woman	Straight woman	Gay woman	Bisexual woman

The heterosexual matrix becomes naturalized through social institutions, and all new members of a society are socialized to view the world through this matrix. Societies are so successful at naturalizing the heterosexual matrix that even very young children reflect its categorization system in their interactions with peers, teachers, and family members (Martin, 1998). And here's the genius behind the heterosexual matrix: Anything that doesn't fall squarely into one of those six cells is either difficult to see or targeted for obliteration—and sometimes both (Bettcher, 2007; BreakOUT!, 2015; Spade, 2014). The heterosexual matrix is reflected not only in broader cultural norms, but also in local systems of activity. Community values and goals, and the cultural artifacts that members draw upon to achieve shared goals, have gendered norms baked into them. The heterosexual matrix can be said to mediate all human activity. Among the tools for preserving the sanctity of the heterosexual matrix are laws, social institutions like schools and prisons and hospitals, fists, any household object that can be turned into a bludgeon, and guns.

As mediator, the matrix affords a possible space of identities, but as queer theory reminds us, it constrains who we can become. This is an essential property of mediation (Wertsch, 1998) and a reminder of what literary analyst W.J.T. Mitchell (1995) calls "no representation without taxation" (p. 21). Meaning, there is no way to employ mediational means to define an identity in ways that does not simultaneously enable us to become particular kinds of people and limit who we can become.

Queer theorists, then, work from an assumption that it's gender and sexuality all the way down. They are interested in exploring how the heterosexual matrix infuses social practice and how it can be reinforced and challenged through interactions with people and cultural artifacts across communities and time.

Queer theory takes an especial interest in identity and works in sympathy with those scholars in the learning sciences who treat identity as interactionally produced. The scholars have challenged dominant models that define identity as "a stable sense of one's goals, beliefs, values, and life roles" (Dillon, Worthington, & Moradi, 2011, p. 649; citing Erikson, 1950; Marcia, 1980). For example, Hand and Gresalfi (2015) position identity as a collaborative endeavour, produced jointly through interaction. Barton and Tan (2010), drawing on Holland, Lachicotte, Skinner, and Cain (1998), frame identity as what emerges when novices take on "positional identities" made available in a particular practice (Holland et al., 1998, p. 125). Identity-in-practice develops through "how novices choose to accept, engage, resist, or ignore" social cues about appropriate dispositions within the practice (Barton & Tan, 2010, p. 193). Nasir and colleagues (Nasir, 2011; Nasir & Hand, 2004; Nasir & Saxe, 2003) have explored how racial, ethnic, and cultural identities become sedimented on bodies as those bodies engage in culturally valued (or devalued) practices.

The above scholars represent a perspective that frames identity as multiple, intersectional, and performed (rather than owned). Queer theorists, too, embrace multiplicity and intersectionality. Gender and sexuality are not stable identities but performances: We "do," or perform, gender and sexuality across contexts and time. Some of these performances are easier to perceive than are others. A queer perspective investigates the identity positions that are rendered invisible by the heterosexual matrix, aiming to disrupt the treatment of these categories as natural and intuitive. Some of the work of queer theory involves introducing new terms, like queer, genderqueer, genderfluid, pansexual, asexual, agender, and so on. Queer theorists also often try to show how identity labels work as a cultural deception, by tricking people into thinking we have stable identities that are fully captured by the language of the heterosexual matrix. For example: Gender variance isn't something that only trans-identified people experience—even people who identify as cisgender women or cisgender men vary their gender over time and in different situations. A person might identify as a lesbian, even while dating a man. And so on.

Queer perspectives can support and extend scholarship addressing issues of identity and identity development, in several ways. First, a queer framework advances an approach to identity that centralizes concerns about sexuality, gender, and erotic desire. These are concerns that have traditionally been relegated to one side, examined only as one aspect of identity—and treated as the domain primarily of adolescents and people who will come to identify as LGBTQ. Queer frameworks position erotic desire as the domain of all people, regardless of age or current or eventual sexual or gender identity. A queer approach to identity begins from an assumption that identities are neither stable nor fully knowable—that all of us move across a range of identity positions throughout our lifespans and, indeed, throughout any given period of time in our lives (Britzman, 1998; Butler, 2004). Because queer theory is particularly interested in the operations of gendered and sexual norms, this approach takes an especial interest in how people perform a variety of gender and sexual identities across contexts and across time. The heterosexual matrix renders some of these performances invisible, marginalizes other types of performances, and legitimates those that most align with dominant cultural norms. Queer theoretical perspectives aim at making visible how social systems accomplish this form of normalization, and at offering strategies for disrupting the process. In this way, queer theory has the potential to offer key insights for learning scientists who investigate identity development—even if those investigations are not explicitly focused on gender and sexual identities.

A queer perspective on identity resists the canonical assumption that as children develop into adults, they also develop an increasingly stable, increasingly coherent identity. A queer approach to human experiences invites us to consider how varied and multiple are the identity positions that are taken up by people across their lifetimes (Britzman, 1998; Kumashiro, 2000, 2002). On a broad level, the labels a culture confers on people change over their lifetimes. For example, a child who is designated female at birth may be described as a girl, and later may embrace the label of a "tomboy." Later in life, she will be referred to as a "young woman," and later, as simply a "woman." Even later than that, she may be referred to as a "middle-aged woman" or an "old woman." Each of these terms carries explicit and tacit expectations about who a person is, how they will appear to others, and what kinds of desires and experiences they are likely to have.

Label changes interact with more minute, situational shifts that people make to their performances of gender and sexuality. A woman changes a child's diaper, then hands the child off to its other mother before leaving for work. At work, the woman updates code for the company's payroll system and, in the bathroom before a staff meeting, notices another dark hair sprouting from her chin. She has recently decided to stop plucking stray facial hairs and touches the new hair lightly. In the staff meeting, a coworker asks her whether her child's "real mother" is recovering well from childbirth. She chooses to pretend not to hear the question, focusing instead on gathering everybody's coffee orders for the afternoon trip to Starbucks.

Each of the actions and interactions described above represent variations on the theme of "woman"—and varied performances of gender and sexual identity. These performances exist in synergy and at times in tension with the heterosexual matrix, and with each other.

Queer perspectives aim at "queering" the notion of identity as stable and coherent, by accounting for the multitudes of identity positions we inhabit across moments, days, months, years, and lifetimes. Doing so opens opportunities to disrupt the heterosexual matrix and envision alternative identities, experiences, and performances that are either invisible or unperformable when straight, cisgender identities are considered the desired norm.

Queering Design Practices

Learning scientists have developed a family of approaches to designing learning environments alternately referred to as design research, design-based research, and design experimentation. Design research is an approach that aims to build theory and practice by organizing conditions to support new learning goals and analyzing when and how these conditions help accomplish those goals (Bell, Hoadley, & Linn, 2004; Cobb, Confrey, diSessa, Lehrer, & Schauble, 2003). Variations of design research emphasize to a greater or lesser degree the centrality of identity to learning and the broader cultural, institutional, and political contexts in which design takes place (Penuel & Spillane, 2014). In our view, design research approaches that foreground political aspects of design and promote equity provide the strongest foundation for integrating queer theory into design (e.g., Bang, Medin, Washinawatok, & Chapman, 2010; Gutiérrez & Vossoughi, 2010).

In this connection, we adopt here an *activist* stance toward learning sciences research, as some other scholars in the learning sciences have recently done. Booker, Vossoughi, and Hooper (2014) advocate for learning scientists to attend directly to political commitments toward human dignity and social equity. We agree with their argument that:

> . . . with this commitment comes a more explicit attention to the kind of future that is embodied and potentially engendered by alternative educational designs and practices. Where new social and political visions are made explicit, research on deepening conceptual understanding and expertise also takes shape differently: intellectual activity is understood as embedded in social relations; those social relations can either reproduce or reimagine and transform the hierarchies (raced, classed, gendered, aged, nationalized, etc.) and forms of competition that uphold the status quo.
> (Booker et al., 2014, p. 920)

For us, learning involves the collective organizing of social futures (O'Connor & Allen, 2010). Because these organizing efforts are often animated by aims such as justice and freedom, accounts of learning must give an account of how these aims gain legitimacy and how they represent "bets" on a particular vision of how society ought to be and who people should become (Penuel & O'Connor, 2010).

We propose an approach to the activist stance toward design that *queers* the assumptions of the design process. A queered approach begins by uncovering what gendered or sexualized practices are privileged by a given design or design process, and challenging collaborators to expand the forms of gender and sexual identity that can be made visible through a given practice. This approach invites a consideration of how "normal" learners are envisioned and enacted through design, and offers strategies for disrupting normativity throughout the design process.

We see our own interrogation of how queer theory can inform learning sciences as an explicit effort to transform learning spaces with and for queer youth, to help bring about a world that does not yet exist. By expanding and making visible alternative forms of identity performance, we can work toward new possibilities in community-building, teaching, and learning. As Muñoz (2009) points out, a sense of possibility for the future sits at the centre of queer theory:

> We may never touch queerness, but we can feel it as the warm illumination of a horizon imbued with potentiality. . . . The future is queerness's domain. Queerness is a structuring and educated mode of desiring that allows us to see and feel beyond the quagmire of the present.
>
> *(p. 1)*

Our aim of presenting a way forward for queer theory in the learning sciences is linked to nothing short of creating liveable educational spaces for queer and transgender/gender non-conforming learners. Further, we hope to demonstrate how queer perspectives can unhitch the hegemonic force of gender and sexual norms from learning in a way that benefits *all* learners, regardless of gender or sexual identity. Gender and sexual identity are, after all, simultaneously flimsy fictions and powerful realities for us all.

Research Contexts—Role of Queer Theory, Activism, Embodiment

We draw on the interdisciplinary work in queer theory to set forth an argument for integrating queer perspectives in the specific efforts of learning scientists. Specifically, we are concerned with the efforts within the field to link learning theory, pedagogy, and design. In the section that follows, we highlight several principles for designing with queer theory. These principles are supported with evidence drawn from two recent research contexts: An undergraduate teacher education course, and an elementary school classroom. Both contexts involved queer undertakings: The goal in each was to design LGBTQ-inclusive pedagogies and learning contexts. In the sections that follow, we first describe the two contexts, then describe key principles in practice.

Context 1: Education 4112

The example of an educational design that I (Bill) share is part of my undergraduate teaching at the University of Colorado Boulder. In this class, on the very first day, I disclose to students the fact that my own perspective on learning and development is shaped by being brought up in a queer household. I grew up in Nashville, Tennessee, in the 1970s and 1980s, a place that was hardly welcoming to lesbian parenting, yet I experienced tremendous love from my mother and her partner throughout my adolescence. I also faced many dilemmas of self-disclosure, hardly ever feeling safe, at my all-boys school or at church, to share that my mom was gay. Many of her partner's friends worked in counselling and social work, and they were a profound influence on my own choice of psychology as a discipline. My experience growing up, and the silence that surrounded me, is a deep motivation for creating safe spaces for queer youth in my classroom today.

Education 4112, Educational Psychology and Adolescent Development, is a course for upper-level undergraduates interested in careers in teaching and in psychological aspects of adolescences. The course is a required part of CU School of Education's minor in education, and each year it also draws a small number of older students returning to school to complete undergraduate degrees on the way to becoming teachers. For many years, the course had been taught as a lecture course for between 85 and 100 students and emphasized traditional educational psychology topics, such as motivation and learning theory. In 2011, Ben Kirshner and I (Bill) began to redesign the course around three broad domains of development: identity, learning, and sociopolitical development.

In the reflections on this course below, I (Bill) draw from evidence collected as part of the course. Specifically, support for claims about what aspects of the course have been most successful draw on written arguments students develop in response to prompts about how they would prepare a group of teachers or volunteers in a school to develop safe and supportive learning spaces for queer youth. I also draw from themes extracted from students' learning reflections written at the end of each semester of the course. As in other forms of design research, I draw on post-class teaching team reflections developed each week from the course. The teaching team is comprised of the instructor, a graduate teaching assistant, and five undergraduate "learning assistants" (Otero, Pollock, & Finkelstein, 2010).

One of the more successful aspects of the redesigned course from our point of view was a week that involved a visit from a local high school Gay-Straight Alliance (GSA). The GSA faculty advisor would bring six to eight young people who were members of the alliance to be part of a panel during a week when we discussed "gender and sexual identity development," the last in a series of weeks focused on the domain of identity development. The youth from the GSA sometimes served on a panel in front of the whole class. Other semesters, we had GSAs go in pairs to small group discussions led by undergraduate learning assistants. Each time they came, we thought our students benefited from hearing first-person stories of queer youth and their experiences in high school. In their essays for the course, our students referred back to the visits frequently, and the questions they posed of panellists when they visited reflected what we saw as a genuine interest in their stories.

In fact, the experiences of those involved were more varied than we had suspected, and not all were positive. Some of the GSA members felt uncomfortable in the smaller groups. Not all were identified as queer or identified at all in a way they felt safe disclosing to our students. Queer students in our class did not always feel safe, either, when the visits happened. The way we represented queer youth in the class—foregrounding issues of promoting safety through GSA—was an important but limited focus. We began to see what we came to call a "tour of identities" approach to organizing the class as insufficient to address important issues at the intersections of identity and that encompassed a full range of concerns of queer youth growing up today.

We set out to redesign the class around some different principles. We did want to keep safe spaces in the foreground of the course, but in the broader context of helping our students build *developmental alliances* with queer and other youth; that is, to join youth in their own developmental processes in a relationship of reciprocal influence "accompanying youth rather than directing them, listening to them as much as we speak to them, and being open to the changes they inspire in us just as we hope they'll be open to the changes we may inspire in them" (Nakkula & Toshalis, 2006, p. xii). We decided that rather than organize the course around different developmental domains, we would organize it into phases of relationship development: building an alliance, growing and developing it, and transitioning out of it (as was necessary for us, because the course includes a strong service-learning component). We reasoned that this approach would allow us to weave aspects of queer youth development throughout the course, emphasizing the diverse concerns of youth across many different domains of their lives, from academics to friendship and family. We also thought that by juxtaposing the experiences of queer youth with traditional positive youth development ideas, we could queer notions of positive developmental settings (National Research Council and Institute of Medicine, 2002) and trouble the idea that there is a single set of strategies that will work for building developmental alliances with youth.

To accomplish the course transformation, we enlisted the support of two students taking the class and leaders of a new initiative in the school focused on supporting teachers and school communities around topics of gender and sexual diversity called *A Queer Endeavor* (http://aqueerendeavor.org/). The students in the course were part of a "special projects" offering for people whose schedule prevented them from taking part in the service-learning component of the course. They worked with Ben Kirshner, my co-instructor in the course, to identify new course readings. They also conducted interviews with faculty and members of the LGBTQ community in the CU Boulder School of Education. In parallel, we worked with the new leadership of *A Queer Endeavor* to restructure our GSA visits to provide a more structured, and hopefully safer arrangement for their visits to class. We set up a process for crowdsourcing student questions to panellists, allowing for a selection of questions that at once reflected the breadth of interests of class members but also a filtering that could minimize risk of "spotlighting" (Carter, 2008) queer youth.

The new class structure in fact enabled us to weave readings, lectures, and small group discussions that made the lives of queer youth come alive throughout the course. When presenting on features of positive developmental settings for youth (National Research Council and Institute of Medicine, 2002), we now highlight ways that GSA foster "support for efficacy and mattering" through leadership activities. We trouble the notion of creating physically and psychologically safe spaces by highlighting ways that safety requires attention to difference and specifically to the diverse concerns of queer youth, through specific readings, media (e.g., the "T Word," www.logotv.com/video/laverne-cox-presents-the-t-word/1731865/playlist.jhtml), and class discussions. Readings and media highlight the experience of queer youth who are homeless (Cruz, 2011), youth engaged in GSA activity, and queer youth as adults looking back at their relationships to parents (e.g., Richman & Kramer, 2013). Perhaps most importantly, we challenge narratives of identity that fix what it means to be a healthy queer youth in the class (Talburt, 2004).

A driving question in the course overall is how we can design settings that can engage and empower young people, and one of the culminating tasks for the course is an essay where students respond to how they would re-design a particular setting. I always include a choice of prompts relating to how safe spaces can be designed to better support queer youth, because it gives students a chance to apply their readings to a practical task. The framing of the driving question and this task are purposeful—it focuses on settings, not youth, and we encourage students to size up settings with respect to their qualities, while not assuming much about the particular youth who they see in the settings. We encourage them to ask how they can be allies in these settings and also to take an active—even activist—stance toward setting re-design.

Context 2: The Trans*Literacies Project

In the 2013–2014 academic year, I (Jacob) worked with a pair of teachers at the "Social Justice Academy" (SJA), a social justice-themed charter school in the Midwestern United States. "Elly," a first-year teacher at the school, invited me to work with her to develop a curriculum focusing on gender diversity, and we collaborated with her co-teacher, "Rick," who was in his first year as a teacher at SJA but who had been a teacher and administrator in the district for more than two decades. The "gender diversity" unit was implemented in SJA's mixed-age, fourth/fifth-grade classroom, which consisted of 53 students (34 male-identified children and 19 female-identified children), Elly and Rick, and three teaching assistants. The unit was implemented over approximately ten weeks during the middle third of the 2013–2014 academic year, beginning in early November and continuing through mid-February.

Elly and Rick expressed an interest in supporting students in developing a critical perspective on gender, gender norms, and social expectations about gender performance. Together, we designed and implemented a unit that invited students to both "read" and "write"—that is, interpret and perform—gender across multiple media platforms.

Queer theory led design in this context in three ways. First, the unit itself was designed to challenge dominant values about "normal" gender and sexual identities, and to invite learners to investigate the various identity positions they take on over the course of a day, a week, a school year, or a lifetime. Second, I developed a queer research design that centralized participants' gender and sexual identities. I also sought to establish and disrupt the design collaborators' (Elly's, Rick's, and my) assumptions about "normal" learning trajectories and about students' identities. I undertook a data collection process that looked for what escaped easy categorization. Third, I developed a queer analytic approach that drew on discourse analytic methods and mediated discourse analysis to highlight how gender and sexual norms emerged and were challenged throughout the unit.

Design Principles

Below, we highlight three design principles that have emerged through implementation of LGBTQ-inclusive curriculum at the research sites described above. These principles emerged through our separate work at these sites and from cross-site comparison conducted from a queer perspective.

Principle 1: Highlight Identity Variance and Varied Identities

Dominant approaches to LGBTQIA-supportive education tend to position learners (and all people) inside of a binary: Either they are LGBTQIA or they are straight/cisgender. While this framing makes it possible to recognize students who might be more vulnerable to harassment, discrimination, and violence, it also effaces the ways in which identity labels can shift, as well as the ways we vary our performances of sexuality and gender regardless of the words we use to identify ourselves.

Queer perspectives view identities as multiple, varied, and constantly shifting. Queerness is, from the view of queer theory, the birthright of us all; and we are united by the experience of running the gauntlet of the heterosexual matrix (Bruhm & Hurley, 2004; Kincaid, 1998). From this standpoint, identity is not innate—we are not "born this way," but instead collect a variety of experiences of attractions and reactions (Barale, Goldberg, Moon, Sedgwick, & Stockton, 2009; Sedgwick, 1993). These experiences are mediated by the gendered and sexual norms that are built into the cultural tools and artifacts we draw upon to create our communities and worlds (Bornstein, 2013; McWilliams, 2016); the experiences accrete over time and sediment around the terms our culture has developed to give name to ourselves and each other.

These terms, however, not only fall short in describing our identities and experiences, but they also smooth out the edges of our experiences. Someone who identifies as a gay man might, for example, experience attraction to people who do not identify as men; but the terms of his identification require him to ignore or reject those attractions. (The same is true, to much more detrimental effect, of people who identify as straight and experience attraction to people of the same gender—in cultures wherein heterosexuality is treated as the desired norm, queer desires are often perceived as perverted, dangerous, and immoral (Bettcher, 2007; Fassinger & Arseneau, 2007; Graves, 2009).) Transgender people receive pressure to embrace the narrative that they were "born in the wrong body" and to reject any experiences, preferences, or orientations that align with the gender they were designated at birth. Likewise, people who identify as cisgender are expected to reject any gender variant tendencies, despite the evidence that we all vary our gender performances across contexts and time.

Take, for example, the "gender line" activity that was implemented in SJA's fourth/fifth-grade classroom. In this activity, students were invited to identify moments in their lives during which they experienced *gender dissonance*: tensions between their actions and cultural messages about gender appropriate behaviour. Students were given post-it notes on which to describe these tensions. They then placed their post-it notes on two gender continua. One continuum was labelled the "your experience" line, and the other was labelled "what the world thinks." Students placed their experiences in different positions on each of these lines—for example, for one student "a boy playing My Little Pony" fell squarely on the "boy" side of the "your experience" continuum even though the same activity landed on the "girl" side of the "what the world thinks" continuum.

Once students had placed their post-it notes, a clear trend was visible: Both female- and male-assigned students felt very comfortable engaging in traditionally masculine activities, but male-assigned students perceived a pressure to avoid traditionally feminine activities. When prompted to reflect on the gender lines, students noticed this trend. Emily, a female-assigned fifth grader, notes that masculinity is valued while femininity is less valued:

Emily: I remember a bit ago how we talked about how it's ok for, um, for girls to wear more, for girls to wear things that would be considered boy things?
Elly: Yeah.
Emily: Things that would be considered boy things? Because, um, on the your opinion line, it, it's, it's more towards the boys' section of everything and toward the middle, and then, there's a lot of stuff on the boy part, and then there's hardly anything on the girl part? Cause it's more okay, it's okay for girls to wear, and do things that are more boy stuff.

Certainly, this activity provided a rich opportunity for exploring how masculinity is valued and placed in binary opposition to the far less valued femininity (Serano, 2009). The activity also, however, highlighted a key principle undergirding queer frameworks: that gender variance is a common, shared experience. The fourth- and fifth-grade students who participated in this activity had no trouble identifying moments when they had varied their performance of gender, and most also quickly identified times in their lives when their performances of gender had been policed by others. This activity created opportunities for students to consider how gender norms are enforced through not only social institutions but also the interactions we have with others—and to come to see that violating gender norms can trigger anger and aggression. Sarah, a female-assigned fourth grader, was so eager to tell her story of gender policing that she had trouble sitting still:

> *I've* been called a boy before a *lot*? Because one, *I* wear clothes that are from the boys' aisle and, I used to have my hair short like *Jenna's* and so, I remember having the experience of one time walking into a girls' bathroom and everybody screaming ah, it's a *boy*.

It should be noted that neither Emily nor Sarah identified as gender variant. No student in this class disclosed a transgender or gender variant identity to Jacob (although some students did say they wished they could perform their gender differently). It's important to emphasize that creating a trans-inclusive classroom should not, and does not need to, wait until a transgender student walks through the classroom door. Highlighting and investigating identity variance and varied identities can be a powerful place to begin this work.

In the undergraduate class, we highlight variations in identity by emphasizing specifically the fluidity of gender identities in the life experiences of adolescents. We feature and discuss media related specifically to the stories of transgender youth and how they are positioned within and resist organizational processes and structures in schools. For a presentation on intersectional identities, we rely on the compelling testimony of Laverne Cox, a transgender woman, addressing a Harvard audience about her experience of intersectionality as African American, transgender, and a woman (Le & Schacter, 2014). Identity is presented as situated within changing cultural and historical contexts and institutions.

Across both these contexts, a common theme is that a queer approach to design emphasizes the varied identities and identity variances that exist within a given community, as well as the vast possibilities for identity that exist in broader communities and cultures. This approach also foregrounds questions of safety—exploration of identity variance requires a fluency with the terms under which one can survive this exploration. Queerness and gender non-conformity are more than intellectual or emotional risks: In some contexts, they also put a person's physical safety on the line. Inviting learners to embrace queerness and gender variance, then, requires a simultaneous attention to helping learners assess when, where, and how queer performances of identity may be met with hostility.

Principle 2: A Telos of Freedom (Designing for Contradiction and Resistance)

Although *telos* can be conceived of as any kind of transformation of human activity (Beach, 2003; Lave, 1996), some have noted a consistent emphasis in the social sciences on a progress-oriented telos (Mbembe & Meintjes, 2003; Morrell, 2008; Puar, 2007). Educational theories typically conceive of learning as featuring "increase"—an increase in opportunities for action (Boyer & Roth, 2005), for example, or increased attunement to or facility with the affordances of cultural tools, knowledge-as-tools, and language-as-tools (Brown, Collins, & Duguid, 1989; Greeno & Middle School Mathematics through Applications Project Group, 1998). Lave (1996) frames telos as movement toward increasingly full participation within one or more communities of practice—a conceptualization that is taken up by many educators and researchers who work from a sociocultural or situative perspective (e.g., Barab & Duffy, 2000; Brown & Duguid, 1991; Harris & Shelswell, 2005). This perspective enables educators to privilege transformations that fit into a narrative of positive development: Over time, learners should "advance" toward a more complex, more sophisticated view of their social world and should act in ways that recognizably and consistently reflect increased complexity in cognition (Lave & Wenger, 1991; Vygotsky, 1978; Wertsch, Tulviste, & Hagstrom, 1993).

The queer perspective resists the characterization of learning as positive change over time, for several reasons. First, queer frameworks are critical of narratives of progress; Britzman (1998), outlining this critique, argues that "we should be wary of the promise of progress, not because development does not occur but because progress must forget the conflicts it requires" (p. 51). Second, the emphasis on positive change normalizes one learning trajectory, as a result obscuring or effacing other possible pathways including resistance, rejection, refusal, or failure (Britzman, 1998; Britzman & Gilbert, 2004). Queer history, indeed, is heavily populated with individuals or groups whose purpose was to insist on *un*intelligibility—behaving in ways that so deeply reject assumptions about what humans want or how they "should" behave that dominant theories of culture, identity, and learning have no utility (Edelman, 2004). Halberstam (2011) frames failure as a wholly valid response to a broken society:

> Perhaps most obviously, failure allows us to escape the punishing norms that discipline behavior and manage human development with the goal of delivering us from unruly childhoods to orderly and predictable adulthoods. . . . And while failure certainly comes accompanied by a host of negative affects, such as disappointment, disillusionment, and despair, it also provides the opportunity to use these negative affects to poke holes in the toxic positivity of contemporary life.
>
> *(p. 3)*

In rejecting the progress narrative, queer perspectives instead take an interest in how bodies resist regulation—how they kick back against clean classification, how they refuse new, "better" knowledge. Analytically and pedagogically, the production of knowledge is most richly visible in moments of contradiction, resistance, and refusal.

A queer approach to educational design rejects the notion of an ideal pathway through curricula. For design researchers, this means resisting an implicit and sometimes overt emphasis on the kinds of learning gains that align with a progress-oriented approach to learning: more knowledge, applied better, and transferred faster to new contexts. Instead, a queer design process seeks alternate forms of engagement.

Known-answer questions, perhaps obviously, have only the most marginal place in a queer pedagogy. In fact, if the answer to a question seems obvious, then that suggests that the answer and the question itself can and perhaps should be "queered." In the fourth/fifth-grade classroom where Jacob collaborated with Elly and Rick on the gender diversity unit, students agreed that American culture has become less sexist and that girls and women have more freedom today in school, careers, and family life. Without disagreeing with this consensus, we traced with them the gendered messages of commercials targeting children. We focused specifically on Lego commercials, which in the early decades (1950s–1970s) of the franchise showed boys and girls playing with the same Lego kit and creating the same kinds of projects. By the 1990s and 2000s, however, children in Lego commercials had become increasingly segregated by gender: Girls were rarely present at all in most Lego commercials, and eventually they were given their own pastel-coloured kit called Lego Friends. Boys, meanwhile, were shown building trucks and tanks and dinosaurs.[1]

Both "truths" can coexist: Laws and policies can exist that combat sexism and misogyny, and gendered cultural messages can become increasingly powerful and increasingly anti-woman. Laying these "truths" alongside each other without attempting to resolve them invited students to interrogate their assumptions about anti-sexism and gender (in)equality, and to sit within the contradictions that emerge.

One of the ways we problematize progress narratives in the undergraduate course is to emphasize repeatedly how laws and institutions constrain possible futures of young people. Students read about queer homeless youth, and the problematic of "identifying" youth putting them at risk of harm and discrimination while at the same time also potentially enabling them to access resources and support. We link these to other stories that trouble progress narratives, such as the pathways (not) available to undocumented youth.

Principle 3: The Activist Stance

Queer perspectives on education adopt an explicitly activist stance. This means, in part, that educational designs work toward a liberatory vision in which justice, equity, generosity, and joy can be achieved. It means, too, that the designers are bodies, claim and resist identities; that they engage disruption and contradiction.

A queer perspective means that researchers and designers embrace a gay agenda: A vision and practice that work toward a queer- and gender-inclusive world. It should be emphasized that although LGBTQIA concerns were the explicit focus of both research contexts described in this chapter, these commitments extend beyond curricular content and into the practices that research collaborators establish in learning contexts. For example, the terms and pronouns we use for each other in collaborative meetings and interactions with learners matter. The assumptions we make about a person's gender and sexual identity lead us to orient toward others in ways that can validate or challenge the heterosexual matrix. And the ways in which we talk about our lives, histories, and experiences can resist the narratives of normalcy that surround all of us working in and around educational contexts.

Additionally, queer perspectives invite intersectional perspectives. Not discussed in this chapter, but essential to the work of social transformation, are investigations into the ways in which gender and sexuality interact with other forms of identity, including race/ethnicity, socioeconomic status, disability status, and age. The absence within the heterosexual matrix of these forms of identity categories is not an accident, and its refusal to account for intersectionality places it in a default position of valuing White, middle/upper class, non-disabled, and youth-positive identities—thereby reinforcing a vast range of inequalities across social and cultural groups. Others have taken up the need to adopt intersectional perspectives on queerness, and their work offers important insights into how a queer lens can inform and be informed by investigations into other forms of identity and experience (e.g., Barnard, 2004; Bucholtz, 1999; Clare, 2015; Eng, 1997; Johnson, 2001; Kumashiro, 1999; McRuer, 2006; Muñoz, 1999).

The activist stance calls on all researchers working in sympathy with queer commitments to take a stand on behalf of themselves, on behalf of the collaborators and stakeholders in their specific research contexts, and on behalf of all those who struggle inside of matrices of normativity—that is, on behalf of all of us living, loving, and learning in this world.

Conclusion

In this chapter, we argue for an approach to learning sciences-focused research that embraces the commitments of queer theory. We call for activist-focused scholarship that aims to open up new opportunities for safety, identity, and learning, and that troubles assumptions about the role of gender and sexual norms in educational communities. The learning sciences as a whole has embraced a focus on designing and bringing about "new forms of learning." Queer perspectives, too, centre on the "new"—new spaces of safety, new forms of engagement and identity, and new frameworks for theorizing learning and development. But the queer frame is not just about a positive trajectory toward some shiny new ideal; it is about challenging, resisting, troubling, and queering notions of normalcy and what we take for granted about the world and our place in it. It is about unlearning and reshaping gendered ways of knowing and about shattering the containers we're given to hold our desires (Britzman, 1998; Spivak, 2012).

In some ways, the commitments of queer theory find synergy with some strands of learning theory. Certainly, many queer theorists would express sympathy with the Engestromian view of "development or learning as breaking away" (Engeström, 1996), although the queer form conceptualizes a version of breaking away that *maintains* relations, even as those relations are always shifting in embodiment and identification (Britzman, 1998). To view identity, development, and learning as a steady trajectory toward something more solid, more coherent, is in opposition to the queer project; but re-envisioning these aspects of education from a queer perspective opens up spaces of freedom—of movement, of identification, of learning, and relationship-building.

Note

1. The commercials used for this trace activity included the following: 1955 black and white commercial with a boy and a girl (http://youtu.be/C1gmrgnYD5A); 1973 two children building a bridge, helicopter, ambulance, tow truck (http://youtu.be/U5u0Hmkh1JM); 1970s young child and older sibling playing with LEGOs (http://youtu.be/JvkiDkMGDqg); 1980s Zack the LEGO maniac (http://youtu.be/pDH3AoOQzE0); 1991 Pirate LEGOmaniac commercial (http://youtu.be/7eFNaloQWsY); 1993 Ice Planet LEGOmaniac commercial (http://youtu.be/BvUhaMnTuPk).

References

Bang, M., Medin, D., Washinawatok, K., & Chapman, S. (2010). Innovations in culturally based science education through partnerships and community. In M. S. Khine & M. I. Saleh (Eds.), *New science of learning: Cognition, computers, and collaboration in education* (pp. 569–592). New York, NY: Springer.

Barab, S. A., & Duffy, T. (2000). From practice fields to communities of practice. *Theoretical Foundations of Learning Environments*, *1*(1), 25–55.

Barale, M. A., Goldberg, J., Moon, M., Sedgwick, E. K., & Stockton, K. B. (2009). *The queer child, or growing sideways in the twentieth century*. Durham, NC: Duke University Press.

Barnard, I. (2004). *Queer race: Cultural interventions in the racial politics of queer theory* (Vol. 3). New York, NY: Peter Lang.

Barton, A. C., & Tan, E. (2010). We be burnin'! Agency, identity, and science learning. *The Journal of the Learning Sciences*, *19*(2), 187–229.

Beach, K. (2003). Consequential transitions: A developmental view of knowledge propagation through social organizations. In T. Tuomi-Grohn & Y. Engeström (Eds.), *Between school and work: New perspectives on transfer and boundary-crossing* (pp. 39–62). London, UK: Pergamon.

Bell, P., Hoadley, C., & Linn, M. C. (2004). Design-based research in education. In M. C. Linn, E. A. Davis & P. Bell (Eds.), *Internet environments for science education* (pp. 73–88). Mahwah, NJ: Erlbaum.

Berlant, L., & Freeman, E. (1992). Queer nationality. *Boundary 2*, *19*(1), 149–180.

Berlant, L., & Warner, M. (1995). What does queer theory teach us about X? *PMLA, 110*(3), 343–349.

Bettcher, T. M. (2007). Evil deceivers and make-believers: On transphobic violence and the politics of illusion. *Hypatia, 22*(3), 43–65.

Booker, A. N., Vossoughi, S., & Hooper, P. K. (2014). Tensions and possibilities for political work in the learning sciences. *Proceedings of the 11th International Conference of the Learning Sciences (ICLS 2014)—Volume 2* (pp. 919–926). Boulder, CO: International Society of the Learning Sciences.

Bornstein, K. (2013). *My new gender workbook: How to become a real man, a real woman, the real you, or something else entirely.* New York, NY: Routledge.

Boyer, L., & Roth, W. M. (2005). Individual/collective dialectic of free-choice learning in a community-based mapping project. *Environmental Education Research, 11*(3), 335–351.

BreakOUT! (2015). Statement from BreakOUT! on death of black transgender youth in New Orleans. *Youth BreakOUT!* Retrieved from http://www.youthbreakout.org/content/breaking-statement-breakout-death-black-transgender-youth-new-orleans

Britzman, D. P. (1998). *Lost subjects, contested objects: Toward a psychoanalytic inquiry of learning.* New York, NY: SUNY Press.

Britzman, D. P., & Gilbert, J. (2004). What will have been said about gayness in teacher education. *Teaching Education, 15*(1), 81–96.

Brown, J. S., Collins, A., & Duguid, P. (1989). Situated cognition and the culture of learning. *Educational Researcher, 18*(1), 32–42.

Brown, J. S., & Duguid, P. (1991). Organizational learning and communities-of-practice: Toward a unified view of working, learning, and innovation. *Organization Science, 2*(1), 40–57.

Bruhm, S., & Hurley, N. (Eds.) (2004). *Curiouser: On the queerness of children.* Minneapolis, MN: University of Minnesota Press.

Bucholtz, M. (1999). You da man: Narrating the racial other in the production of white masculinity. *Journal of Sociolinguistics, 3*(4), 443–460.

Butler, J. (1993). Critically queer. *GLQ: A Journal of Lesbian and Gay Studies, 1*, 17–32.

Butler, J. (1999). *Gender trouble.* New York, NY: Routledge.

Butler, J. (2004). *Undoing gender.* New York, NY: Routledge.

Carter, D. J. (2008). On spotlighting and ignoring racial group members in the classroom. In M. Pollock (Ed.), *Everyday anti-racism: Getting real about race in school* (pp. 230–234). New York, NY: New Press.

Clare, E. (2015). *Exile and pride: Disability, queerness, and liberation.* Durham, NC: Duke University Press.

Cobb, P. A., Confrey, J., diSessa, A. A., Lehrer, R., & Schauble, L. (2003). Design experiments in educational research. *Educational Researcher, 32*(1), 9–13.

Cruz, C. (2011). LGBTQ street youth talk back: A meditation on resistance and witnessing. *International Journal of Qualitative Studies in Education, 24*(5), 547–558.

Dilley, P. (1999). Queer theory: Under construction. *International Journal of Qualitative Studies in Education, 12*(5), 457–472.

Dillon, F. R., Worthington, R. L., & Moradi, B. (2011). Sexual identity as a universal process. In S. J. Schwartz, K. Luyckx & V. L. Vignoles (Eds.), *Handbook of identity theory and research* (pp. 649–670). New York, NY: Springer.

Dobber, M. (1995). SexCrime. *Alternative Law Journal, 20*(6), 285–287.

Edelman, L. (1998). The future is kid stuff: Queer theory, disidentification, and the death drive. *Narrative*, *6*(1), 18–30.

Edelman, L. (2004). *No future: Queer theory and the death drive*. Durham, NC: Duke University Press.

Eng, D. L. (1997). Out here and over there: Queerness and diaspora in Asian American studies. *Social Text*, *52/53*, 31–52.

Engeström, Y. (1987). *Learning by expanding*. Helsinki, FI: Orienta-Konsultit Oy.

Engeström, Y. (1996). Development as breaking away and opening up: A challenge to Vygotsky and Piaget. *Swiss Journal of Psychology*, *55*, 126–132.

Erikson, E. H. (1950). *Childhood and society*. New York, NY: Norton.

Fassinger, R. E., & Arseneau, J. R. (2007). "I'd rather get wet than be under that umbrella": Differentiating the experiences and identities of lesbian, gay, bisexual, and transgender people. In K. J. Bieschke, R. M. Perez & K. A. DeBord (Eds.), *Handbook of counseling and psychotherapy with lesbian, gay, bisexual and transgender clients* (pp. 19–49). Washington, DC: American Psychological Association.

Gould, D. B. (2009). *Moving politics: Emotion and ACT UP's fight against AIDS*. Chicago, IL: University of Chicago Press.

Graves, K. (2009). *And they were wonderful teachers: Florida's purge of gay and lesbian teachers*. Urbana, IL: University of Illinois Press.

Green, A. I. (2007). Queer theory and sociology: Locating the subject and the self in sexuality studies. *Sociological Theory*, *25*(1), 26–45.

Greeno, J. G., & Middle School Mathematics through Applications Project Group. (1998). The situativity of knowing, learning, and research. *American Psychologist*, *53*(1), 5–26.

Gutiérrez, K. D., & Vossoughi, S. (2010). Lifting off the ground to return anew: Mediated praxis, transformative learning, and social design experiments. *Journal of Teacher Education*, *61*(1–2), 100–117.

Halberstam, J. (2011). *The queer art of failure*. Durham, NC: Duke University Press.

Hand, V. M., & Gresalfi, M. (2015). The joint accomplishment of identity. *Educational Psychologist*, *503*(3), 190–203.

Harris, S. R., & Shelswell, N. (2005). Moving beyond communities of practice in adult basic education. In D. Barton & K. Tusting (Eds.), *Beyond communities of practice: Language, power and social context* (pp. 158–179). New York, NY: Cambridge University Press.

Herek, G. M., & Glunt, E. K. (1988). An epidemic of stigma: Public reactions to AIDS. *American Psychologist*, *43*(11), 886–891.

Holland, D., Lachicotte, W., Jr., Skinner, D., & Cain, C. (1998). *Identity and agency in cultural worlds*. Cambridge, MA: Harvard University Press.

Jagose, A. (1996). *Queer theory: An introduction*. New York, NY: New York University Press.

Johnson, E. P. (2001). "Quare" studies, or (almost) everything I know about queer studies I learned from my grandmother. *Text and Performance Quarterly*, *21*(1), 1–25.

Kaptelinin, V., & Nardi, B. (2006). *Acting with technology: Activity theory and interaction design*. Cambridge, MA: MIT Press.

Kincaid, J. R. (1998). Producing erotic children. In H. Jenkins (Ed.), *The children's culture reader* (pp. 241–253). New York, NY: New York University Press.

Kozulin, A. (1986). The concept of activity in Soviet psychology: Vygotsky, his disciples and critics. *American Psychologist*, *41*(3), 264.

Kumashiro, K. K. (1999). Supplementing normalcy and otherness: Queer Asian American men reflect on stereotypes, identity, and oppression. *International Journal of Qualitative Studies in Education*, *12*(5), 491–508.

Kumashiro, K. K. (2000). Teaching and learning through desire, crisis, and difference: Perverted reflections on anti-oppressive education. *The Radical Teacher, 58*, 6–11.
Kumashiro, K. K. (2002). *Troubling education: "Queer" activism and anti-oppressive pedagogy.* New York, NY: Routledge.
Lave, J. (1996). Teaching, as learning, in practice. *Mind, Culture, and Activity, 3*(3), 149–164.
Lave, J. (2012). Changing practice. *Mind, Culture, and Activity, 19*(2), 156–171.
Lave, J., & Wenger, E. (1991). *Situated learning: Legitimate peripheral participation.* Cambridge, MA: Harvard University Press.
Le, Q.-N., & Schacter, J. R. (2014, Feb. 24). Actress Laverne Cox discusses identity, trans issues. *Harvard Crimson.* Retrieved from http://www.thecrimson.com/article/2014/2/24/laverne-cox-trans-event/
Marcia, J. (1980). Identity in adolescence. In J. Adelson (Ed.), *Handbook of adolescent psychology* (pp. 159–187). New York, NY: John Wiley and Sons.
Martin, K. A. (1998). Becoming a gendered body: Practices of preschools. *American Sociological Review, 63*(4), 494–511.
Mbembe, J.-A., & Meintjes, L. (2003). Necropolitics. *Public Culture, 15*(1), 11–40.
McRuer, R. (2006). Queer/disabled existence. In L. J. Davis (Ed.), *The disability studies reader* (pp. 301–308). New York, NY: Routledge.
McWilliams, J. J. (2016). Queering participatory design research. *Cognition and Instruction, 34*(3).
Mitchell, W. J. T. (1995). Representation. In F. Lentricchia & T. McLaughlin (Eds.), *Critical terms for literary study* (pp. 11–22). Chicago, IL: University of Chicago Press.
Morrell, K. (2008). The narrative of "evidence based" management: A polemic. *Journal of Management Studies, 45*(3), 613–635.
Muñoz, J. E. (1999). *Disidentifications: Queers of color and the performance of politics.* Minneapolis, MN: University of Minnesota Press.
Muñoz, J. E. (2009). *Cruising utopia.* New York, NY: NYU Press.
Nakkula, M. J., & Toshalis, E. (2006). *Understanding youth: Adolescent development for educators.* Cambridge, MA: Harvard Education Press.
Nasir, N. (2011). *Racialized identities: Race and achievement among African American youth.* Stanford, CA: Stanford University Press.
Nasir, N., & Hand, V. M. (2004). *From the court to the classroom: Managing identities as learners in basketball and classroom mathematics.* Paper presented at the annual meeting of the American Educational Research Association, San Diego, CA.
Nasir, N., & Saxe, G. B. (2003). Ethnic and academic identities: A cultural practice perspective on emerging tensions and their management in the lives of minority students. *Educational researcher, 32*(5), 14–18.
National Research Council and Institute of Medicine. (2002). *Community programs to promote youth development.* Washington, DC: National Academy Press.
O'Connor, K., & Allen, A. (2010). Learning as the organizing of social futures. *Yearbook of the National Society for the Study of Education, 109*(1), 160–175.
O'Connor, K., & Penuel, W. R. (2010). Introduction: Principles of a human sciences approach to research on learning. *Yearbook of the National Society for the Study of Education, 109*(1), 128–143.
Otero, V., Pollock, S., & Finkelstein, N. (2010). A physics department's role in preparing physics teachers: The Colorado learning assistant model. *American Journal of Physics, 78*(11), 1218–1224.

Packer, M. J., & Goicoechea, J. (2000). Sociocultural and constructivist theories of learning: Ontology, not just epistemology. *Educational Psychologist*, *35*(4), 227–241.

Penuel, W. R., & O'Connor, K. (2010). Learning research as a human science: Old wine in new bottles? *Yearbook of the National Society for the Study of Education*, *109*(1), 268–283.

Penuel, W. R., & Spillane, J. P. (2014). Learning sciences and policy design and implementation: Key concepts and tools for collaborative engagement. In R. K. Sawyer (Ed.), *Cambridge handbook of the learning sciences* (2nd edn., pp. 649–667). Cambridge, UK: Cambridge University Press.

Pinar, W. (1998). *Queer theory in education*. Mahwah, NJ: Lawrence Erlbaum.

Puar, J. (2007). *Terrorist assemblages: Homonationalism in queer times*. Durham, NC: Duke University Press.

Queer Nation. (1990). *Queers read this* [Brochure]. New York, NY: Queer Nation.

Richman, J., & Kramer, S. K. (Producers). (2013). *Amanda: 16 years later*. Retrieved from http://www.radiodiaries.org/amanda-16-years-later/

Sannino, A., Daniels, H., & Gutiérrez, K. D. (2009). *Learning and expanding with activity theory*. Cambridge, UK: Cambridge University Press.

Sedgwick, E. K. (1993). How to bring your kids up gay: The war on effeminate boys. In M. Warner (Ed.), *Fear of a queer planet: Queer politics and social theory* (pp. 69–81). Minneapolis: University of Minnesota Press.

Serano, J. (2009). *Whipping girl: A transsexual woman on sexism and the scapegoating of femininity*. Emeryville, CA: Seal Press.

Shilts, R. (2007). *And the band played on: Politics, people, and the AIDS epidemic, 20th-anniversary edition*. New York, NY: Macmillan.

Spade, D. (2014). Their laws will not make us safer. In R. Conrad (Ed.), *Against equality: Prisons will not protect you* (pp. 1–12). Oakland, CA: AK Press.

Spivak, G. C. (2012). *In other worlds: Essays in cultural politics*. New York, NY: Routledge.

Stetsenko, A., & Arievitch, I. M. (2004). The self in cultural-historical activity theory reclaiming the unity of social and individual dimensions of human development. *Theory & Psychology*, *14*(4), 475–503.

Talburt, S. (2004). Constructions of LGBT youth: Opening up subject positions. *Theory into Practice*, *43*(2), 116–121.

Vygotsky, L. S. (1978). *Mind in society*. Cambridge, MA: Harvard University Press.

Warner, M. (1993). *Fear of a queer planet: Queer politics and social theory* (Vol. 6). Minneapolis, MN: University of Minnesota Press.

Wertsch, J. V. (1998). *Mind as action*. New York, NY: Oxford University Press.

Wertsch, J. V. (2005). Vygotsky's two approaches to mediation. In S. Norris & R. H. Jones (Eds.), *Discourse in action: Introducing mediated discourse analysis* (pp. 52–61). New York, NY: Taylor & Francis.

Wertsch, J. V., Tulviste, P., & Hagstrom, F. (1993). A sociocultural approach to agency. In E. Forman, N. Minnick & C. A. Stone (Eds.), *Contexts for learning: Sociocultural dynamics in children's development* (pp. 336–356). New York, NY: Oxford University Press.

7
TOWARDS AN ETHIC OF DECOLONIAL TRANS-ONTOLOGIES IN SOCIOCULTURAL THEORIES OF LEARNING AND DEVELOPMENT

Megan Bang

The socio-ecological challenges of the 21st century will likely mark an important time in the evolution, adaptation, and reimagining of human communities. These cultural shifts will also be consequential for more-than-human life and the natural world upon which humans depend. The construction of relations between human worlds and the more-than-human natural world—human–nature relations for short—lives at the centre of these challenges as well as the possible futures humans might make and live. Seriously examining the ways in which constructions of human–nature relations have shaped societies—that is, understanding the socio-historical development of our current times—is critical if humans are to engage in the kind of social change making demanded of us.

We need social change making that at its heart asks us to reimagine relationships and constructions of freedom that have depended on domination—of people and of nature. While this change is needed across many sectors of societies, this chapter focuses on the ways that construction of human–nature relations have shaped our theories of learning and development. I argue that there is a need to examine how colonial and settler-colonial histories may have and currently are shaping our theories and approaches to learning and development.

My motivations to become a scholar have been deeply driven by the need to contribute to the collective continuance (Whyte, 2013) of Indigenous people with an eye towards the broader socio-ecological issues of our times, as well as my love and experience teaching from formal pre-K and middle school settings to informal and inter-generational settings. Whyte (2013) defines collective continuance as "a community's capacity to be adaptive in ways sufficient for the livelihoods of its members to flourish into the future" (p. 518). More specifically, with respect to Indigenous peoples, Whyte contends that "tribal collective continuance can be seen as a community's aptitude for making adjustments to current or predicted change in ways that contest colonial hardships and embolden comprehensive aims at robust living" (p. 518). These forms of robust living necessitate relationships to place (lands and waters) that make continuance possible. Note that the evaluation criteria in collective continuance stands in significant distinction to a quest for freedom and self-regulation, one that Jovanović (2015) suggests rests on modernist agendas in which human beings are orientated to conquering nature. In examining evaluations criteria and the historical in Vygotsky's theory, Jovanović (2015) writes:

> Ideally, conquering nature means liberation from necessity and entering the 'kingdom of freedom.' The same model applies to relation to internal nature. . . . There are already many doubts as to whether such a model of progress is acceptable—in the relation of human beings to 'external' nature and society, as well as to their psychic, subjective world.
>
> *(pp. 26–27)*

In short, the construction of "external" human–nature relations and "internal" psychological worlds (and our constructions of such worlds) are consequentially linked. For Jovanović, consequentiality implies those of socio-ecological challenges—which I extend to those of colonialism.

Although it is unlikely that any human community will not undergo some shifts because of the current socio-ecological challenges, not all communities contend with the present external challenges equally. Indigenous communities across the globe tend to be on the front lines of these issues, though by and large they are responsible for little to none of the human-produced factors causing the socio-ecological changes (Wildcat, 2009). Some of these inequities occur because of geography, wherein many Indigenous peoples' homelands are in climate change hot spots. However, much of the inequity is entrenched in colonial difference reflected in infrastructure (economic, industrial, political), uses of lands by people and nation states, and the ways in which people reason, value, and engage in and with the natural world (e.g. Agyeman, Cole, Haluza-DeLay, & O'Riley, 2010; LaDuke, 1999; Whyte, 2016). These three factors—social infrastructure, land use and relations, and epistemology–ideology dynamics—perpetuate particular forms of historically shaped power and invisibility of land, water, and Indigenous peoples, and therefore challenge Indigenous collective continuance—and perhaps, as Jovanović seems to suggest, human collective continuance more broadly.

Learning, and the possibilities for social change that learning entails, continue to be, in my opinion, the most compelling places of change and possibility in ensuring collective continuance. Sociocultural theories of learning have fed the social dreaming I engage in as a scholar. However, in my development as a scholar, I have encountered sources of tension in sociocultural theory that sometimes silenced questions, critiques, and possibilities. In part this occurred because

I often was asked to read past some of the significant problems in foundational texts in the field. Put candidly—we are often asked to ignore the characterizations of Indigenous peoples and the inherent coloniality in some of the foundational texts and broader theories of sociocultural learning, presumably in service of understanding or to buffer good ideas from the times in which the thinker lived. While this is reasonable to an extent, doing so without critically understanding the impacts is counter-productive.

Towards these ends, in this chapter I consider how core ontological claims about relations between people and the natural world have tended to reflect Western perspectives that not only extend coloniality but also have narrowed the possible space of imagining and knowing human learning and development within sociocultural theory. Richardson (2012), building with Maldonado-Torres's (2007, 2009) "decolonial attitude" and Mignolo's (2000) "decolonial dialogues," proposes that "a decolonial trans-ontology is an emergent form of being stemming from a border thinking and bilanguaging" (p. 550), one in which "European ontologies lose something of their habitability" (p. 550). These scholars all note the need to articulate a trans-ontology that opens the possibilities for plurality of ontologies beyond the West to distinguish it from the notion of ontology steeped in Western intellectual traditions. Such trans-ontologies undermine the coloniality of being[1] and create space for more than Western intellectual traditions and new forms of thought and education. I aim to raise questions that may contribute to developing a "de-colonial ethic" for cultivating "trans-ontologies" applied to sociocultural theories of human learning and development—an ethic that can contribute to the social change demanded of our times.

Importantly, sociocultural theories of learning are by far the most productive for me because they have made significant progress in eroding foundational premises embedded in much of Western thought by repatriating thought to dialogical social activity. However, colonial premises, like human exceptionalism, remain embedded in much of contemporary Western thought, including sociocultural theory. My aim in this chapter is not to reject sociocultural theory in totality. Rather, I intend to begin to unearth the historicized tensions, reflective of the colonial insistence on an essentialized difference between colonizer and colonized, that live in some of the foundational texts of Vygotsky. I argue that issues of coloniality and settler-coloniality manifest in our theories of learning in at least three ways: 1) the dominant focus and characterizations of human–human interactions; 2) the minimal focus on interactions in and with the natural world; 3) the decoupling of subject–object relations from subject–subject relations. To make this argument I first review some tenets of coloniality within an historical context that established human exceptionalism as the central grounds for claims about human thought. I describe how coloniality manifests in Vygotsky's treatment of so-called primitive thought. Then I review core aspects of settler-coloniality to explain why the considerable focus on human–human interactions found in Western ontologies, and their relatively minimal focus on human–nature relations, are consequential and politically weighted. Specifically, I focus on how human–human interactions privilege a focus on temporality as distinct from space, and explain how this disregard for space/land works against collective continuance. I explore why the need for expanded focus on subject–subject relations from multiple ways of knowing is necessary ground for the socioculturalists to take up seriously. Finally, given the readings of colonial and settler-colonialism, whose distinctions rely on the relation of settlers to colonized lands and positioning of Indigenous people, I raise questions about potential directions for seriously developing decolonial ontologies in sociocultural theories of learning. It is my intent that this exploration of ideas may contribute to the field additional ways we can to continue to build with Vygotsky and others—but with expanded sensibilities and questions towards new possible futures.

Beginning to see Colonialism in Vygotskian Thought

Developing decolonial trans-ontologies of learning requires significant work in tracing how the foundations of sociocultural theories reflect cultural and institutional practices (Cole, 1996; Rogoff, 2003) in particular political contexts, and examining the impact of these contexts on constructions of difference and theories of change. For example, Daniels (1996) notes:

> Whilst attempts to develop Vygotsky's work in Russia have not foregrounded semiotic mediation but have foregrounded the analysis of social transmission in activity settings, much of the work in the West has tended to ignore the social beyond the interactional and to celebrate individual and mediational processes at the expense of a consideration of socio-institutional, cultural and historical factors. Ideological differences between the West and the East have given rise to differences in theoretical development and of course pedagogical application.
>
> (p. 9)

In other words, political and ideological contexts influence scholarly work in the present, as well as interpretations of the scholarly work that preceded it.

More recently, Matusov (2008) worked to trace the ways in which different ontological projects have emerged within what he calls "Vygotskian academia." He says: "We should see conceptual struggles within Vygotskian academia not just as a struggle of ideas but also as a struggle of diverse social orders, diverse supertasks, and diverse sociocultural conditions under which Vygotskian scholars live" (p. 7).

Matusov (2008) argues that there were substantive distinctions between "cultural-historical" and "sociocultural" projects and theories of change or strategies towards equity that were reflected in neo-Vygotskian scholarship.[2] He links these distinctions to differences in where and when scholars were engaged in work (South African cultural-historical versus US-based sociocultural scholars). He suggests that both camps of scholars were interested in cultural difference but with distinctly different sensibilities around characterizing cultural differences and its consequences as well as subsequent theories of change. For example, he says: "Cultural-historical approaches see cultural difference as negative—something that disempowers 'historically backward' social groups—and temporary" (p. 20). He continues on to suggest that cultural-historical scholars (locating this originally with Vygotsky, 1994) believed social engineering, in the form of providing access to "modern cultural tools" (p. 19), was necessary for societal transformation and empowerment of marginalized communities. Importantly, Matusov locates social engineering efforts as emergent from South Africa's racialized system and suggests that the cultural-historical camp has emerged in dialogic opposition to biological apartheid ideologies.

In contrast to cultural-historical approaches, Matusov (2008) argues that sociocultural approaches emerged as a dialogical opposition to economic neoliberalism as located in "**standards**, **testing**, and **a system of punishments and rewards**" (p. 21, emphasis in original). Further, he characterizes neoliberalism as promoting a deficit model of students and their communities—particularly non-dominant communities. He suggests that in socioculturalists' dialogic reply to neoliberalism, scholars have worked to demonstrate how non-dominant communities are "differently capable" (p. 25), and argued that institutions need to change to accommodate those strengths and capacities.

While Matusov's characterizations are certainly incomplete with respect to the ontological projects of Vygotskian scholars (Vygotskian academia contains many layered ontological projects), I nonetheless have found it a useful analysis and agree with the challenge he poses to Vygotskian academia: "We have to situate our research questions in our ontological projects and dialogical opponents and relate our own ontology with the different ontological projects of other scholars" (p. 28).

Building from both Daniels and Matusov, I aim to take up Matusov's challenge and work to unearth the ways in which logics of colonialism are embedded in Vygotskian approaches. I suggest that colonialism and settler-colonialism continue to shape both cultural-historical and sociocultural approaches. While both camps of Vygotskian scholars challenge and seek to transform power differences between dominant and non-dominant human communities, the foundational hierarchical ordering of human domination over nature has not been a central focus of scholarship.

My view, however, is that the presumed human domination over nature, closely related to the philosophy of human exceptionalism, sits at the heart of the power differential that Vygotskian scholars often seek to transform. To support this argument, I review the work of several scholars who have developed a succinct analysis of the historical unfoldings of colonial logics and construction of thought. Briefly, I will discuss the development of the concept of human exceptionalism over the course of the 16th century. According to this ontology, inferior subjects (non-humans) do not think and thus are not worthy of the rights of humans. The historical development of this ontology is fundamentally rooted in colonial ideology, or what we might call the colonial difference, and manifests in what Maldonado-Torres (2008) named the coloniality of being. To be clear, I am not suggesting that there are not differences between humans and other forms of life. However, there is a significant distinction between assertions that humans are different from other life forms, and that difference manifesting as human exceptionalism defined by coloniality. Following the historical background, and in an attempt towards a decolonial social order, I consider dimensions in Vygotsky's work that reflect the colonial logics of human exceptionalism and human domination over nature.

Brief Overview of the Historical Developments of the Coloniality of Human Exceptionalism

Scholars across disciplines have formulated a remarkable historical analysis of the influence of 16th century world affairs on present-day ideologies. Indeed, the 16th century saw the creation of a fundamental colonial logic, through a grammar of human exceptionalism, that continues to undergird contemporary Western thought (e.g. Dussel, 1992, 1995, 2008; Grosfoguel, 2013; Mignolo, 2013). Various scholars have articulated the ways in which European men's claims to epistemic authority drove and were driven by desires to apply, impose, and force Western epistemologies on other locations in the name of superiority and need for resources creating fundamental constructions of Cartesian time/space relations (e.g. Deloria, 1969; Deloria, Deloria, & Foehner, 1999; Grosfoguel, 2013; Mignolo, 2012). Importantly, claims of epistemic authority created a dialogic inevitability—the construction of epistemic inferiority—and gave rise to epistemic racism and sexism (i.e., a stance that "privileges as superior Western male knowledges and treats as inferior knowledges that are women centered and non Western," Grosfoguel, 2012, p. 83). The dialogic of epistemic authority and inferiority also drove what has come to be called "epistemicide": "the extermination of knowledge and ways of knowing" (Grosfoguel, 2013, p. 74). Grosfoguel suggests that the prevailing logic during colonial expansion can be defined as "I conquer, therefore I am" but the four genocides/epistemicides of the "long 16th century" (1450–1650) created an intermediary "I exterminate, therefore I am." This intermediary provided the foundations and conditions under which Descartes's famous "I think, therefore I am" in 1637, became possible.

Just how did the transformation to "I think, therefore I am" occur? Grosfoguel reviews four key historical genocides/epistimicides and traces the evolution of this logic. He starts with the first epistemicide: the conquest of Al-Andalus and the physical and cultural genocide imposed on Jews and Muslims by the Catholic Monarch, done under the slogan of "purity of blood." Grosfoguel suggests that though this slogan invokes the notion of biology, the genocide was based in religious superiority and did not (yet) question the humanity of the victims at a fundamental level.

However, Grosfoguel suggests that the second epistemicide, the conquest of the Americas, gave rise to a new racial imaginary. Indigenous peoples' heterogeneity was collapsed into the category Indian, and simultaneously Indians became expelled from the category of human because of the absence of a god and therefore a soul. Grosfoguel points to the ways in which the dehumanization of Indians was a necessary logic that gave moral pardon to colonialism and slavery in the Americas. European arguments about the ethics of enslaving and exterminating Indigenous peoples focused on the soul and on Indigenous knowledge systems and economic practices. Those in favour of enslaving Indians argued that they were inferior because they "have no sense of private property and no notion of markets because they produce through collective forms and distribute wealth through reciprocity" (Grosfoguel, 2013, p. 83). Opponents who believed that Indians did have souls argued that slavery was a sin in the eyes of God, but believed that barbarian (godless) Indians should be "Christianized." These two arguments reflect both the biological and cultural racist discourses that provided justification for epistemicide.

Grosfoguel (2013) goes on to argue that the third epistemicide, the African holocaust, further solidified these logics and the intertwining of biological and culturally racist discourses with epistemicide. Africans, like Indigenous peoples of the Americas, were forbidden to pray or practice their ways of knowing—"a regime of epistemic racism that forbade their autonomous knowledge production" (Grosfoguel, 2013, p. 84). Finally, Grosfoguel details the witch trials in Europe as a fourth important event aiming to decimate forms of knowing outside of the Cartesian logics.

The justification for conquering, and for exterminating, was by then solidly linked to European conceptions of logical thought. Importantly, the critical turning point of the "conquest of the Americas giving rise to a new racial imaginary" first rested on the Western invader's claims that Indigenous peoples' "religious" beliefs were illegible. Such claims produced "Indian simulations" (Vizenor, 1999, 2000, 2008) based on primitiveness. The settlers' rendering of Indigenous peoples as illegible gave rise to racial domination and debates about human status that carried forward into the 19th century and beyond. This claimed illegibility extended beyond religious beliefs and included claims about the illogicality of Indigenous peoples' knowledge systems and the need for Indigenous peoples to be assimilated into Western forms of knowing.

So far we have unearthed the history of Cartesian logics, and made their coloniality clear. However, it is important to also acknowledge how these logics are narrated and live in contemporary approaches. Grosfoguel (2013) argues that there are two key points in Cartesian racist and sexist epistemology that continue a coloniality of being.

First, he suggests that Descartes's move from God to the "I" (the "I" that thinks, that exists), rests on ontological dualism (mind is different than body, thus mind can soar) and allows for claims to universal forms of knowledge not tethered to place or perspective. Mignolo and Tlostanova (2006) have called such claims the "epistemology of the zero point" (p. 207), in contrast with decolonial or "border thinking" that recognizes that knowledge is always related to the "geo- and corporal location of the thinker" (p. 214). This first move effectively relieved the power of God and the perceived competition of the superiority of thought between humans and God and embedded human exceptionalism at the core of Cartesian thought.

Second, Grosfoguel argues that Descartes rejected the notion that humans produced knowledge dialogically—or in social relations. Instead, Descartes argued that humans relied on internal monologues or epistemic solipsism. From this view, knowledge was not placed and specifically inter-personed but rather was located in the exceptional human capacity for thought. From this view, coloniality simultaneously asserts the epistemic superiority of Western intellectual traditions granting assimilative authority to the non-Western (by any means necessary) and the reduction of non-Western humanity and capacity. This simultaneity reflects an incommensurable recognition of Indigenous difference and denial of Indigenous peoples' humanness.

Sociocultural theories have importantly not only rejected but made significant progress in eroding the foundational premises of coloniality embedded in Cartesian logics. These theories have done so through claims that social relations and activity are central to thought. However, human exceptionalism remains embedded in much of contemporary Western thought, including sociocultural theory. Indeed, the ontological projects of contemporary Vygotskian scholars, as Matusov (2008) lays out, seem to largely work to create or perhaps restore an inclusive form of human exceptionalism. At the very least, the field has largely not acknowledged how Vygotsky himself continued much of the positioning of Indigenous peoples reflected in the history I have just reviewed. On the one hand, perhaps one might suggest that the text's latent colonialism and racism towards Indigenous peoples is simply an historical relic that has no serious bearing on the foundation of the claims or theory put forth. On the other hand, it may be important to understand how the need for human exceptionalism has narrowed the way we study and know learning. In the next section, I begin articulating the coloniality in Vygotsky by examining the positioning and characterization of Indigenous peoples in his work. In doing so, I open space for potential questions about the theoretical impacts and consequences.

Readings of Indigenous Peoples in Vygotsky

The treatment and readings of Indigenous peoples (named primitive peoples) in Vygotsky is reflective of the unfolding colonialism detailed above. Though Vygotsky uses the word primitive man or primitive people (see Scribner, 1985, for another account), for my purposes I write Indigenous peoples in their place as a refusal of the historical positioning that primitive entails. Consider the following quotes, which exemplify several ways in which Vygotsky reproduced colonial understandings of Indigenous peoples:

> There is another very interesting trait of primitive thought that shows us complex thinking in action and points up the difference between pseudo-concepts and concepts. This trait—which Levy-Bruhl was the first to note in primitive peoples, Alfred Storch in the insane, and Piaget in children—is usually called participation.
>
> *(Vygotsky, 2012, p. 136)*

First, Vygotsky mobilized research that found Indigenous peoples illegible and lacking in logic; he names Indigenous peoples' ways of knowing "primitive thought." This tendency plays out across much of his writing. Second, Vygotskian thought is built around the need to distinguish between lower-order mental functions and higher-order mental functions (Vygotsky, 1978, 2012). He used primitive peoples (as well as the "mentally ill") positioned in lesser categories as a starting ground for making many arguments. This routinized positioning echoed claims about Indigenous peoples' lack of humanness. These points raise broader questions about how the construction of Vygotskian theory may be restricted by this colonial logic.

One set of claims in need of further scrutiny involves the trajectory and distinction between complexes and concepts. Vygotsky argues that Indigenous peoples only have the capacity for thinking in complexes, not concepts, and that complexes are of a less sophisticated or developed nature. Vygotsky repeatedly claimed that the key distinction between complexes and concepts is that complexes allow for a heterogeneity of subjective connections (or empirical connections) between elements, whereas concepts rely on logical, objective, causal connections. Vygotsky contended that these were significant differences in the internal structure of was complexes and concepts, which manifest in differences in activity. He suggested that concepts had homogenous relational definitions, and that as children ascended from thinking in complexes to thinking in concepts, they were able to overcome their "ego-centricism" (i.e., "mistak[ing] connections between his own impressions for connections between things," Vygotsky, 2012, p. 120). Of course, if Indigenous peoples reasoned in ways that Vygotsky considered normative, then he would have recognized their conceptual development, potentially changing the course of his theory. A difference in ways of knowing was considered a deficit that reflects colonial history and logics. Further, in these assertions there are hints of and perhaps even outright alignment with Cartesian thought, in which knowing becomes dislocated from place and perspective.

The coloniality embedded in the distinction between concepts and complexes is further exemplified in Vygotsky's discussion of pseudoconcepts (a specific type of complex). Vygotsky takes up the Bororo people's relationship to red parrots, as characterized in the work of von den Steinen and Levy-Bruhl, in which Bororo people have a symbiotic reincarnated relationship with parrots. Vygotsky (2012) used the Bororo people as an example to support his claim that complexes are based on a form of reasoning that he called participation. He described participation as characteristic of children's thinking "in bonds unacceptable to adult logic" (p. 137), and in which "a particular thing may be included in different complexes on the strength of its different concrete attributes and consequently may have several names" (p. 137). Vygotsky suggests that participation is emblematic of children's thought *and* Indigenous thought, and that it is an impossibility for "our own logic" (p. 138). In other words, there is an illegibility to participation when measured against Western logic; participation results in words having an entirely different functional application for Indigenous peoples. He finds Indigenous thought to be illegible, compares it to the thinking of Soviet children, and therefore assigns it to a lower category of development than concept.

> [Levy-Bruhl] approaches the Bororo statements about being red parrots from the point of view of our own logic when he assumes that to the primitive mind, too, such an assertion means identity of beings. But since words to the Bororo designate groups of objects, not concepts, their assertion has a different meaning: The word for parrot is the word for a complex that includes parrots and themselves.
>
> *(2012, pp. 138–139)*

Indeed his reading places Indigenous people's thought, specifically in this case the functional role of words, into an ontologically distinct category that echoes historical distinctions that were discussed earlier in relation to Indigenous people's humanity. He says:

> The key to understanding participation and the thinking of primitive peoples is the fact that this thinking is carried out in complexes rather than concepts. Consequently, in these languages the functional application of the word is entirely different than it is in our own. The word is used in a different manner. It is not a means for forming and carrying concepts.
>
> *(Vygotsky, 1962, p. 146)*

The distinction between complexes and concepts is based in epistemic superiority and is reflective of the logics of the conquest of the Americas. The explanation echoes colonial constructions of differences in human status based on the denial of Indigenous people's souls. Here, instead, Indigenous people are denied the capacity to use words to carry concepts, via the claimed illegibility of Indigenous ways of knowing.

What questions and possibilities arise if we question the logic that gave rise to such distinctions? I am not suggesting that there are not developmental trajectories. Instead, I ask whether our ways of imagining such trajectories may be deeply transformed if they are not grounded in colonial logics. Without a presumption of Indigenous inferiority, it is possible to study Indigenous and non-Indigenous (or between different Indigenous) peoples' knowledge and knowledge organization in ways that expand what we know about human cognition broadly. Recent research suggests that there are important differences in knowledge organization and patterns of reasoning, whereby Western knowledge systems tend towards taxonomic organization of knowledge, and where Indigenous knowledge systems tend towards ecological or systems-level organization of knowledge (Medin & Bang, 2014; Medin, Ross, Atran, Cox, Coley, Proffitt, & Blok, 2006). Interestingly, these differences in logics may in some ways already be reflected in how Vygotsky describes complexes; the heterogeneity in complexes may actually be more reflective of ecologically organized thought that reflects systems-level understandings (i.e. concepts).

Further, the past decade has seen major advances in theory and observations on causal reasoning (e.g., Griffiths & Tenenbaum, 2009; Holyoak & Cheng, 2011; Tenenbaum, Kemp, Griffiths, & Goodman, 2011; Waldmann & Hagmayer, 2013). This work has included attention to cultural differences (e.g., Bender & Beller, 2011; Morris & Peng, 1994) and considered complexities such as multiple explanatory frameworks within a single individual (see Gelman & Legare, 2011, for a review). These theoretical expansions suggest the need for careful reworking of the trajectories laid by Vygotsky.

While contemporary sociocultural theorists might be reluctant to argue that present-day Indigenous peoples exhibit primitive reasoning, the uptake of Vygotsky's theory of complexes reflects the epistemic racism that presumed the epistemic inferiority of Indigenous peoples. To put it simply, scholars who would never label an entire group of Indigenous people as cognitively inferior, might still stand by theories and coding schemes that are premised on and label large numbers of individual Indigenous people as such. Vygotsky's characterization of concepts as the apex of linguistic reasoning creates a kind of "concept exceptionalism" in which only concepts qualify as full status human thought. I suggest that Vygotsky's coupling of colonial human exceptionalism with concept exceptionalism codifies the position of epistemic superiority in sociocultural theories of learning. If we continue to accept that complexes are "less than" concepts, then we will continue to find that Indigenous people—or others that don't reflect the Western normative forms of concepts—don't measure up and potentially perpetuate the epistemic racism inherent in those judgements.

In his theory of concept development, Vygotsky (2012) constructed distinctions between chimpanzees, Indigenous peoples, and humans with higher-order mental functions based on distinctions in the use of signs and mediation.

> The process of concept formation, like any other higher form of intellectual activity, is not a quantitative overgrowth of the lower associative activity, but a qualitatively new type. Unlike the lower forms, which are characterized by the *immediacy of intellectual processes, this new activity is mediated by signs.*
>
> (p. 116)

Here he suggests that the associative nature of complexes is based in the differences between mediated and unmediated activity. He then goes on to suggest that Indigenous people are a useful data source for studying unmediated thought based in complexes, a type of thought that he locates at an earlier stage of phylogenetic (i.e., evolutionary) development.

> To the extent that we can explore the phylogenetic development of intellect by studying the mind and thinking of primitive man, we again find little evidence in this domain that would indicate that the path of development moves from lower to higher forms through a quantitative increase in the number of associations.
>
> (Vygotsky, 1962, p. 127)

The classification of mediated thought as the most sophisticated, and as reserved to humans, led Vygotsky to focus on human–human interactions as the place of psychological frontier and possibility. I suggest that this positioning meant that attempts to understand relations between humans and more-than-humans could never entertain the existence of communicative functions between humans and more-than-humans—in part because more-than-humans have no meaning-making capacity in Vygotskian thought.

This form of human exceptionalism contributes to epistemicide (Grosfoguel, 2013) for those communities and ways of knowing that have always been based in more-than-human ontologies (ontologies that are being problematically called "posthumanism," as if the idea is new). More concretely, the human exceptionalism driving sociocultural theory may be perpetuating or creating a silencing—or epistemicide—of relational ontologies focused on multiplicities of vibrant forms of life and land/natural world. This possibility reflects coloniality, and in particular, the social orders of settler-colonial nations.

Settler-Colonialism in Sociocultural Theories?

In this section I begin to unpack how spatial and temporal constructs carry political inflections reflective of settler-colonialism, and consider how these constructs are embedded in sociocultural theories of learning and development. I review some key tenets of settler-colonial theory with respect to land and human exceptionalism and suggest that these two tenets may help to expand the mediational focus of sociocultural theories towards a decolonial ethics of trans-ontologies. I will then provide an analysis of two ways in which Vygotskian thought is reflective of settler-colonial constructs: the invisibility of the natural world, and the temporal positioning of Indigenous peoples. Sociocultural theory's subject–object focus, especially when decoupled from subject–subject relations and the designation of objects, is reflective of settler-colonial ideologies. (Note here I am using "subject–subject," in contrast to "human–human relations," where subjects can be humans or more-than-humans.) When these settler-colonial constructions are interrogated, they may allow us to expand our fundamental understandings of learning and development, and to create more socially just and ecologically sustainable communities.

Settler-Colonialism

The study of settler-colonialism is a robust interdisciplinary field with origins in history, anthropology, and political theory (see Deloria & Lytle, 1984; Veracini, 2010; Wolfe, 2006). Settler-colonialism is a form of colonialism but carries significant distinctions that influence the logics and practices in settler-colonial nations. In both colonialism and settler-colonialism, the colonizers aim to establish dominion over the desired homelands. A key distinction in settler-colonialism is that settlers also stay, live, and become the norm. As a result, colonialism is an event and settler-colonialism is an on-going structural process (Wolfe, 2006), in which the primary focus of settler-colonial societies is the acquisition of land as property, followed by the establishment of settler lifeways as normative. Both colonialism and settler-colonialism employ a grammar of race and inferiority to justify colonization—as detailed earlier. However, settler-colonialism employs this grammar in service of elimination or assimilation of the original inhabitants of the desired homelands (Deloria, 1969; Veracini, 2011; Wolfe, 2006).

In settler-colonial societies, settler normativity is constructed through a set of dialectic relationships between settlers and Indigenous others. In these relations, settlers are positioned not only as normative, but also as superior to the Indigenous people. According to settler-colonial theory, the positioning of settlers is structurally maintained by employing a set of rules that reify circles of inclusion and exclusion (e.g., hypodescent and blood quantum[3]). Core processes of inclusion and exclusion enabling settler normativity are: (1) erasure of Indigenous presence, (2) erasure of relocated Indigenous people's humanity through the *structuration* of chattel slavery and resultant reduction to and control of bodies (Wolfe, 2006). I suggest that the construction of human exceptionalism and the simultaneous exclusion of Indigenous peoples from this exceptionalism is reflective of settler normativity as well.

There is significant complexity in each of these processes, which are co-constituted and dynamically shape each other. I will show how these dynamics manifest in the ways space and time are constructed in sense-making. Settler-colonialism constructs space/land through a grammar of time, and the privileging of temporality perpetuates the epistemicide of Indigenous ways of knowing that are based in land. I further explore each point.

The Erasure of Indigenous Presence

The erasure of Indigenous presence is a complex phenomenon that affects conceptualizations of the past, present, and future. The temporal positioning of Indigenous peoples as primitive or as less developed constructs a cultural-historical temporality in the service of settler-colonialism that enables the erasure of Indigenous peoples in the present. This erasure involves reconstructing space, to imply that Indigenous peoples no longer occupy lands in the present and forgo the possibility of Indigenous futures (Tuck & Yang, 2012).

In other words, settlers use concepts of time to make sense of land: Indigenous occupation of homelands is constructed as a thing of the past, irrelevant to the present and the future. This ontological register contrasts with many Indigenous ontologies that are founded on land. In such land-based ontologies, space is emphasized over time. Put simply, "Places produce and teach particular ways of thinking about and being in the world. They tell us the way things are, even when they operate pedagogically beneath a conscious level" (Bang, Curley, Kessel, Marin, Suzukovich, & Strack, 2014, p. 44). This is not to suggest that a spatially prioritized ontology doesn't construct temporality (or vice versa). It certainly does (e.g. Massey, 2005), but still the foundational ontology—land-based or time-based—has cascading ramifications in the way place is lived (e.g. Cresswell, 2014; Ingold, 2000). In sum, settler-colonial time-based ontologies contribute to the erasure of Indigenous presence across all aspects of life (political, economic, social, etc.), with consequences for theories of learning and development that need to be explored more fully.

For current purposes I focus on how settler-colonial time-based ontologies shape practices (in the sense of Bourdieu, 1977) across historical time (Smith, 1999) and how these create frames and potential lines of flight for sense-making in the moment-to-moment unfolding of interaction (Giddens, 1984; Goffman, 1974). Linda Smith (2012) writes:

> Different orientations towards time and space, different positioning within time and space, and different systems of language for making space and time 'real' underpin notions of past and present, of place and of relationships to the land . . .
>
> *(p. 113)*

Settler-colonial legitimacy rests on the need to disavow Indigenous presence and to construct meanings of land as vast, uninhabited spaces ripe for discovery and endless possibility (Deloria et al., 1999; Veracini, 2011). Thus, the varying forms of absence (complete or partial) and presence of Indigenous peoples teaches conceptions of place that legitimize settler colonialism; if Indigenous people are absent, then the land can/must "belong" to the settlers. When land is constructed as vast and uninhabited, settler-colonial constructions and perception of people and lands persist, and even shape the ways of knowing and possible identities that can be cultivated in learning environments. More specifically, images of land as vast and uninhabited enable dispossession from place as part of identity. These images also position the desire for perpetual frontiers (including frontiers of knowledge) as the normative and desired form of sense-making (Tuck & Yang, 2012).

Educational standards and legislation ensure that Indigenous erasure persists and thus reinforces settler normativity. As an example, consider the ways in which Native people are (or are systematically not) part of school curricula in the U.S. Recent work by Shear, Knowles, Soden, and Castro (2015) examined history and social studies standards in all 50 states across all grade levels. They found that 86.6% of the standards dictated teachers to teach about Native peoples only in the time period before 1900. Further, there were 17 states that did not have any standards at all with respect to Native people. In short, in many states Native people are completely erased from curriculum, and when they are present, Native people tend to disappear from history after 1900. Shear and colleagues also conducted an analysis of the nature of the standards and note that studies of Indigenous cultures pre-1900 tend to be romanticized. In addition, standards typically describe initially cooperative relations between Europeans and Natives that then become conflictual. This is followed by the settlers' westward expansion; the removal of Native people from land for settler inhabitation; and is often positioned as the logical and inevitable outcome to conflictual tensions. Note that these curriculum standards reinforce both the erasure of Indigenous peoples, and a sense of vast uninhabited lands ripe for settler futures.

An additional increasingly important example of legislation that erases Indigenous presence is reflected in the changing diaspora of Indigenous children and dynamics of racialization. More than 72% of school age Native American children do not live on reservations, and yet the majority of Native American services are focused on reservation communities. While this pattern is importantly linked to current forms of sovereignty, those political dynamics impact learning and development for the vast majority of Native children, because from the perspective of broader systems, Native children not on reservations become a racial category dislocated from land. This process is an example of the impact of time–space relations: A settler, time-based perspective fundamentally presumes that non-reservation lands are rightly settler lands, not Indigenous lands. Thus the construction of urban Indigenous peoples as not Indigenous is simultaneously an issue of race and of land. This demonstrates how Indigenous erasure from lands and concomitant views of naturalized settler futures are intertwined (Tuck & Yang, 2012).

Structuration of Chattel Slavery

The second fundamental process of settler-colonialism is the structuration of chattel slavery, which erases people's humanity and turns them into material resources. In the United States, Indigenous African peoples and their descendants have been the primary target of this process, but in recent decades Indigenous peoples from Central and South America, often racialized as Latin@, are increasingly being placed in analogous structural positions. Further, urban dwelling Indigenous people, if visible at all, are increasingly being positioned in racialized terms. Importantly from settler-colonial perspectives the construction of race emerges from dynamics of land and settler normativity. Race becomes the primary discourse of difference (instead of discourses whose grammar acknowledges the heterogeneity of Indigenous peoples or a focus on relations to land) contributing to the invisibility of both Indigenous peoples and land.

These dynamics become codified in what Cheryl Harris (1993) calls settled expectations or "the set of assumptions, privileges, and benefits that accompany the status of being white . . . that whites have come to expect and rely on" (p. 1713) and are adjudicated and protected by law (as reflected in the standards example above). Importantly, the maintenance of settler normativity and resultant settled expectations, requires the *structuration of time–space relations* in ways that make the inseparable dynamics of acquisition of land, Indigenous erasure, and the domination of black people (in the US) appear as an inevitable, unconnected, and natural course of development rather than socio-politically engineered to support and foster white claims, entitlement and privilege.

From Indigenous perspectives, white claims to land remains a—if not the—key axis of concern. Importantly, claims to land are not just about the materiality of land—for Indigenous people claims to land are also centrally about our knowledge systems, sovereignty, and "collective continuance" (Whyte, 2013).

Settler-Colonialism and Conceptions of Nature and Culture

These two tenets of settler colonialism have broad implications for human–nature relations. Settler-colonial societies are premised on the idea that nature and culture are separate and distinct realms (e.g., Cajete, 2000; Kawagley, 1993; Latour, 2013), and that humans (owners of culture) should have domination over the natural world. Indeed this sentiment is reflected in Vygotsky and his constructions of freedom and progress.

The centrality of subject–object relations (mediated activity) to Vygotskian thought has perpetuated nature–culture relations that reflect human domination and entitlement, thus contributing to the epistemicide of Indigenous peoples. For example, the study of mediational means constructs the person as subject, and mediational means as object. In contrast, Indigenous ways of knowing would construct some of these mediational means as subjects, and understand the relation between person and mediator as subject–subject relations (Bang & Vossoughi, 2016; Packer, 2011). To be clear, I am not disputing the importance of subject–object relations. Instead, I am suggesting that the focus on construction of objects without simultaneous attention to relations between subjects has privileged Western knowledge systems, narrowed how we imagine learning and development, and minimized our conceptions of relational agency, especially with respect to the natural world.

Scholars of settler-colonialism have argued that the conceptual construction of land as uninhabited (one aspect of the settler's time–space construction) allows settlers to position themselves as entitled to lands based in their own ways of knowing, doing and being (Veracini, 2011). To say this another way, settler time–space constructions are defined by genesis amnesia[4] (the creation and history of these constructions are masked) and manifest destiny[5] (constructions appear God-given and right) (Bourdieu, 1977). These time–space constructions set in motion settler ways of knowing that position humans as separate from the rest of the natural world. (Latour (2013) calls this the "nature-culture boundary.")

The separation between humans and the rest of the natural world results in asymmetrical forms of reasoning, and ontological claims that are characterized by human exceptionalism (i.e., claims that relegate all non-humans to material resource). In other words, this separation transforms non-human forms of life into objects for human use. As Latour (2013) articulates, Western ontologies retain the persistent orientation that non-humans are without agency and intent, making such domination more palatable. Further, recall that the same Western ontologies construct Indigenous peoples as less than human.

The subject of more-than-human agency marks a critical ontological difference in Western scientific ways of knowing and Indigenous ways of knowing. As described above, in many Indigenous ways of knowing (though maybe not all) humans are not the only intentional and agentic actors in the world, nor do humans occupy a privileged status that divests us of responsibility, humility, and reciprocity (Cajete, 2000; Kawagley, 1993, 2006). Settler conceptual dynamics are reflected in curricular constructions and modes of inquiry/pedagogies typically employed in science learning environments. For example, in Western science classrooms, most representations of ecosystems fail to include humans. When humans are present in these representations, they often reflect frames of extraction or pollution—manifestations of nature–culture relations reflecting human domination and entitlement (Medin & Bang, 2014).

Research into how people reason about, with, and in the natural world (including, but not limited to, research on biological cognition) also tends to reflect Western epistemologies and ontologies. Indeed, much of what we know about these topics is based on children from middle-class, urban populations typically from Western, Educated, Industrialized, Rich, and Democratic (WEIRD) societies (Henrich, Heine, & Norenzayan, 2010) although there are important exceptions (e.g., Carey, 1985; Chavajay & Rogoff, 1999, 2002; Coley, 2012; Correa-Chávez, Rogoff, & Mejía Arauz, 2005; Gelman & Wellman, 1991; Hatano & Inagaki, 1999; Hirschfeld, 1995; Keil, 1989, 2007). Further, developmental trajectories of biological cognition have been conceptualized through a lens of Western epistemic traditions, norms, problems, and more specifically, understandings of the domain of biology (Medin, Waxman, Woodring, & Washinawatok, 2010; Ojalehto & Medin, 2015).

Recent research, even from settler perspectives, has demonstrated that Western ways of reasoning about the natural world are inadequate to address current socio-ecological challenges. Indeed, the fields of psychology and linguistics have documented a devolution of knowledge about the natural world over the last 20–30 years. Over this time period, the average [white] American and college-going student's reasoning about the specifics of the natural world has become more generic, and less connected to the real world. Specifically, many people have lost knowledge about particular plant and animal species, and are unable to distinguish different species in specific places (Wolff & Medin, 2001; Wolff, Medin, & Pankratz, 1999). Further, there has been a decline in people's understandings of dynamics in complex ecologies, and a tendency to increasingly reason through one-way causal hierarchies (Atran, Medin, & Ross, 2004). In short people's knowledge has become more generic, and they are less able to detect nuance and interactions in places.

Not only is this devolution of knowledge a product of settler conceptions of the natural world, I suggest this devolution is an outcome of the politicized erasure of Indigenous peoples in settler-colonial societies. That is, settler-colonialism minimizes the importance of the natural world, and constructs narrow relations between humans and the natural world. Nature's ontological status is relegated to that of a resource. The devolution and devaluing of knowledge and reasoning may indeed contribute to our collective inabilities to make decisions (including policy) that could prevent the broad-scale destruction of the natural world and by result human worlds.

To address contemporary socio-ecological challenges in ways that bring about more socially and ecologically just forms of life, we must challenge perspectives that position the more-than-human world as object or as a material mediation in service of humans. When the construction of more-than-humans expands beyond that of mediational tool, it becomes possible to develop theories of learning that emerge from perspectives of relational dwelling in and across places. This expansion allows us to reconsider issues of agency—or potentials for change—for humans, and makes visible the change potentials for all life. Further, this expansion refuses settler colonialism's foundational constructions of land and Indigenous peoples.

Thus, while scholarship has rightly focused on the ramifications of settler-colonialism for Indigenous people, I want to also consider its ramifications for the more-than-human world. Settler colonialism does not position the more-than-human world as capable of co-constructing meaning and sociocultural perspectives have so far been complicit. There is a danger in raising this issue: Engaging more deeply with Indigenous conceptions of place and land may result in a shift in relations to land, but inertia in the inequitable social and power relations between peoples. Indeed the uptake of Indigenous and decolonizing perspectives in scholarship suggests that this is a significant concern (Tuck & Yang, 2012). While addressing settler constructions of the more-than-human world is necessary for creating sustainable forms of human communities—which is an increasingly attractive course of action for Western thought—it must also be done from a recognition of the colonial power differential between humans that Western thought is predicated on. Thus in my view, seriously addressing settler constructions of the more-than-human world will also necessitate a reworking of settler relations with Indigenous peoples. Emergent then are questions about what such reworkings mean for the development of decolonial ethics and trans-ontologies in sociocultural theories of learning? Or further, what forms of learning and education might emerge?

Directions and Questions for Cultivating Decolonial Ethics Towards Trans-Ontologies

This chapter has only barely begun to scratch the surface of unearthing the under-explored colonial difference that is embedded in sociocultural theory. In my view, sociocultural theory has long taken steps towards the possibility of a decolonial ethic, by centring learning theory around culture and dialogic development. However, these constructs have remained largely defined through Western constructions of human exceptionalism. The unearthing and questioning of human exceptionalism may help to open new recognition of mediated activity reflective of trans-ontologies previously unseen. Such inquiries will likely reimagine the co-construction of signs between subjects, will designate more-than-humans as subjects, and consider the inter-animation of humans and more-than-humans as part of development (Kohn, 2013). These opened grounds of mediated activity may be taken up as new forms of bilanguaging. We may reimagine the ways in which the internal structures of concepts are developed and manifest in activity, particularly when grammars of time and space are taken up as central constructs. Seriously grappling with the colonial difference may also mean considering the incommensurability of ontological claims, and charting new communicative forms that are not reliant on agreement. The development of such communicative forms may indeed be necessary for a collective continuance that reflects cultural heterogeneity and can develop sustainable forms of human and more-than-human relations. On the one hand, the work is somewhat daunting. On the other, it could help to evolve the design of forms of education that emerge from decolonial ethics of trans-ontologies and invite collective dreaming towards social and ecological transformations. Such collective reimaginings could cultivate a deep sense of hope and possibility in a time when narratives of division, dread, and despair are too common.

Notes

1. Coloniality of being refers to "the lived experience of colonization and its impact on language" (Maldonado-Torres, 2007, p. 242).
2. Matusov's use of the terms cultural-historical and sociocultural differ from their use elsewhere in this volume. Matusov (2008) used cultural-historical to describe "South African Vygotskian scholars like Ian Moll [who] saw their ontological project as how to help Blacks to overcome their cultural deprivation and transform their traditional practices in order to prepare them for modern schooling and the corporate world" (p. 13). He used sociocultural to describe research whose main ontological commitment is to "the problem of disproportional institutional failure" (p. 14), or, alternatively "how to eliminate the institutional failure from schooling rather than to make sure that the failure is proportionally distributed among culturally diverse social groups" (p. 15).
3. Both hypodescent and blood quantum rules apply to children born to a mixed union (one parent is of a dominant social group, and one is a member of a subordinate group). The rule of hypodescent states that the child is automatically a member of the subordinate group. In the rule of blood quantum, a person's Indigenous identity is defined by the percent of their ancestors who were "full-blood" Indigenous people.
4. Genesis amnesia refers to the obliteration (or forgetting, amnesia) of the creation and development (genesis) of a concept or discipline.
5. Manifest destiny is the European settlers' belief that they were destined to inhabit and control all of North America.

References

Agyeman, J., Cole, P., Haluza-DeLay, R., & O'Riley, P. (Eds.). (2010). *Speaking for ourselves: Environmental justice in Canada.* Vancouver, BC: UBC Press.
Atran, S., Medin, D., & Ross, N. (2004). Evolution and devolution of knowledge: A tale of two biologies. *Journal of the Royal Anthropological Institute, 10*(2), 395–420.

Bang, M., Curley, L., Kessel, A., Marin, A., Suzukovich, E. S. III, & Strack, G. (2014). Muskrat theories, tobacco in the streets, and living Chicago as indigenous land. *Environmental Education Research, 20*(1), 37–55.

Bang, M., & Vossoughi, S. (2016). Participatory design research and educational justice: Studying learning and relations within social change making. *Cognition and Instruction, 34*(3), 173–193.

Bender, A., & Beller, S. (2011). The cultural constitution of cognition: Taking the anthropological perspective. *Frontiers in Psychology, 2*(67), 1–6.

Bourdieu, P. (1977). *Outline of a theory of practice* (Vol. 16). Cambridge, UK: Cambridge University Press.

Cajete, G. (2000). *Native science: Natural laws of interdependence*. Santa Fe, NM: Clear Light Publishing.

Carey, S. (1985). *Conceptual change in childhood*. Cambridge, MA: MIT Press.

Chavajay, P., & Rogoff, B. (1999). Cultural variation in management of attention by children and their caregivers. *Developmental Psychology, 35*(4), 1079–1090.

Chavajay, P., & Rogoff, B. (2002). Schooling and traditional collaborative social organization of problem solving by Mayan mothers and children. *Developmental Psychology, 38*(1), 55–66.

Cole, M. (1996). *Cultural psychology: A once and future discipline*. Cambridge, MA: Harvard University Press.

Coley, J. D. (2012). Where the wild things are: Informal experience and ecological reasoning. *Child Development, 83*(3), 992–1006.

Correa-Chávez, M., Rogoff, B., & Mejía Arauz, R. (2005). Cultural patterns in attending to two events at once. *Child Development, 76*(3), 664–678.

Cresswell, T. (2014). *Place: An introduction*. New York, NY: John Wiley & Sons.

Daniels, H. (1996). Introduction: Psychology in a social world. In H. Daniels (Ed.), *An Introduction to Vygotsky* (pp. 1–27). London, UK: Routledge.

Deloria, V., Jr. (1969). *Custer died for your sins: An Indian manifesto*. Norman, OK: University of Oklahoma Press.

Deloria, V., Jr., Deloria, B., & Foehner, K. (1999). *Spirit & reason: The Vine Deloria, Jr., reader*. Golden, CO: Fulcrum Publishing.

Deloria, V., Jr., & Lytle, C. M. (1984). *The nations within: The past and future of American Indian sovereignty*. Austin, TX: University of Texas Press.

Dussel, E. (1992). *Historia de la iglesia en América Latina: Medio milenio de coloniaje y liberación (1492–1992)*. Madrid: Mundo Negro-Esquila Misional.

Dussel, E. (1995). *The Invention of the Americas*. New York, NY: Continuum.

Dussel, E. (2008). A new age in the history of philosophy: The world dialogue between philosophical traditions. *Prajñā Vihāra: Journal of Philosophy and Religion, 9*(1), 1–21.

Gelman, S. A., & Legare, C. H. (2011). Concepts and folk theories. *Annual Review of Anthropology, 40*, 379–398.

Gelman, S. A., & Wellman, H. M. (1991). Insides and essences: Early understandings of the non-obvious. *Cognition, 38*(3), 213–244.

Giddens, A. (1984). *The constitution of society: Outline of the theory of structuration*. Berkeley, CA: University of California Press.

Goffman, E. (1974). *Frame analysis: An essay on the organization of experience*. Cambridge, MA: Harvard University Press.

Griffiths, T. L., & Tenenbaum, J. B. (2009). Theory-based causal induction. *Psychological Review, 116*(4), 661–716.

Grosfoguel, R. (2012). The dilemmas of ethnic studies in the United States: Between liberal multiculturalism, identity politics, disciplinary colonization, and decolonial epistemologies. *Human Architecture, 10*(1), 81–90.

Grosfoguel, R. (2013). The structure of knowledge in westernized universities: Epistemic racism/sexism and the four genocides/epistemicides of the long 16th century. *Human Architecture*, *11*(1), 73.

Harris, C. I. (1993). Whiteness as property. *Harvard Law Review*, *106*(8), 1707–1791.

Hatano, G., & Inagaki, K. (1999). A developmental perspective on informal biology. In D. L. Medin & S. Atran (Eds.), *Folkbiology* (pp. 321–354). Cambridge, MA: MIT Press.

Henrich, J., Heine, S. J., & Norenzayan, A. (2010). The weirdest people in the world? *Behavioral and Brain Sciences*, *33*(2–3), 61–83.

Hirschfeld, L. A. (1995). Do children have a theory of race? *Cognition*, *54*(2), 209–252.

Holyoak, K. J., & Cheng, P. W. (2011). Causal learning and inference as a rational process: The new synthesis. *Annual Review of Psychology*, *62*(1), 135–163.

Ingold, T. (2000). *The perception of the environment: Essays on livelihood, dwelling and skill.* London, UK: Routledge.

Jovanović, G. (2015). Vicissitudes of history in Vygotsky's cultural-historical theory. *History of the Human Sciences*, *28*(2), 10–33.

Kawagley, A. O. (1993). *A Yupiaq world view: Implications for cultural, educational, and technological adaptation in a contemporary world* (Doctoral dissertation). University of British Columbia.

Kawagley, A. O. (2006). *A Yupiaq worldview: A pathway to ecology and spirit.* Long Grove, IL: Waveland Press.

Keil, F. C. (1989). *Concepts, kinds, and conceptual development.* Cambridge, MA: MIT Press.

Keil, F. C. (2007). Biology and beyond: Domain specificity in a broader developmental context. *Human Development*, *50*(1), 31–38.

Kohn, E. (2013). *How forests think: Toward an anthropology beyond the human.* Berkeley, CA: University of California Press.

LaDuke, W. (1999). *All our relations: Native struggles for land and life.* New York, NY: South End Press.

Latour, B. (2013). *An inquiry into modes of existence* (C. Porter, Trans.). Cambridge, MA: Harvard University Press.

Maldonado-Torres, N. (2007). On the coloniality of being: Contributions to the development of a concept. *Cultural Studies*, *21*(2–3), 240–270.

Maldonado-Torres, N. (2008). La descolonización y el giro des-colonial. *Tabula Rasa*, *9*, 61–72.

Maldonado-Torres, N. (2009). Rousseau and Fanon on inequality and the human sciences. *The CLR James Journal*, *15*(1), 113–134.

Massey, D. (2005). *For space.* London, UK: SAGE.

Matusov, E. (2008). Applying a sociocultural approach to Vygotskian academia: "Our tsar isn't like yours, and yours isn't like ours". *Culture & Psychology*, *14*(1), 5–35.

Medin, D. L., & Bang, M. (2014). *Who's asking?: Native science, western science, and science education.* Cambridge, MA: MIT Press.

Medin, D. L., Ross, N. O., Atran, S., Cox, D., Coley, J., Proffitt, J. B., & Blok, S. (2006). Folkbiology of freshwater fish. *Cognition*, *99*(3), 237–273.

Medin, D., Waxman, S., Woodring, J., & Washinawatok, K. (2010). Human-centeredness is not a universal feature of young children's reasoning: Culture and experience matter when reasoning about biological entities. *Cognitive Development*, *25*(3), 197–207.

Mignolo, W. (2000). The many faces of cosmo-polis: Border thinking and critical cosmopolitanism. *Public Culture*, *12*(3), 721–748.

Mignolo, W. (2012). *Local histories/global designs: Coloniality, subaltern knowledges, and border thinking*. Princeton, NJ: Princeton University Press.

Mignolo, W. (2013). Geopolitics of sensing and knowing: On (de) coloniality, border thinking, and epistemic disobedience. *Confero: Essays on Education, Philosophy and Politics*, 1(1), 129–150.

Mignolo, W. D., & Tlostanova, M. V. (2006). Theorizing from the borders: Shifting to geo- and body-politics of knowledge. *European Journal of Social Theory*, 9(2), 205–221.

Morris, M. W., & Peng, K. (1994). Culture and cause: American and Chinese attributions for social and physical events. *Journal of Personality and Social Psychology*, 67(6), 949–971.

Ojalehto, B., & Medin, D. (2015). An ecological perspective on culture and concepts. *Annual Review of Psychology*, 66, 249–275.

Packer, M. (2011). *The science of qualitative research*. Cambridge, UK: Cambridge University Press.

Richardson, T. A. (2012). Disrupting the coloniality of being: Toward de-colonial ontologies in philosophy of education. *Studies in Philosophy and Education*, 31(6), 539–551.

Rogoff, B. (2003). *The cultural nature of human development*. New York, NY: Oxford University Press.

Scribner, S. (1985). Vygotsky's uses of history. In J. V. Wertsch (Ed.), *Culture, communication, and cognition: Vygotskian perspectives* (pp. 119–143). Cambridge, UK: Cambridge University Press.

Shear, S. B., Knowles, R. T., Soden, G. J., & Castro, A. J. (2015). Manifesting destiny: Re/presentations of indigenous peoples in K–12 US history standards. *Theory & Research in Social Education*, 43(1), 68–101.

Smith, L. T. (1999). *Decolonizing methodologies: Research and indigenous peoples*. London, UK: Zed Books.

Smith, L. T. (2012). *Decolonizing methodologies: Research and indigenous peoples* (2nd edn.). London, UK: Zed Books.

Tenenbaum, J. B., Kemp, C., Griffiths, T. L., & Goodman, N. D. (2011). How to grow a mind: Statistics, structure, and abstraction. *Science*, 331(6022), 1279–1285.

Tuck, E., & Yang, K. W. (2012). Decolonization is not a metaphor. *Decolonization: Indigeneity, Education & Society*, 1(1), 1–40.

Veracini, L. (2010). *Settler colonialism*. New York, NY: Palgrave Macmillan.

Veracini, L. (2011). Introducing: Settler colonial studies. *Settler Colonial Studies*, 1(1), 1–12.

Vizenor, G. R. (1999). *Manifest manners: Narratives on postindian survivance*. Lincoln, NE: University of Nebraska Press.

Vizenor, G. R. (2000). *Fugitive poses: Native American Indian scenes of absence and presence*. Lincoln, NE: University of Nebraska Press.

Vizenor, G. (Ed.). (2008). *Survivance: Narratives of native presence*. Lincoln, NE: University of Nebraska Press.

Vygotsky, L. S. (1962). *Thought and language* (E. Hanfmann & G. Vakar, Trans.). Cambridge, MA: MIT Press.

Vygotsky, L. S. (1978). *Mind in society: The development of higher psychological processes*. Cambridge, MA: Harvard University Press.

Vygotsky, L. S. (1994). The socialist alteration of man. In L. S. Vygotsky, R. van der Veer & J. Valsiner (Eds.), *The Vygotsky reader* (pp. 175–184). Oxford, UK: Blackwell.

Vygotsky, L. S. (2012). *Thought and language* (Revised and expanded edition, E. Hanfmann, G. Vakar & A. Kozulin, Trans.). Cambridge, MA: MIT Press.

Waldmann, M. R., & Hagmayer, Y. (2013). Causal reasoning. In D. Reisberg (Ed.), *Oxford handbook of cognitive psychology* (pp. 733–752). Oxford, UK; New York, NY: Oxford University Press.

Whyte, K. P. (2013). Justice forward: Tribes, climate adaptation and responsibility. *Climatic Change*, *120*(3), 517–530.

Whyte, K. (2016, April). Indigenous experience, environmental justice and settler colonialism. *Environmental Justice and Settler Colonialism*. Retrieved from http://papers.ssrn.com/sol3/papers.cfm?abstract_id=2770058

Wildcat, D. R. (2009). *Red alert: Saving the planet with indigenous knowledge*. Golden, CO: Fulcrum Publishing.

Wolfe, P. (2006). Settler colonialism and the elimination of the native. *Journal of Genocide Research*, *8*(4), 387–409.

Wolff, P., & Medin, D. L. (2001). Measuring the evolution and devolution of folk-biological knowledge. In L. Maffi (Ed.), *On biocultural diversity. Linking language, knowledge, and the environment* (pp. 212–227). Washington, DC: Smithsonian Institution Press.

Wolff, P., Medin, D. L., & Pankratz, C. (1999). Evolution and devolution of folkbiological knowledge. *Cognition*, *73*(2), 177–204.

8
CRITICAL PEDAGOGY AND SOCIOCULTURAL THEORY

Shirin Vossoughi[1] *and Kris D. Gutiérrez*

Introduction

Paulo Freire's pedagogical approach was intimately related to critical approaches to knowing and learning. While Freirean scholars have most often focused on elaborating the importance of critical pedagogies, the unmistakable object of these pedagogies is robust, equitable, and transformational learning capable of reshaping lived social realities. Yet, less attention has been paid to the implications of Freire's work for understanding consequential forms of learning. In this chapter, we argue that Vygotsky's theories of learning are aligned in important ways with Freire's persistent focus on pedagogies of hope and possibility.

It is the emphasis on prolepsis, that is, "the cultural mechanism that brings the end into the beginning" (Cole, 1998, p. 183), within learning arrangements that we seek to highlight in both critical pedagogical and sociocultural traditions. Prolepsis is best understood as a nascent experience of the future in the present (Cole, 1998, p. 184). In both traditions, prolepsis is not simply a theoretical term but a consequential everyday practice of learning and sociopolitical activity. Consider the role of prolepsis in the ways families across the globe draw on their pasts to negotiate present activity and socialize their children through the practices and family routines they arrange (Gutiérrez, Izquierdo, & Kremer-Sadlik, 2010; Weisner, 1998). This everyday example of arranging for sustained well-being in the present "for the future" is consistent with Freirean and Vygotskian perspectives; however, for Freire it was expressed both as a sociopolitical and humanizing aim. Prolepsis is central to contemporary work that draws on these traditions, insofar as learning is organized around imagining what is "not yet" (Gutiérrez, 2016). Hope and possibility are materialized when learning is organized as a formative anticipation of a possible future (Vossoughi, 2011). To this end, we note Freire's own interest in elaborating learning dimensions in his work.

One of us (Gutiérrez) had the opportunity to engage in a discussion of Vygotskian theory on one of Freire's last trips to UCLA.[2] Professor Carlos Torres, a close colleague and a longtime collaborator of Freire's,[3] invited me to join him for a day of conversation with Paulo before his public lecture that evening. We listened and learned and engaged in collective discussion about his work and its specific implications for Latinx youth in Los Angeles and the U.S. It was during this particular visit that I mustered the courage to ask Paulo about my study of Vygotsky and its potential for elaborating discussions of learning in critical pedagogy. Before I could even finish my sentence on Vygotsky, Paulo eagerly overlapped, "Yes, Vygotsky! He is the missing link. I have been reading Vygotsky." That evening Paulo mentioned Vygotsky's work in his talk.

This vignette illustrates two issues with which we continue to grapple: how to make issues of learning more salient in the theory and practice of critical pedagogy, and how to contribute to a more critical sociocultural theory of learning and development. Our goal is to bring these two bodies of work into conversation, and to highlight their shared focus on the role of historicity and futurity in pedagogies of possibility. Our own collective work views learning as the organization of possible futures and has focused on how attention to history in the present can open up proleptic visions. We have drawn both from cultural historical approaches to learning and critical pedagogies to design and study newly imagined futures for youth from nondominant communities.

Before illustrating the ways critical pedagogy and sociocultural theory can be brought together to create a more expansive set of tools for analysis and design, we present our understanding of critical pedagogy. We then locate areas of potential alignment with Vygotskian perspectives, while identifying the points of tension and potential growth across the two traditions. We view the insights gained from bringing these traditions into greater dialogue as essential to the design and study of intellectually generative and politically grounded learning environments. Our discussion therefore offers conceptual and methodological resources for educators and researchers grappling with what sociocultural theory and critical pedagogy mean in practice, particularly for nondominant youth. Ultimately, we aim to contribute to public debates about the place of education in a democratic society, and the creative practice of pedagogy towards liberatory ends.

Critical Pedagogy and the Freirean Tradition

Critical pedagogy is a multi-voiced field and movement that analyzes the relationship between education and oppression in order to help bring about social transformation. The theoretical, pedagogical, and political tradition galvanized by the work of Brazilian educator and activist Paulo Freire represents one genealogy of critical pedagogy (alongside the foundational contributions of W.E.B. Du Bois, Frantz Fanon, Gloria Anzaldúa, Antonio Gramsci, Augusto Boal, and others) that has shaped our own research on learning and equity.

Paulo Freire's (1970/2002) analysis of the relationship between "banking education" and oppression sheds light on the role schools play in social reproduction, particularly the ways dominant ideas and practices become a part of who we are (Mendoza, 2014). Banking education refers specifically to the narrative process through which teachers (the primary *subjects* of the pedagogical process) deposit knowledge in the heads of students (passive *objects* of educational activity). In this model, students play their role most successfully by memorizing facts that are often disconnected from their lived experiences. Interweaving pedagogical and political critique, Freire drew a direct connection between banking education and authoritarian political systems:

> It is not surprising that the banking concept of education regards men [sic] as adaptable, manageable beings. The more students work at storing the deposits entrusted to them, the less they develop the critical consciousness which would result from their intervention in the world as transformers of that world. The more completely they accept the passive role imposed on them, the more they tend simply to adapt to the world as it is and the fragmented view of reality deposited in them.
>
> *(2002, p. 73)*

Banking education offers a window into the role teaching and learning practices play in socializing students to accept the "world as it is," rather than to imagine and enact the world as it could be (Boal, 1995/2015). Freire's response to banking education was "problem posing education," a humanizing pedagogical approach that engages social reality as transformable and treats students as *historical actors*, subjects rather than objects of pedagogy and history (Freire, 1970/2002).

Freire's seminal work, *Pedagogy of the Oppressed*, also appeared as a warning: educators and activists invested in the creation of a more just world must be careful not to replicate the pedagogical forms of the present social order—such as banking, sloganism, and authoritarianism. In other words, simply replacing the *content* of teaching (from hegemonic to counter-hegemonic ideas) does not unsettle the social and intellectual relations that sustain an unequal society. Instead, Freire insisted on the need to transform both the means and ends of schooling, treating classrooms as arenas for the analysis of social life and the *practice* of more liberatory forms of thought and action. From this vantage point, Freire's work was geared towards multiple audiences: those who knowingly or unknowingly engaged in banking education on behalf of an oppressive system, and those who engaged in similar pedagogical methods (treating students as passive objects in need of the teacher's knowledge) *within* revolutionary projects. The treatment of students as passive is sometimes present in Freire's own writings as well, where descriptions of problem-posing education and a spirit of dialogue appear alongside seemingly linear marches towards "critical consciousness." This tension is reflected in some of Freire's diverse intellectual descendants and represents one of the core issues we take up in this chapter.

Emerging in the wake of Freire, Marx, and the Frankfurt School, critical pedagogy defined education as an inherently political practice that shapes how we think about and move within the social world. Critical pedagogues argue that the knowledge and cultural ways of being taught in school (through manifest and hidden curricula) often serve to reproduce unequal social conditions (Apple, 1990; Giroux, 1981). This tendency includes devaluing the cultural practices of historically marginalized groups, thereby predicating academic success on cultural assimilation. While offering powerful analyses of schooling and its relationship to social reproduction, critical pedagogy also articulates an alternative: schools can and should become transformative spaces where teachers and students work together to develop "a deepening awareness of the social relations that shape their lives and their own capacities to re-create them" (Darder, Baltondano, & Torres, 2003, p. 15). Becoming critically conscious involves developing tools to analyze and transform the world through social action. As McLaren writes, "Critical educators argue that any worthwhile theory of schooling *must be partisan*. That is, it must be fundamentally tied to a struggle for a qualitatively better life for all through the construction of a society based on non-exploitative relations and social justice" (1998, p. 172).

Critical pedagogy also elucidates the relationships between cultural and economic capital and questions what is treated as legitimate knowledge in schools (Apple, 1990). Rather than taking the value of school knowledge for granted, scholars within this tradition pose a different set of questions: what is the nature of school knowledge? Whose knowledge is it? Why is it being taught in the first place? (Apple, 1990; Giroux, 1988). For educators working to create an alternative, these questions push us to articulate the epistemological genealogies and values of our own curriculum, and to define intellectual activity as a collective practice aimed at producing emancipatory understandings: knowledge directed at eliminating pain, oppression, and inequality, and at promoting justice and freedom (hooks, 1994; McLaren, 1998). Echoing Freire (1970/2002), this approach is centrally concerned with *praxis*: the generative relationship between reflection and action.

Drawing from Hegelian–Marxist philosophy and the European tradition of Critical Theory, this continual movement between reflection and action is grounded in dialectical thinking. Recognizing the dangers of authoritarianism, positivism, and more orthodox forms of Marxism, the Frankfurt School sought to develop a form of self-conscious critique that averted the tendency to "cling dogmatically to our own doctrinal assumptions" (Giroux, 2003, p. 27). Borrowing from Held (1980), Giroux defines dialectics as revealing "the insufficiencies and imperfections of 'finished' systems of thought . . . it reveals incompleteness where completeness is claimed. It embraces that which is in terms of that which is not, and that which is real in terms of potentialities not yet realized" (2003, p. 36). This insistence on an epistemic mode that embraces contradictions, genetic analysis, and the processual development of thought suggests that no ideology, theory, or politics is pristine. Rather, theory is and must be treated as an unfolding *moment* that aims to interpret a world itself always in movement. Rooted in this dialectical approach to knowledge, Darder et al. argue that critical pedagogy seeks to support "the dynamic interactive elements, rather than participate in the formation of dichotomies and polarizations in thought and practice . . . hence, all theorizing and truth claims are subject to critique" (2003, pp. 13–15).

Critical pedagogues have therefore developed powerful analyses of the relationship between schooling and the current social order, and proposed alternative conceptualizations of what teaching and learning ought to look like. Yet, when alternative pedagogical forms are researched, there is often a focus on *what* is to be taught (alternative curriculum, social theory, critical texts, and social consciousness) rather than the parallel question of *how* we teach—the organization of learning, social relations, and forms of mediation that constitute the means through which we engage students towards these objects. If we focus on the organization of learning, then we become attuned to more than one aspect of a robust humanizing pedagogy; instead the focus is necessarily on a constellation of influences on learning, such as social and spatial relationships, tools, processes, and aims. Thus, what is taught (e.g., the curriculum) can become a potentially powerful mediating tool, rather than the end point of critical pedagogy. In our view, a focus on the micro-processes of critical pedagogy involves documenting and analyzing 1) how social relations are constituted; 2) how power and ideologies are imbued in practices; 3) how tools expand or limit opportunities for the development of critical thought; and, 4) how students develop as thinkers and historical actors. These are some of the methodological lenses and units of analysis that emerge when sociocultural theory is leveraged to analyze the micro-genetic layers of critical pedagogical practice and how they are imbued with history.

In practice, analytic emphasis on alternative pedagogical ends (rather than means) opens critical pedagogy to teaching methods that may contradict its goals of humanization and social transformation. For example, narratives that emphasize students' *arrival* at critical understandings risk obscuring the pedagogical process and constraining the space for transparent discussions of the tensions that inevitably emerge in the moment-to-moment interactions that constitute critical educational practice. We believe that a more empirically detailed engagement with the practices of critical teaching and learning will therefore raise important new theoretical insights and questions. These questions can help us move beyond critique and toward the creative development, analysis, and amplification of efforts to engender "qualitatively different social relations" (Giroux, 2003, p. 24).

To further illustrate the pedagogical and political tensions that can emerge when micro-practices are not treated as explicit objects of analysis, consider the following passage from Peter McLaren's seminal *Life in Schools*:

> Not all prevailing ideas are oppressive. Critical educators, too, would like to secure hegemony for their own ideas. The challenge for teachers is to

recognize and attempt to transform those undemocratic and oppressive features of hegemonic control that often structure everyday classroom existence in ways not readily apparent. These oppressive features are rarely challenged since the dominant ideology is so all inclusive that individuals are taught to view it as natural, commonsensical and inviolable.

(1998, pp. 179–180)

On the one hand, we may interpret the notion of "securing hegemony for our own ideas" as an attempt to engender a future where humanizing, non-exploitative values become normalized as common-sense. Indeed, one can imagine a teacher deliberately organizing a classroom environment where such values are treated as given. However, two aspects of this concept remain troubling. First, while the notion that "dominant ideology is so all inclusive that individuals are taught to view it as natural" speaks to the pervasiveness of hegemonic narratives, it also risks painting students (prior to their engagement with critical pedagogy) as void of "critical consciousness." Narratives of "false consciousness" gloss over the intellectual resources young people bring to the classroom based on their complex engagement with the social world, and the subtle ways these resources may be cultivated or stifled within classroom discourse. We prefer to interpret hegemony as perpetually open to contestation from below, rather than all encompassing or impenetrable (de Certeau, 1984; Erickson, 2004; Scott, 1990). Further, the concept of "securing hegemony for our own ideas" suggests that engaging in humanizing practices may not require conscious reflection. Drawing from critical pedagogy's own emphasis on dialectical thinking, we argue that conscious reflection recognizes the persistent tensions that can emerge between word and deed, and opens these practices to continual development.

This discussion bleeds into one of our central concerns about critical pedagogy: a tendency towards ideological heavy-handedness that may, at times, limit the development of thought and action. This heavy-handedness can ebb and flow within the micro-moments of classroom life—the kinds of assistance teachers offer, the ways they form objects of analysis, respond to student questions, and determine what counts as "critical." For example, we recall a classroom discussion where a teacher employed what we would characterize as overly simplified theories of race, conflating race and ethnicity with culture, and glossing over the heterogeneity within cultural communities. When one student raised a question about how people of colour have sometimes occupied exploitative roles within historical systems of oppression, the teacher sought to realign the student's comment with his own theory. Rather than treating her nuanced intervention as a productive tension and a potential resource for expansive learning (Engeström & Sannino, 2010), the teacher read her comment as hegemonic. Such oversimplified typologies can constrain the non-linear and often vulnerable movements of genuine sense making (Philip & Zavala, 2015). Indeed, the search for right answers, so common in banking education, can easily replicate itself in critical pedagogical settings, where teachers may explicitly or implicitly communicate expectations for what is acceptably critical. Consider, for example, the difference between a teacher designating a student as "colonized" and a teacher working with students to analyze colonial *talk*—an approach that acknowledges the ways all participants (teachers and students) may step in and out of hegemonic forms of thinking (Espinoza, personal communication, May, 2009). This approach also avoids positioning the teacher as one who has "arrived" in critical consciousness, and resonates more closely with Freire's critique of the teacher–student binary (Freire, 1970/2002).

There are conceptual and political traps that can lead inadvertently to enacting critical consciousness as a "state of grace" in critical pedagogy, and in critical approaches more generally, if theory becomes rule instead of tool. As discussed above, some of these traps exist within the text itself, and some emerge when critical frameworks are implemented with a kind of orthodoxy, thereby constraining agency, imagination, and sociopolitical action. Further, when the development of new understandings is understood outside of practice, then the theory loses its transformative potential. Finally, if the locus of change is in the individual, rather than viewing change as implicating the individual and the practices of which she is a part, a new kind of individualism can ensue, one that is antithetical to Freire's intention and to notions of mediation and learning in cultural historical activity theory.

Critical Pedagogy and Sociocultural Theory: Points of Resonance

During their respective historical moments, Paulo Freire, Lev Vygotsky, and their collaborators offered a critique of reigning psychological and sociological approaches to education, and developed their own conceptualizations of what teaching and learning could be. In bringing these traditions into dialogue, we started by pursuing a comparison of key similarities and differences. However, our reengagement with primary sources led us to shift our analysis; instead, we seek to identify points of tension and potential for mutual growth *within* points of resonance. This view avoids oversimplifying differences across the two or erasing productive areas of resonance.

We highlight three central points of resonance that are consequential to the development of a critical cultural historical approach to learning, development, and pedagogy: 1) Marxist definitions of the human as a sociohistorical being; 2) the centrality of cultural and pedagogical mediation; and 3) the relationship between the scientific and the everyday. We also highlight distinctions *within* these points—particularly with regards to the ways Freire's overt political analyses might extend core conceptions of learning within sociocultural theory.

The Human as Social and Historical Being

In tandem with the strong humanist currents running under each of these traditions, both theories attend to the relationship between sociohistorical contexts and individual thought and action. In their own ways, Freire and Vygotsky drew from Marx's historical materialism to distinguish human cognition from that of animals,[4] thereby challenging behaviourist conceptions of learning as the accumulation of predetermined reflexes. They also defined human activity in terms of praxis: humans change the environment through tools; in turn, the use of tools and the new environments they engender *change us back*, influencing the forms of activity made possible over time. In *Education for Critical Consciousness*, Freire (1973) writes:

> Human relationships with the world are plural in nature. Whether facing widely different challenges of the environment or the same challenge, men are not limited to a single reaction pattern. They organize themselves, choose the best response, test themselves, act, and change in the very act of responding. They do all this consciously, as one uses a tool to deal with a problem. Men [sic] relate to their world in a critical way . . . through reflection—not by reflex, as do animals. And in the act of critical perception, men discover their own temporality. Transcending a single dimension, they reach back to yesterday, recognize today, and come upon tomorrow.
> (p. 3)

Similarly, in *Cultural Psychology*, Cole draws from anthropologist Leslie White's work to describe how cultural mediation influences temporality: the world is "not made up of the present only but of a past and a future as well" (1998, p. 120). Cole then presents Alexander Luria's description of this 'double world':

> The enormous advantage is that their world doubles. In the absence of words, human beings would have to deal only with those things which they could perceive and manipulate directly. With the help of language, they can deal with things that they have not perceived even indirectly and with things which were part of the experience of earlier generations. Thus, the word adds another dimension to the world of humans. . . . Humans have a double world.
> (Luria, 1981, p. 35 as cited in Cole, 1998, p. 120)

One can sense the ways these thinkers were traveling similar conceptual paths, in search of theoretical resources to elucidate the distinct, historical qualities of human cognition and development. In both bodies of work, the potential for human thought and action is *expanded* through tools, which provide access to the history of ideas developed by prior generations. One also senses a shared concern with the forms of agency that emerge through the human ability to draw from this historical inheritance, and to do so *consciously*. As Freire writes, "*Integration* with one's context, as distinguished from *adaptation*, is a distinctively human activity. Integration results from the capacity to adapt oneself to reality *plus* the critical capacity to make choices and to transform that reality" (1973, p. 4). Another point of resonance can be seen between Luria's discussion of the "word adding another dimension to the world of humans" and Freire and Macedo's (1987) articulation of the dialectical relationship between "reading the word" and "reading the world." In both cases, language is not merely descriptive or referential; it fundamentally mediates and transforms human activity.

Finally, Freire and Vygotsky both drew from Marxist theory while defying some of its more orthodox strands. In Vygotsky's case, the highly politicized context within which he was working[5] may have limited him to drawing from the psychological and cultural dimensions of Marxist theory, as opposed to its more overtly political stances. In contrast, the aforementioned passages from Freire's work convey a greater emphasis on "critical perceptions of reality," or the "critical capacity to make choices and transform that reality." This language of critique points to Freire's greater willingness to connect historical materialist conceptions of human development with the more politicized Marxist notion of revolutionary praxis. For Freire, sociohistorical definitions of the human were coupled with overtly political analyses of oppression. Put differently, the human capacity for changing the environment through tools (including language) was not, for Freire, a politically neutral or benign process. His notion of praxis invoked a continuous movement towards more just and humanizing social relations. We believe this distinction can help grow sociocultural theories of learning and development, which have brought much needed analytic attention to the process of learning but could benefit from a more critical engagement with the ends of learning.

The Centrality of Cultural and Pedagogical Mediation

Both Freire and Vygotksy challenged behaviourist and individualist conceptions of human learning and the didactic forms of pedagogy they engender. However, unlike some of their European contemporaries (e.g., Piaget, Montessori) they did not swing to the other extreme of child-centred approaches, which tend to minimize the role of the teacher in favour of "self-directed learning," or conflate all forms of direct assistance with the stifling of student autonomy. Instead, both theorists took a more *dialectical* approach and saw pedagogical and cultural mediation as a generative conduit between historical tools and student creativity.[6]

For Vygotsky (1978), optimal contexts for learning are created when students, with the assistance of more experienced others, engage in practices they are not yet ready to do alone. But rather than limiting learning to the shift from assisted to independent performance, Vygotsky privileged joint activity; "good" learning is aimed not at what is already known, but at what participants (students and teachers) are in process of knowing. The assistance of more expert others creates a context for students to "act a head taller than themselves" (1978, p. 102) and for teachers to see and support developmental changes. Vygotsky referred to these changes as the "buds of development" (1978, p. 86): emergent practices that signal the dawning of a future self. Importantly, Griffin and Cole (1984) argue that this future self is not simply a reflection of the teacher's past. Rather, the guidance of an expert provides a structure within which a novice may gain mastery and make a given practice her own: "Adult wisdom does not provide a teleology for child development, social organization and leading activities provide a gap within which the child can develop novel creative analysis" (1984, p. 62). Similarly, John-Steiner and Meehan define learning as the transformation (rather than transmission) of knowledge, and suggest that "a sufficiently deep familiarity with what is known is a constituent part of the dynamics of transformation" (2000, p. 35). The teacher's role is to organize the learning environment and to develop a skilled sensitivity to moments when novices are ready to take on more responsibility (Rogoff, 2003), or when students' forms of dissent might open up novel solutions (Engeström, 2007).

While Freire's critiques of banking education are sometimes interpreted as akin to student-centred models, key passages within early texts belie this interpretation and mirror core constructs within sociocultural theory: mediation, object-oriented activity, intersubjectivity, and cognition as a joint or shared accomplishment. For example, Freire (1970/2002) writes:

> Liberatory education consists in acts of cognition, not transferals of information. It is a learning situation in which the cognizable object (far from being the end of the cognitive act) intermediates the cognitive actors. . . . Dialogical relations—indispensable to the capacity of cognitive actors to cooperate in conceiving the same cognizable object—are otherwise impossible. . . . The teacher is no longer merely the-one-who-teaches, but one who is himself taught in dialogue with the students, who in turn while being taught also teach. They become jointly responsible for a process in which they all grow.
>
> *(pp. 79–80)*

The interpretation of Freire as a constructivist is not unfounded, particularly in the ways he centres the active construction of knowledge as counterpoint to the passive reception of information characteristic of banking education. However, the subject of knowledge construction, for Freire, is not the individual learner, but the teacher and students working in dialogical relations. Perhaps even more so than sociocultural theorists, Freire seeks to foreground moments when teachers are learning and students are teaching, and highlight the ways liberatory teaching always simultaneously involves learning. Some of the more nuanced interpretations of the zone of proximal development within sociocultural theory also privilege the bi-directional learning that can emerge within joint, mediated activity (Chaiklin, 2003; Griffin & Cole, 1984; Gutiérrez, 2008).

Freire was aware that some scholars interpreted his words as a call to minimize the role of the teacher. In a conversation with Donaldo Macedo in the *Harvard Educational Review* (1995), he sought to clarify his position: "What one cannot do in trying to divest of authoritarianism is relinquish one's authority as teacher. In fact, this does not really happen. Teachers maintain a certain level of authority through the depth and breadth of knowledge of the subject matter that they teach" (p. 378). Here, Freire makes an important distinction between acting as an authority (i.e., having the responsibility to leverage expertise in equitable and respectful ways) and engaging in pedagogical authoritarianism. This was a distinction Gutiérrez heard him emphasize repeatedly in his lectures and discussions. Just as Vygotsky emphasized the importance of historical tools and forms of knowledge, Freire argued against denying the teacher's greater familiarity with the subject matter. In fact, he directly challenged the notion that teachers should be non-directive:

> To the extent that all educational practice brings with it its own transcendence, it presupposes an objective to be reached. Therefore, practice cannot be nondirective. . . . The facilitator who claims that "since I respect students I cannot be directive, and since they are individuals deserving respect, they should determine their own direction," does not deny the directive nature of education that is independent of his own subjectivity. Rather, this facilitator denies himself or herself the pedagogical, political, and epistemological task of assuming the role of a subject of that directive practice. . . . To avoid reproducing the values of the power structure, the educator must always combat a laissez-faire pedagogy, no matter how progressive it may appear to be.
>
> *(Freire & Macedo, 1995, p. 378)*

The idea of educational practice bringing with it "its own transcendence" clearly resonates with the aforementioned interplay of structure and creativity within sociocultural theory. This sensibility frees teachers to guide students towards particular objectives, because the objectives themselves are always seen as horizons that are both intellectually generative and soon-to-be transcended through shared engagement with their contradictions (Engeström & Sannino, 2010). Indeed, Freire argues that a lack of direction is not a politically neutral or benign position, but one that likely allows for (or makes invisible) normative relations and ways of knowing. Thus, for Freire, the task of mediating educational practice is also the teacher's *political* responsibility; teachers must be vigilant to challenge the reproduction of social hierarchies, and to intentionally guide collective activity towards humanizing social and intellectual possibilities.

Freire contended "educators should never allow their active and curious presence to transform the learners' presence into a shadow of the educator's presence" (1995, p. 379), an argument reminiscent of Cole and Griffin's assertion that a student's future is not simply a reflection of the teacher's past. However, Freire added, "Nor can educators be a shadow of their learners. The educator who dares to teach has to stimulate learners to live a critically conscious presence in the pedagogical and historical process" (1995, p. 379). In *Pedagogy of Freedom*, Freire (1998) connected this stance to the "unfinished" character of human beings: "both the authoritarian teacher who suffocates the natural curiosity and freedom of the student as well as the teacher who imposes no standards at all are equally disrespectful of an essential characteristic of our humanness, namely, our radical (and assumed) unfinishedness, out of which emerges the possibility of being ethical" (p. 59). Thus, similar to the ways Freire's attention to politics expanded his application of historical materialism in the educational realm, so too did his insistence on connecting pedagogical mediation to ethical practice.

The Scientific and the Everyday

A final point of resonance involves the dynamic relationship between everyday and scientific concepts or practices. Sociocultural theorists developed this set of ideas as a tool for design and research, while Freire defined everyday knowledge as a crucial resource for the development of critical social consciousness. In order to consider the implications of these ideas for the organization of disciplinary activity, we focus on the ways both traditions analyzed the scientific and everyday practices of literacy learning.

Grounded in the assumption that *mind* and *culture* are deeply interwoven, sociocultural theorists define literacy as a situated, social practice. For example, Scribner and Cole (1988) used a series of ecologically valid tasks to study the cognitive consequences of literacy aside from schooling, documenting the cognitive dimensions of everyday tasks to learn how people apply their knowledge for specific purposes in specific contexts of use. Rejecting homogenous views of "non-literate" populations, they concluded that cognitive skills are intimately bound up with the practices that require them. This approach challenged monolithic views of reading and writing as discrete *skills* that can be understood outside their contexts of use, advancing a new definition of literacy as a set of socially organized practices.

According to Erickson (1984), Scribner and Cole's findings also challenged the "fallacy that school-like learning tasks require greater capacity for higher order thinking than do everyday tasks in home, community and work-like settings" (p. 531). By disentangling cognitive development from literacy and modern schooling, Scribner and Cole were able to critically reframe a central challenge in the teaching of literacy: "the kinds of literacy practices that go on in school generate products that meet teacher demands and academic requirements but may not fulfill other instrumental ends" (1988, p. 69).

Cole and Griffin sought to address this problem through the establishment of the Fifth Dimension model in the late 1980s (described in Cole, 2006). The intention was to create a model learning environment that allowed for the systematic study of social and intellectual development. Explicit goals involved 1) using computer technologies in the learning environment "to invite the inclusion of girls and minorities into the program" (p. 5); 2) providing a rich educational setting for children during after-school hours that did not replicate school; 3) creating a structure for interactions that promoted cultural, economic, religious, and age diversity; 4) creating a program that was mutually beneficial to community and university; and 5) developing such partnerships to be sustained over time (Cole, 2006). In Gutiérrez' 5th Dimension Program, "*Las Redes*," elementary students worked with undergraduates to play computer and board games, and communicated through letter writing using hybrid language practices with a bilingual wizard named "*El Maga*" (Vasquez, 2009). Here, reading, writing, mathematical, and strategic thinking were developed within the context of play; skills were embedded in the meaningful practices that required them (Gutiérrez, Baquedano-López, Alvarez, & Chiu, 1999).

In ways that resonate with a Freirean approach, Yrjö Engeström (1991) used the notion of encapsulation to analyze the ways schools separate learning from purposes that connect with students' everyday practices. Engeström also criticized learning environments that define texts as the *object* of activity rather than as a tool for engaging meaningfully in the world (Engeström, 1991; Smagorinsky, 2001). Engeström advanced a model of "expansive learning," which seeks to "expand the object of learning to include the relationships between traditional school texts, the context of discovery and the context of practical application, thus *transforming the activity of school learning itself from within*" (1991, p. 256). Bearing in mind criticisms of the sociocultural school for "tending to shy away from broader political and ideological questions" (Street, 2007, p. xii), it is important to note that expansive learning engages students in the analysis of contradictions within schooling in order to collectively "re-mediate" educational activity (Griffin & Cole, 1984; Gutiérrez, Hunter, & Arzubiaga, 2009).

Such collective re-mediation in service of expansive learning can be seen in scholarly-pedagogical projects that challenge the dichotomy between the academic and the everyday, including work on funds of knowledge (González, Moll, & Amanti, 2006), hybridity (Gutiérrez, Baquedano-López, & Tejeda, 1999), cultural modelling (Lee, 2001), and sociocritical literacy (Gutiérrez, 2008). By reframing students' language, literacy, and cultural practices as powerful *resources* for learning, these scholars have challenged deficit views of nondominant students, as well as the inequitable schooling systems that are often offered as their contexts for learning.

This work does not merely valorize local literacies (Gutiérrez, 2008), nor does it simply draw on the everyday as a scaffold for normative forms of academic achievement. Rather, these scholars treat school as a space for developing a conscious, expanded awareness of everyday practices, including language and literacy itself. As Vygotsky wrote, "scientific concepts may therefore *grow down into* the everyday" (1986, p. 219). In Lee's cultural modelling work, African American students work with their teacher to examine the cognitive resources embedded within African American English Vernacular, including historically developed practices such as signifying. Students uncover and name everyday linguistic tools (such as symbolism or metaphor), and then use these everyday tools to analyze canonical texts. As Moll argued, "schooled discourses represent a qualitatively different form in that the means of communication become an object of study . . . through formal instruction, children develop the capacity to consciously manipulate the symbolic system" (1990, p. 10).

In contrast to approaches that dichotomize home and school (or youth culture and school), syncretic approaches to literacy acknowledge the importance of bringing together and reorganizing vertical and horizontal forms of expertise towards consequential forms of learning (Gutiérrez, 2014). Vertical expertise, particularly in school contexts, involves building increasing amounts of disciplinary knowledge. Horizontal expertise develops as people move across everyday contexts, and is rarely factored into school-based concepts of learning. As Engeström (1996) has theorized, "instead of just vertical movement across levels, development should be viewed as horizontal movement across borders" (p. 4). Syncretic learning reorganizes everyday and school-based literacy practices to support the development of powerful literacies that challenge traditional models of academic literacy and, in doing so, develop horizontal forms of expertise within and across an individual's practices. In this way, syncretic approaches not only seek to expand learning; they seek to rupture the in-school and out-of-school learning dichotomy (Gutiérrez, 2014).

Turning now to Freire's work on the scientific and the everyday, scholars working in the tradition of *critical literacy* view educational settings as both socially reproductive and potentially emancipatory spaces. Freire and Macedo (1987) were particularly concerned with the political dimensions of the relationship between reading the word and reading the world, and argued that reading and writing ought to be aimed at critically understanding and "re-writing" the social world (p. 35). This approach supports students to perceive the social world as "something dynamic that we constitute through our encodings and decodings of everyday practice" (Peters, 1996, p. 53).

Offering an example of the relationship between reading the word and reading the world, Freire shared the reflections of a student in an adult literacy circle: "'I like talking about this,' a woman said, pointing to the codification of her own living situation, 'because that's the way I live. But while I am living this way, I don't see it. Now, yes, I can see the way I am living'" (1985, p. 15). For Freire, the guided opportunity to reflect, codify, and examine one's life with new conceptual tools had the potential to reshape people's relationships with everyday experiences of oppression, which become increasingly perceived as open to resistance and change.

Critical pedagogy argues for teaching school-based reading and writing in ways that make substantive contact with students' everyday experiences. However, similar to the move beyond valorization in syncretic approaches to literacy learning, critical pedagogy understands itself as responsible for extending these practices, helping to develop students as intellectuals and social actors. In this vein, Freire argues that "the concept of voice should never be used to restrict students to their own vernacular. Rather, students should be empowered to interrogate and selectively appropriate aspects of the dominant culture that help to define and transform, rather than merely serve, the wider social order" (1985, p. 152). Developing a capacity to think critically *about* literacy practices (including dominant discourses) is fundamental to appropriating these practices in emancipatory ways, what Luke refers to as "critical vocabularies for talking about what reading and writing and texts and discourses can do in everyday life" (2000, p. 453). Critical pedagogy views the development of meta-languages for talking about literacy as an important pedagogical practice.

Thus, Freire would likely be skeptical of approaches that leverage the relationship between the everyday and the scientific without 1) turning a critical eye towards the disciplines themselves as historical artifacts, 2) guarding against erasure of the everyday by maintaining the tension that necessarily exists between the two, and 3) supporting young people to both enter into and transform disciplinary practices in order to help create a more just world (Medin & Bang, 2014; Nasir, Rosebery, Warren, & Lee, 2006). This understanding of power can help push the learning sciences to take a more critical stance towards expanding student achievement in conventional disciplinary domains.

Freire also proposed a distinction between "ingenious" and "epistemological" curiosity that resonates with the Vygotskian focus on the everyday and the scientific. As Freire (1998) wrote:

> The difference and the distance between ingenuity and critical thinking, between knowledge resulting from pure experience and that resulting from rigorous methodological procedure, do not constitute a rupture but a sort of further stage in the knowing process. This further stage, which is a continuity rather than a rupture, happens when ingenious curiosity, while remaining curious, becomes capable of self-criticism. In criticizing itself, ingenious curiosity becomes 'epistemological curiosity,' as through greater methodological exactitude it appropriates the object of its knowing.
>
> *(p. 37)*

For Freire, the distinction between everyday ingenuity and epistemological curiosity rested on the ability to approach one's own thinking as an object of analysis. Similar to the ideas presented by Engeström, Moll, and others, this practice opens up new possibilities for critically engaging with both school-based curriculum and everyday forms of knowing. Syncretic approaches make these moves explicit by "bringing together and reorganizing different, contradictory and discrete cultural practices that are generally incompatible or in tension with one another; preserving and foregrounding the tension between everyday and scientific practices; and seeking to maintain the value, history, and integrity of the everyday genre vis-à-vis the dominant form, especially in light of historical power relations" (Gutiérrez, 2014, p. 49). Similarly, Freire (1998) asked: "Why not establish an 'intimate' connection between knowledge considered basic to any school curriculum and knowledge that is the fruit of the lived experiences of these students as individuals? Why not discuss the implications, political and ideological, of the neglect of the poor areas of the city by the constituted authorities?" (p. 36). These questions align with sociocultural research on learning and equity, in that both are rooted in respect for what students know.

The continuity Freire describes between everyday ingenuity and more self-reflective forms of epistemology hinges on the practice of *curiosity*. As he stated, "Curiosity as restless questioning, as movement towards the revelation of something hidden, as a question verbalized or not, as search for clarity, as a moment of attention, suggestion, and vigilance, constitutes an integral part of the phenomenon of being alive" (Freire, 1998, pp. 37–38). This emphasis on curiosity may help address a persistent tension in the ways sociocultural work on everyday practices is sometimes taken up in educational settings. Too often, young people's everyday experiences become incorporated in tokenized ways, or are treated as "raw material" to be polished and made meaningful through their connection to normative disciplinary ideas. In *Unspeakable Things Unspoken* Toni Morrison (1988) wrote about a similar problem in the interpretation of African American art and literature. Writing against normative bestowals of artistic value in the context of white supremacy, she stated,

> When Afro-American art is worthy, it is because it is "raw" and "rich," like ore, and like ore needs refining by Western intelligences. Finding or imposing Western influences in or on Afro-American literature has value, but when the sole purpose is to *place* value only where that influence is located it is pernicious. My unease stems from the possible, probable, consequences these approaches may have upon the work itself. They can lead to an incipient orphanization of the work in order to issue its adoption papers.
>
> *(pp. 134–135)*

For Morrison, combatting such "orphanization" requires both historicized interpretations of African American artistic practice *on its own terms*, as well as the critical examination of the Western "canon" itself, including the ways it is always already shaped by racial hierarchies.

Here, Freire's decision to name everyday and scientific practices as *forms of curiosity* provides an additional resource for critical pedagogy and research. Rather than treating everyday knowledge as settled or static (which may lend itself to the "raw material" approach Morrison criticized), attending to everyday forms of curiosity considers young people's everyday *ways of knowing* and *asking* as substantive intellectual resources such that the questions students are already asking about their everyday lives can be fruitfully connected to systematic forms of social analysis. In this view, the scientific or academic concepts made available in critical pedagogical spaces may be reframed as tools for deepening students' curiosities. Thus, for Freire, a focus on curiosity moves beyond the "rupture" between the everyday and the scientific, towards a continuum defined by various forms of critical inquiry.

At the same time, Freire's distinction between "ingenious" and "epistemological" curiosity also suggests that everyday forms of knowing/asking are somehow less epistemological, a belief that may exclude forms of curiosity or dissent that productively complicate critical texts. Recall Erickson's (1984) discussion of the "fallacy that school-like learning tasks require greater capacity for higher order thinking than do everyday tasks in home, community and work-like settings" (p. 531). We are interested in the ways Freirean scholars might learn from this stance, and from the sociocultural emphasis on extensive ethnographic inquiry into community-based forms of intellectual activity. In the realm of political education, we wonder how further inquiry into the forms of critical social consciousness *already present in* communities might help to expand critical pedagogy.

Conclusion

In this chapter, we have examined three central points of resonance across Freirean and Vygotskian traditions: 1) Marxist definitions of the human as a sociohistorical being; 2) the centrality of cultural and pedagogical mediation; and 3) the relationship between the scientific and the everyday. We have also sought to highlight tensions *within* these points of resonance, with a particular emphasis on the ways critical pedagogy might push sociocultural theories—and more broadly the learning sciences—to critically examine the purposes of learning. While sociocultural approaches are already future-oriented, as reflected in concepts such as the zone of proximal development and prolepsis, Freirean ideas might sharpen our articulations of the sociopolitical relations embodied by particular visions for the future.

While this chapter has therefore largely considered the ways sociocultural theories might grow from deeper engagement with critical pedagogy, we conclude by elaborating how critical pedagogy might also grow from deeper engagement with sociocultural theories of learning. To this end, we describe a social design experiment (Gutiérrez & Vossoughi, 2010) that was in many ways a historical descendant of both Freirean and Vygotskian legacies.

The Migrant Student Leadership Institute

The Migrant Student Leadership Institute (MSLI) was a summer academic program for high school aged migrant students that worked to 1) apprentice participants into university level literacy, social scientific, and scientific practices, and 2) develop academic, artistic, and political tools to transform the university. Drawing from the Freirean tradition, students were introduced to complex social theoretical texts, such as Eduardo Galeano's *Open Veins of Latin America*, Gloria Anzaldúa's *Borderland/La Frontera* and Freire's *Pedagogy of the Oppressed*. As Vossoughi (2015) has written:

> These texts were framed as tools for collectively wrestling with the social problems that directly affected students' lives: migration, economic exploitation, racism, patriarchy. Yet the ways we engaged these texts mattered more than their mere presence in the curriculum. Teachers often read together, working to craft generative prompts, interpretive paths and metaphors. In moment-to-moment discussions of complex passages, students were treated as fellow thinkers, poised to contribute weighty questions and ideas. They were also encouraged to ask for help.
>
> *(n.p.)*

In other words, the social organization of reading drew heavily from Vygotskian understandings of re-mediation. While "remedial" models are organized around reductive conceptualizations of skills, narrow forms of assistance, and deficit ideologies, re-mediation involves a reorganization of the ecology: "a shift in the way that mediating devices regulate coordination with the environment" (Griffin & Cole, 1984, p. 70). Key here is the coupling of rich intellectual tasks with ample and strategic forms of support that allow students to experience the whole activity of reading. Thus, where critical pedagogy might emphasize texts and the critical consciousness such texts work to mediate, a sociocultural sensibility is also concerned with what reading means, looks, and feels like for participants, and how collective experiences of close textual analysis might re-mediate students' relationships with texts, and with the act of reading more broadly.

In our experiences, critical educational settings that do not explicitly attend to ideas about learning can sometimes reproduce remedial models. For example, instructors who make the guiding assumption that primary texts will be "too difficult" might introduce critical social theoretical concepts through more simplified, "accessible" versions or by drawing primarily on secondary readings. These teaching strategies highlight the political tensions that can emerge when texts are used as vehicles towards particular ideas, rather than as mediating tools to aid the joint development of new ideas, questions, and forms of acting in the world. To borrow from Cole (1995): in the latter approach, the process through which students and teachers grapple with complex texts *becomes the product*.

Similar possibilities for theoretical dialogue emerge when we consider research methodologies. In MSLI, our research was concerned in part with better understanding the specific qualities of political education that were developed in this setting, and the possibilities for learning that emerged therein. This focus led us to study the moment-to-moment affordances of pedagogical talk. Analyzing the "pedagogical grammar" of the Migrant Program, Gutiérrez (2008) argued that certain speech acts (giving advice, proffering suggestions, proposing possible solutions, using modal verbs [may, would, could] to engage in proleptic discourse) oriented students towards possibility, organizing a dialogue with future action. Similarly, Vossoughi (2014) found that teachers in MSLI consistently used phrases like "here is one suggestion," "tal vez" *(perhaps)*, "what if we think about it this way," or "that's one interpretation." The language of assistance was *subjunctive* in the sense that it tended towards opening up multiple conceptual paths, providing a range of possibilities for students to play with in crafting an essay, interpreting text, or designing a *Teatro* scene. To the extent that students began taking on some of these discourse forms within their own speaking and writing, studying the grammar of teacher talk provided new ways to recognize consequential shifts in participation and identity over time (Vossoughi, 2014). Thus, the phenomena commonly studied by sociocultural researchers (classroom discourse, gesture and multi-modal activity, shifts in participation over time, tensions and contradictions, etc.) might offer fruitful lenses for the study of critical pedagogical environments. In this way, the dialogic quality of teaching and learning so valued by the Freirean tradition becomes an object of analysis (to be studied as it emerges, is sustained or imperiled) rather than an assumed outcome of particular political principles or critical texts.

Sociocultural methodologies can also contribute to the study of schooling as a form of social reproduction and colonial domination. In *Toward a Decolonizing Pedagogy*, Tejeda, Espinoza, and Gutiérrez (2003) argue that

> Within a decolonizing perspective, cultural-historical activity theory can be used to examine and expose the ways the social constructs of race and ethnicity, and its proxies, language and ability, achievement and underachievement, as well as the social practices of racism, discrimination, and privileging mediate the schooling outcomes of working class indigenous and non-white students.
>
> *(p. 36)*

Here theoretical constructs such as mediation, historicity, everyday activity, cultural artifacts, and practices are used to study the workings of hegemony with greater micro-analytic precision, thereby contributing to our understandings of learning as a political and potentially oppressive process, rather than as neutral or benign.

Others have drawn on these traditions to study quotidian forms of resistance in ways that echo the points of resonance we advance here. Pacheco (2012) explored "everyday resistance" to illustrate the value of both recognizing and leveraging the learning that students, families, and communities developed as they negotiated the demands of their "politically charged contexts" (p. 121). Pacheco found that youth and families develop a set of enacted political practices that constituted a form of everyday resistance. These repertoires were developed *in situ*, as the Latinx youth coordinated challenges to particular social and educational policies. Drawing on cultural historical activity theory and Engeström's (1986) use of the notion of "double bind," Pacheco analyzed the cultural resources that were generated in everyday resistance and argued that these cultural repertoires can and should be leveraged in learning and pedagogy.

These contributions serve as models for what becomes possible when we approach the design and study of learning in ways that bring together the political sensibilities advanced within the Freirean tradition with the sociocultural emphasis on cultural mediation and everyday activity. As we have argued throughout, we envision this conversation as a mutually generative endeavour. In the spirit of the syncretic, rather than simply bringing together the respective lenses afforded by Vygotskian and Freirean theories, we are interested in the ways newfound points of resonance might productively reframe each body of work. We are also interested in the ways points of tension might be intentionally held or preserved as a way to continuously surface how each might be pushed by the other, while maintaining the integrity of each as a constellation of ideas born out of its own cultural, historical, and political context.

Notes

1. Vossoughi was both first author and conceptual lead on this chapter.
2. Gutiérrez had the opportunity to interact with him in a variety of venues since the early 1980s.
3. Torres is Director of the UCLA Paulo Freire Institute.
4. This point also reflects the Western epistemological influences on both schools of thought, particularly with regards to human exceptionalism (Bang, this volume), and hierarchical views of human-nature relations (Medin & Bang, 2014).
5. Shortly after his death, Vygotsky's writings were banned for 20 years as part of Stalin's systematic persecution of Soviet intellectuals (Blanck, 1990, p. 43). See also Cole, M. and Levitin, K. (2000). *The autobiography of Alexander Luria: A dialogue with the making of mind*. New Jersey: Lawrence Erlbaum Associates, Inc.
6. This stance resonates with John Dewey's critique of overly individualized approaches to education, particularly in later works such as *Experience and Education* (1938).

References

Apple, M. (1990). *Ideology and curriculum*. New York, NY: Routledge.
Boal, A. (2015). *Rainbow of desire*. London, UK: Routledge. (Originally published in 1995)
Chaiklin, S. (2003). The zone of proximal development in Vygotsky's analysis of learning and instruction. In A. Kozulin, B. Gindis, V. S. Ageyev & S. M. Miller (Eds.), *Vygotsky's educational theory in cultural context* (pp. 39–64). Cambridge, UK: Cambridge University Press.
Cole, M. (1995). From Moscow to the Fifth Dimension: An exploration in romantic science. In M. Cole & J. Wertsch (Eds.), *Contemporary implications of Vygotsky and Luria* (pp. 1–38). Clark University Press.
Cole, M. (1998). *Cultural psychology: A once and future discipline*. Cambridge, MA: Harvard University Press.
Cole, M., & Distributive Literacy Consortium. (2006). *The Fifth Dimension: An after-school program built on diversity:* New York, NY: Russell Sage Foundation.
Cole, M., & Levitin, K. (2000). A cultural-historical view of human nature. In N. Roughley (Ed.), *Being humans: Anthropological universality and particularity in transdisciplinary perspectives* (pp. 64–80). Berlin, DE: Walter de Gruyter GmbH & Co.
de Certeau, M. (1984). *The practice of everyday life*. Berkeley, CA: University of California Press.
Engeström, Y. (1986). The zone of proximal development as the basic category of educational psychology. *Quarterly Newsletter of the Laboratory of Comparative Human Cognition*, *8*(1), 23–42.
Engeström, Y. (1991). Non scolae sed vitae discimus: Toward overcoming the encapsulation of school learning. *Learning and Instruction*, *1*(3), 243–259.
Engeström, Y. (1996). Development as breaking away and opening up: A challenge to Vygotsky and Piaget. *Swiss Journal of Psychology*, *55*(2), 126–132.
Engeström, Y. (2007). Enriching the theory of expansive learning: Lessons from journeys toward coconfiguration. *Mind, Culture, and Activity*, *14*(1), 23–39.
Engeström, Y., & Sannino, A. (2010). Studies of expansive learning: Foundations, findings and future challenges. *Educational Research Review*, *5*(1), 1–24.
Erickson, F. (1984). Literacy, reason and civility: An anthropologist's perspective. *Review of Educational Research*, *54*(4), 525–546.
Erickson, F. (2004). *Talk and social theory*. Cambridge, UK: Polity Press.
Freire, P. (1973). *Education for critical consciousness* (Vol. 1). New York, NY: Bloomsbury Publishing.
Freire, P. (1985). *The politics of education: Culture, power, and liberation*. New York, NY: Bergin & Garvey.
Freire, P. (1998). *Pedagogy of freedom: Ethics, democracy, and civic courage*. Lanham, MD: Rowman & Littlefield.
Freire, P. (2002). *Pedagogy of the oppressed*. New York, NY: The Continuum International Publishing Group Inc. (Original work published 1970)
Freire, P., & Macedo, D. (1987). *Literacy: Reading the word and the world*. London, UK: Routledge.
Freire, P., & Macedo, D. (1995). A dialogue: Culture, language, and race. *Harvard Educational Review*, *65*(3), 377–403.
Giroux, H. (1981). *Ideology, culture and the process of schooling*. Philadelphia, PA: Temple University Press.
Giroux, H. (1988). *Teachers as intellectuals: Towards a critical pedagogy of practical learning*. South Hadley, MA: Bergin and Garvey.

Giroux, H. (2003). Critical theory and educational practice. In A. Darder, M. Baltodano & R. D. Torres (Eds.), *The critical pedagogy reader* (pp. 27–56). New York, NY: Routledge-Falmer Press.

González, N., Moll, L. C., & Amanti, C. (Eds.). (2006). *Funds of knowledge: Theorizing practices in households, communities, and classrooms.* New York, NY: Routledge.

Griffin, P., & Cole, M. (1984). Current activity for the future. In B. Rogoff & J. Wertsch (Eds.), *Children's learning in the "zone of proximal development": New directions for child development* (pp. 45–64). San Francisco: Jossey-Bass.

Gutiérrez, K. (2008). Developing sociocritical literacies in the third space. *Reading Research Quarterly, 43*(2), 148–164.

Gutiérrez, K. (2014). Integrative research review: Syncretic approaches to literacy learning. Leveraging horizontal knowledge and expertise. In P. Dunston, L. Gambrell, K. Headley, S. Fullerton, & P. Stecker (Eds.), *63rd literacy research association yearbook* (pp. 48–61). Alamonte Springs, FL: Literacy Research Association.

Gutiérrez, K., (2016). Designing resilient ecologies: Social design experiments and a new social imagination. *Educational Researcher, 45*(3), 187–196.

Gutiérrez, K., Baquedano-López, P., Alvarez, H., & Chiu, M. (1999). A cultural-historical approach to collaboration: Building a culture of collaboration through hybrid language practices. *Theory into Practice, 38*(2), 87–93.

Gutiérrez, K., Baquedano-López, P., & Tejeda, C. (1999). Rethinking diversity: Hybridity and hybrid language practices in the third space. *Mind, Culture, and Activity, 6*(4), 286–303.

Gutiérrez, K. D., Hunter, J. D., & Arzubiaga, A. (2009). Re-mediating the university: Learning through sociocritical literacies. *Pedagogies: An International Journal, 4*(1), 1–23.

Gutiérrez, K. D., Izquierdo, C., & Kremer-Sadlik, T. (2010). Middle class working families' beliefs and engagement in children's extra-curricular activities: The social organization of children's futures. *International Journal of Learning, 17*(3), 633–656.

Gutiérrez, K., & Vossoughi, S. (2010). Lifting off the ground to return anew: Mediated praxis, transformative learning, and social design experiments. *Journal of Teacher Education, 61*(1–2), 100–117.

Held, D. (1980). *Introduction to critical theory: Horkheimer to Habermas.* Berkeley, CA: University of California Press.

hooks, b. (1994). *Teaching to transgress: Education as the practice of freedom.* New York, NY: Routledge.

John-Steiner, V. P., & Meehan, T. M. (2000). Creativity and collaboration in knowledge construction. In C. D. Lee & P. Smagorinsky (Eds.), *Vygotskian perspectives on literacy research: Constructing meaning through collaborative inquiry* (pp. 31–50). Cambridge, UK: Cambridge University Press.

Lee, C. (2001). Is October Brown Chinese?: A cultural modeling activity system for underachieving students. *American Educational Research Journal, 38*(1), 97–141.

Luke, A. (2000). Critical literacy in Australia: A matter of context and standpoint. *Journal of Adolescent & Adult Literacy, 43*(5), 448–461.

Luria, A. R. (1981). *Language and cognition.* Washington: V. H. Winston; New York, NY: J. Wiley.

Medin, D. L., & Bang, M. (2014). *Who's asking?: Native science, Western science, and science education.* Cambridge, MA: MIT Press.

Mendoza, E. (2014). *Disrupting common sense notions through transformative education. Understanding purposeful organization and movement toward mediated praxis* (Doctoral dissertation). Retrieved from ProQuest Dissertations & Theses Database. (UMI No. 3635879).

McLaren. P. (1998). *Life in schools: An introduction to critical pedagogy in the foundations of education* (3rd edn.). New York, NY: Longman Press.

Moll, L. C. (1990). Introduction. In L. C. Moll (Ed.), *Vygotsky and education: Instructional implications and applications of sociohistorical psychology* (pp. 1–27). Cambridge, UK: Cambridge University Press.

Morrison, T. (1988). Unspeakable things unspoken: The Afro-American presence in American literature. *Michigan Quarterly Review, 28*(1), 1–34.

Nasir, N. I. S., Rosebery, A. S., Warren, B., & Lee, C. D. (2006). Learning as a cultural process: Achieving equity through diversity. In R. K. Sawyer (Ed.), *The Cambridge handbook of the learning sciences* (pp. 489–504). Cambridge, UK: Cambridge University Press.

Pacheco, M. (2012). Learning in/through everyday resistance: A cultural-historical perspective on community resources and curriculum. *Educational Researcher, 41*(4), 121–132.

Peters, M. (1996). Critical literacy and digital texts. *Educational Theory, 46*(1), 51–70.

Philip, T. M., & Zavala, M. (2015). The possibilities of being "critical": Discourses that limit options for educators of color. *Urban Education, 51*, 1–24. First published March 18, 2015. doi:0042085915574523

Rogoff, B. (2003). *The cultural nature of human development*. Oxford, UK and New York, NY: Oxford University Press.

Scott, J. (1990). *Domination and the art of resistance: Hidden transcripts*. New Haven, CT: Yale University Press.

Scribner, S., & Cole, M. (1988). Unpackaging literacy. In E. Kintgen, B. Kroll & M. Rose (Eds.), *Perspectives on literacy* (pp. 57–70). Carbondale, IL: Southern Illinois Press.

Smagorinsky, P. (2001). If meaning is constructed, what is it made of? *Review of Educational Research, 71*(1), 133–169.

Street, B. (2007). Forward. In C. Lewis, P. Enciso & E. B. Moje (Eds.), *Reframing sociocultural research on literacy* (pp. vii–x). Mahwah, NJ: Lawrence Erlbaum Associates.

Tejeda, C., Espinoza, M., & Gutiérrez, K. (2003). Toward a decolonizing pedagogy: Social justice reconsidered. In P. Trifonas (Ed.), *Pedagogies of difference* (pp. 10–40). New York, NY: RoutledgeFalmer Press.

Vasquez, O. (2009). *La Clase Mágica: Imagining optimal possibilities*. Mahwah, NJ: Lawrence Erlbaum.

Vossoughi, S. (2011). *On the formation of intellectual kinship: A qualitative case study of literacy, learning, and social analysis in a summer migrant education program* (Doctoral dissertation). Retrieved from ProQuest Dissertations & Theses Database (UMI No. 3472609).

Vossoughi, S. (2014). Social analytic artifacts made concrete: A study of learning and political education. *Mind, Culture, and Activity, 21*(4), 353–373.

Vossoughi, S. (2015). Intellectual respect: Envisioning alternative educational possibilities. *Equity Alliance Blog*. Retrieved from http://www.niusileadscape.org/bl/shirin-vossoughi/

Vygotsky, L. (1978). *Mind in society*. Cambridge, MA: Harvard University Press.

Vygotsky, L. (1986). *Thought and language*. Cambridge, MA: MIT Press.

Weisner, T. S. (1998). Human development, child well-being, and the cultural project of development. *New Directions for Child and Adolescent Development, 1998*(80), 69–85.

9

TOWARD CRITICAL SOCIOCULTURAL THEORIES OF LEARNING

Indigo Esmonde and Angela N. Booker

Introduction

We began this project because we needed conceptual tools to help us attend to persistent social and historical patterns of exclusion. We believe that our field is well positioned to contend with inequitable distributions of power and privilege and the consequences of those patterns. Within the learning sciences, sociocultural theories have provided our initial foothold. The sociocultural tradition emerged through times of strife and change (Booker, Vossoughi, & Hooper, 2014; Dewey, 1916; Vygotsky, 1978), and as a result, sociocultural theory offers tools to situate individual learners and learning experiences inside of wider sociopolitical contexts. For example, we can examine how and when knowledge is distributed through a group engaged in shared practice (Gutiérrez & Rogoff, 2003; Hutchins, 1995; Saxe, 2012). We can trace moves that reveal relations among people as they begin to participate in a community (Lave & Wenger, 1991; Rogoff, 2003). We can address the design of environments and consider how identities and practices emerge for participants (Holland, Lachicotte, Skinner, & Cain, 2001). We can examine participation in activities with regard to their social and historical roots (Cole, 1996; Engeström, Miettinen, & Punamäki-Gitai, 1999; Vygotsky, 1978). Sociocultural research in the learning sciences has paved the way for us to address how people relate to one another in activity, and opens the door to examining how we produce exclusion and reinforce stratification.

A persistent challenge for learning scientists is how to work effectively across scales, from individual learners to systems organizing the societies in which we live. Despite our field's continued advances in the design of learning environments and in the study of learning across contexts and the life span, hegemony remains a pressing factor for anyone concerned with learning and lived experience. As Apple (2004) points out, we must keep two aspects of hegemony in mind. The first aspect is that "our economic order 'creates' categories and structures of feeling which saturate our everyday lives" (p. 10). In other words, our common sense views of the world mask systems of oppression that uphold an unequal economic order. The second aspect is that "intellectuals," including researchers and scholars, "employ and give legitimacy to the categories, . . . [and] make the ideological forms seem neutral" (p. 10). Our work in the learning sciences can unwittingly uphold the status quo, leaving us unable to truly understand learning or design equitable learning environments.

Equity and inclusion are frequently cited large-scale goals of research in our field, and they require that we address historical patterns of exclusion. Our conversations with colleagues whose work directly responds to these concerns (e.g., community-based and participatory design research, studies of learning among organizers for social change, and studies addressing learning among historically marginalized groups) led us to theoretical models for addressing power and privilege expressed at a macro-scale—what we have referred to here as "critical theories." We have argued that learning scientists can more effectively disrupt broad patterns of exclusion when we seek connections with critical theories. These critical theories can help us to challenge normativity and address how power circulates and sorts.

Our task, then, has been to build bridges between the premises undergirding these theories. In many ways, sociocultural theories did similar bridge-building work by situating individualist understandings of learning within cultural, historical, and community contexts. Sociocultural scholars have called for attention to the conditions in which people's processes of learning unfold, and considered how these processes vary by kinds of experience and ways of knowing. As a result, we know more about which kinds of knowledge and practice tend to get privileged in particular kinds of learning environments, and have improved our ability to recognize diverse ways of knowing and doing. This work has generally addressed micro- and meso-levels of analysis (e.g., from person, family, or neighbourhood to community, tribe, school district, urban or rural territories, etc.). Still, power and privilege operate at systemic scales that are difficult to reckon with in micro- and meso-scales alone. If the learning sciences directly attended to intersections between macro-level relations of power and micro- and meso-levels of practice, we could then more effectively address the maintenance of normativity and the production of differential outcomes that affect learners and their networks of communities.

Our longer-term intent is to make it easier for learning scientists to take up relevant critical theories in our work. In the learning sciences, we acknowledge that we cannot put the onus for learning on individual people. Indeed, we are proposing a shift in direction for an entire community of scholars. The theoretical synthesis that we believe is necessary represents a design problem for our field: how can we purposefully adapt our scholarly activity system, to support the field to conceptualize and study power in relation to learning? Following a brief summary of chapters, we consider how the theories presented here, placed in dialogue, direct our collective attention toward some starting points for centring issues of power and privilege in the learning sciences.

Summary of Chapters

Sociocultural Theory

Esmonde (this volume) summarized six assertions that unite the theories housed under the sociocultural umbrella. Sociocultural theory contends that: 1) cultural artifacts mediate human activity; 2) learning should be studied as it occurs in everyday life; 3) learning both endures and changes as people move across contexts, so the unit of analysis for learning must include some aspects of context; 4) multiple historical timescales are relevant for the study of learning; 5) learning should be studied using a genetic (developmental) method that addresses the process of learning and not just the outcomes; and 6) as they participate in joint activity, people simultaneously exercise agency and are constrained.

Sociocultural theories of learning address power in several ways. When learning is viewed as a process of becoming, social relations between people are foregrounded, as are pathways from peripheral to full participation. Artifacts that carry history into the present mediate those social relations. Individuals are constrained by the traditions of the practices in which they participate, and yet they are capable of changing the practice, simply by participating in it (Rogoff, 2003). While sociocultural theories of learning have been effectively mobilized to address micro- and meso-level analyses of power, macro-level analyses have proven more challenging to integrate into studies of learning and the design of learning environments.

Critical Race Theory

Critical race theory (CRT) developed as an off-shoot of critical legal studies in the late 1980s, and was introduced into education scholarship by Ladson-Billings and Tate (1995). The theory is critical because it centres systems of racial oppression in the United States, as evidenced in the legal system, education system, and other social institutions. Some key tenets of critical race theory include: 1) racism is persistent and endemic in the United States; 2) liberal notions like meritocracy and colour-blindness both mask and facilitate racism in the United States; 3) phenomena in social life should be analyzed from a historical perspective (which includes a historical perspective on race); 4) the experiential knowledge of people of colour in the United States is an essential source of data when studying social phenomena; and 5) scholarship should seek to eliminate racism.

Sociocultural scholars agree on the importance of historical analysis, but have not, thus far, centred race (or any other system of oppression) in analysis. In fact, many sociocultural studies implicitly support notions of meritocracy (assuming that those who achieve success, academically or otherwise, do so on their own merits) and colour-blindness (assuming that race is irrelevant to our analyses). CRT suggests that sociocultural studies should begin by assuming that race and racism are embedded in social interaction, and seek to discover the particulars of white supremacy in a given community of practice, activity system, or figured world. In turn, CRT studies of schooling could be strengthened by sociocultural theory's conceptual and methodological frameworks for analyzing how people learn.

Poststructural Race Theory

Poststructural theory examines the relationship between discourse and power, where discourse refers to processes of meaning making and representations that can be "read" as texts: words, actions, images, and so on. Poststructural race theory (PRT) argues that discourse is the method by which race circulates in society, and that discourse both enables and constrains people's actions. People are understood to be "subject to discourse" in the sense that discourse offers pre-existing subject positions. Whereas sociocultural theory typically asks how people come to take on or resist particular identities, PRT wonders what makes those identities (usually called subject positions or subjectivities) possible, and what is the impact of this set of subject positions on the world.

Both PRT and sociocultural theory are interested in processes of change and agency, with PRT most adept at analysing macro-levels, and sociocultural theory well suited to micro-levels. PRT offers a number of insights that are useful to sociocultural theory. One important insight is that racial discourses mediate interaction at the micro-level. It is significant that the analyst cannot know in advance which moves are racial discourse moves, especially in a context in which explicit race talk is discouraged (as is the case in many U.S. schools). In Shah and Leonardo's chapter (this volume), students were helpful informants about which moments they read as racial. A second insight for sociocultural theory is that race is *learned*. Sociocultural theory's theoretical frameworks, including mediation, figured worlds, zone of proximal development (and others) could be brought to bear on how race is learned so long as we keep in mind that not all racial representations bear the same weight; the paucity of representations of people of colour in the United States means that each representation carries undue weight in influencing racial discourse.

Cultural Historical and Critical Approaches to Disability

In Vygotsky's time, defectology framed disabilities as qualitative (rather than quantitative) differences in human development. Smagorinsky, Cole, and Braga (this volume) bring that conversation forward, using a cultural-historical activity theory approach to distinguish between human difference and the social construction of disability. Vygotsky (1993) pointed out that disabilities are exacerbated by learning environments in which people with disabilities are prevented from full participation. The defectology perspective argues that disabilities emerge as a social problem that is most effectively addressed through cultural development. In this regard, a non-disabled public must be educated in how to support and re-mediate participation of people designated as disabled, via new mediational means—a position both ahead of its time and available for critique from a critical disability studies point of view.

Critical disability studies (CDS) reminds us that disability is actually the more frequent condition, with most humans being temporarily or permanently disabled at some point in their lives. CDS turns our gaze towards the construction of normativity, and asks how the concept of "normal" is used to oppress and dehumanize people who do not meet normal's narrow and ever-changing criteria. Where defectology proposes new and more effective ways to assimilate people with disabilities into normal life, CDS questions the very notion of assimilation, and demands that society accept people with disabilities as they are.

Sociocultural theory could benefit from defectology's emphasis on re-mediation so that people with disabilities can participate more fully in normative contexts, such as the built environment, and educational contexts. Sociocultural theory could also benefit from CDS's critical eye towards disability. In fact, sociocultural theory is well positioned to study "normativity" and to *question* how people learn what normativity is. Given that sociocultural theory insists that almost all human actions are mediated actions, how do we learn that some forms of mediation signify "normal," and some signify "disabled"?

Queer Theory

Queer theory aligns with sociocultural theory in viewing identity as something one *does*, rather than something one *is*. In other words, gender is interactionally produced, and people come to identify (verb) with particular categories that are made available. Queer theory also highlights the insufficiency of any gender or sexual categories that could be used to label people, and opposes binaries (like man/woman, straight/gay) as organizing principles for society. Queer theory is an activist theory, aimed at liberation for all people, while centring the experiences of people living out non-normative gender or sexual identities.

Sociocultural theory conceptualizes identity as multiple, shifting, and relational, but this understanding of identity does not always extend to views of gender. In much of sociocultural theory research, gender is taken for granted and is rarely defined or analyzed. Sociocultural theory could benefit from a closer examination of gender performance in various contexts. In particular, McWilliams and Penuel (this volume) suggest that design processes for instructional contexts can: 1) highlight identity variance and varied identities (for all students, not just students with non-normative gender or sexual identities); 2) design for freedom, contradiction, and resistance; 3) take an activist stance.

Settler Colonialism and Indigenous Ways of Knowing

Colonial and settler colonial epistemologies and ontologies manifest in our theories of learning in at least three ways: 1) the dominant focus is human–human interactions; 2) the natural world is not seen as significant; and 3) more-than-humans are not considered capable of agency or interaction with humans (Bang, this volume). Sociocultural theory, beginning with Vygotsky's work, offers powerful tools to connect human development to its cultural and historical context. Yet, readers are often encouraged to read past colonialist thinking that, on the one hand, describes humans as exceptional and superior to other animals, and on the other hand, describes Indigenous peoples as primitive and less-than-human. If instead of reading past colonial thinking, we directly interrogate our texts to grapple with the influence of colonial and settler colonial epistemologies, we have the opportunity to build a stronger and more equitable theory of learning.

Critical Pedagogy

Although critical pedagogy scholarship typically focuses on teaching, and sociocultural theory on learning, the two fields share deep roots and have much to offer one another. Critical pedagogy is critical in that it critiques prevailing notions of "banking education," in which the teacher's role is to deposit information into a student's mind. This type of education is linked to schooling's role in reproducing systems of oppression. However, critical pedagogy insists that education is capable of leading social transformation if instead of banking, education focuses on "problem-posing," with teachers and students positioned as co-learners about the social world, and historical actors capable of making change.

Critical pedagogy and sociocultural theories of learning share: "1) Marxist definitions of the human as a sociohistorical being; 2) the centrality of cultural and pedagogical mediation; and 3) the relationship between the scientific and the everyday" (Vossoughi & Gutiérrez, this volume). The two theories contain many points of resonance, but, as Vossoughi and Gutiérrez describe, these points of resonance also suggest areas of growth for each of the theories. Ultimately, critical pedagogy encourages sociocultural theory to take a critical approach to the disciplinary knowledge that is usually advanced as the ends of schooling (e.g., state-sanctioned curriculum expectations, school-to-career outcome measures, etc.). Sociocultural theory provides tools and concepts that help critical pedagogues attend more closely to the means of schooling (e.g., specific pedagogical moves, and ways of understanding the give-and-take of dialogical learning).

Towards Synthesis: Power as Always Present and Diffuse

We began this book with a project in mind: we call on scholars in the learning sciences to centre issues of power in our scholarship. As a community, we share a commitment to deepening our understanding of learning and teaching. This commitment extends to self-reflexive analysis of the ways our field supports new and seasoned scholars to build knowledge, and to improve our own teaching and learning practices. These goals cannot be achieved without a direct reckoning with issues of power and privilege, because power is always already there, in our research contexts, in our articles and books, in our conferences, and in our classrooms.

Power is already there in the contexts of learning we study. In various ways, learners are studying normativity: how to recognize it, how to perform it (McWilliams and Penuel, this volume), and even, how to marginalize people who don't meet normative standards (Smagorinsky, Cole, and Braga, this volume). They learn race, and gender, and other systems of oppression that structure their societies and learning contexts.

Power is already there in the explicit and in the hidden curriculum of learning contexts. In all learning contexts, power is involved in the determination of what will or should be learned and in how that learning will be supported and measured. This is most readily seen in government-regulated schooling, in which a vast political process determines the explicit curriculum. This political process extends to the assessment and evaluation process, so that learning is only credentialed if it is expressed in state-sanctioned ways.

Power is already there in our coding schemes. Whenever researchers classify different types of reasoning, or approaches to problem-solving, or levels of disciplinary knowledge, we are sorting and categorizing people or practices and creating normativities. This is how we make people intelligible for our research. Often, our coding schemes are influenced by our notions of normativity, or conceptions of optimal forms of knowledge, optimal identities, optimal discourse patterns. We do not always articulate how we as scholars decide that some discourses, patterns of reasoning, identities, and the like, are more optimal than others.

Power is already there in our research labs, in our conferences, and in our systems for publishing and promotion. Even in an interdisciplinary field like the learning sciences, there is a fuzzy boundary around what scholarship is included (or perhaps, performances of scholarship). We have both been told, at various points in time and in different ways, that our work does not fit in the field, because of a primary emphasis on power and privilege. While we have been nurtured, welcomed, and encouraged, we have also been told, explicitly and implicitly, that we do not fit into the community, because of race, gender, sexuality, disability, nationality. Or, alternatively, that we fit only because of some aspect of diverse experience we represent, even when that is not the focus of our scholarship. To be blunt, and to make it personal: the academy does not always know how to welcome us in all our complexity—as a white, queer, non-binary, sequined and lipsticked, disabled, non-U.S. person . . . or a black, lesbian, mother, spiritual, mystic, justice-seeking, activist scholar.

A Design Challenge

If we want our research to have reach, and we want our community to include a diversity of researchers that will strengthen the field's ways of knowing, then we must deal with power. Again, we emphasize that this is not an individual undertaking, and we are not criticizing any one person for "not knowing enough." The problem: how can we, the learning sciences, create contexts for collective activity that support critical sociocultural analyses of learning? At minimum, this will include making topics of power and privilege a central concern of research, supporting the ongoing growth and development of individuals and groups of researchers, and addressing issues of power, privilege, and systemic oppression within our academic community.

With this volume, we have provided exposure to the ways a set of critical theories are currently being taken up by scholars in the field. The chapters addressed how this set of theories might be engaged within the present foundation of learning sciences work in order to carve a path for graduate students to build a broader foundation of theoretical knowledge while remaining clear about the defining parameters that organize the field. Early career scholars must more directly contend with how to be legible within our field's publishing and presentation venues. In this regard, we intend this volume to catalyze the kinds of theorizing about power and privilege that can be informed by the empirical work of new scholars in the field. Likewise, we see opportunity for collaboration with later career scholars who have established expert practice in a particular domain. Together, the chapters help us identify when and how scholars in the learning sciences can address power and privilege at multiple spokes of the research, writing, and dissemination process: defining research questions, methodological approaches, and strategies for communication. We conclude by considering how key conceptual themes raised in the chapters might contribute to analyzing the problem, and/or developing a design for a more critical learning sciences.

Concerted Attention to Racialized Experience

How would critical race theory analyze and design a solution for the learning sciences? CRT scholarship suggests that the history of race in educational and legal systems has some bearing on the difficulty of integrating critical theories into the learning sciences activity system. Consider the texts that are positioned as "classics" in the field; in the historical period in which these classics were developed, what were the racial politics of the academy? Consider graduate student development today: is there a prevailing discourse of meritocracy and colour-blindness? We believe so, and we believe that this discourse fluidly extends to publication, promotion, tenure, grant awards, and the like. CRT insists that we cannot solve this problem with what are assumed to be race-neutral policies and practices.

How would poststructural race theory analyze and design a solution for the learning sciences? PRT might focus on the hidden racialization embedded in academic discourses. Which work, and which scholarship, is coded as racialized? And (how) does this process function to frame scholarship that addresses race as specialized, rather than mainstream? PRT also pushes us to consider the representations of the academy. How do our conferences, publications, graduate classrooms, put forward a set of representations of the learning sciences and learning scientists? How do these representations function to make some subject positions more intelligible and viable than others?

Challenging Normativity

How would cultural historical psychology and critical disability studies analyze and design a solution for the learning sciences? At all educational levels, people with disabilities are disadvantaged by systems that expect us all to be normates. Cultural historical approaches suggest the importance of re-mediating our academic environments, to provide multiple pathways for participation that can include people with disabilities of various kinds. Inclusion requires both detailed study of the needs of people who cannot currently participate optimally, and the education of the broader field to validate that alternative ways to participate are equally legitimate.

CDS would also suggest the importance of critically examining the value systems underlying academic normativity. Why is unrelenting productivity better than slow scholarship (King, 2012)? Why must we always be experts, and what is wrong with expressing the vulnerability of not-knowing? What do our academic careers demand of us, and what do we lose—who do we lose—when we demand 60-hour work weeks, or 12-hour conference days?

How would queer theory analyze and design a solution for the learning sciences? Queer theory and disability studies have a similar lens. Both can ask: what is academic normativity? Who and what does it exclude? The academy reifies socially meaningful categories of gender, sexuality, race, disability, as well as our own system of categories of graduate student, assistant, associate and full professor, elite university, small liberal arts college, etc. Queer theory highlights the inadequacy of any of these categories to capture our selves and our scholarship, and also delights in the unintelligible, the unknowable. If the learning sciences insists on a clean definition of what is in, and what is out, we lose out on the weird, the new, the blurred boundaries of what counts as important scholarship.

Elevating the Urgency in Engaging Multiple Ways of Knowing

How would colonial and settler-colonial theories analyze and design a solution for the learning sciences? Colonial and settler-colonial theories require that we question the origins of our present commitments to particular ways of knowing, and recognize how these commitments serve to erase Indigenous histories and brutal claims placed on the human and more-than-human world. By coming to understand the painful histories and unavoidable tensions that must be reckoned with, we can begin to recognize how and when learners and educators negotiate intersections between family, culture, epistemologies, and hegemonic systems.

As long as the field continually commits to pursuing equity and recognizes the urgency of remaking our approaches to multiple ways of knowing, we must also contend with real, daily impacts of persistently inequitable social life. This requires more than awareness or acknowledgement. Colonial and settler-colonial theories suggest a direct and collaborative engagement with these erasures, their costs, and ways Indigenous epistemologies can be mobilized as a central way of challenging hegemony. Importantly, Indigenous epistemologies reframe our understandings through human–nature relations and socio-ecological systems. As such, they go beyond opportunity to heal inequity and offer connection to knowledge and practice rooted in commitments to collective continuance.

How would critical pedagogy analyze and design a solution for the learning sciences? Critical pedagogy suggests the need to focus on both the means and the ends of our academic schooling systems (systems that extend well beyond graduate school, to the ranks of full professordom). Let's begin with the ends. If the canon of the learning sciences is encapsulated in books such as the *Cambridge Handbook of the Learning Sciences* (Sawyer, 2005) and *How People Learn* (National Research Council, 2000), then issues of power and privilege—minimally addressed in these texts—cannot be adequately addressed. Topics related to social justice and systems of oppression have thus far been considered peripheral to the field. If the learning sciences maintains a canon, it must be expanded to include critical research.

At the same time, critical pedagogy reminds us of the dangers of selecting a canon. The theory suggests that the learning sciences must be a problem-posing field, one that engages in continued dialogue and in which hierarchies and orthodoxies of all kinds are challenged. We do not suggest that we establish a canon of unquestionable truths; instead, we suggest that doctoral programs in the learning sciences should introduce the broad range of concerns addressed by our field, including critical work.

Re-mediating the Learning Sciences' Relationship to the Study of Power

We see this volume as an invitation to the field. The six critical theory chapters that we have included have presented new ideas to consider, but this is no definitive account. For one, the authors of this volume have all largely been educated in the U.S. context and in U.S. theoretical traditions. For another, all of the theories we have discussed are in a constant process of change through scholarly discourse. Each chapter in this book presents a single story about a single theory, when in fact there are multiple unresolved controversies and debates about each theory. Further, there are myriad other critical theories we could have included. Frankly, we are eager to read and discuss other critical approaches that will allow us to keep growing as scholars and as a field. And finally, as Vossoughi and Gutiérrez (this volume) pointed out, as soon as we believe we have all the answers, we can no longer critique our own work. It is productive, for individual scholars and for the field, to allow contradictions and tensions into our work, and to deny meta-narratives that would tell us there is only one right way to see the world.

That leaves us with a collective opportunity. It is one whose foundation has been carefully laid by scholars working to articulate sociocultural approaches to the study of learning (Cole, 1996; Engeström, 1999; González, Moll, & Amanti, 2005; Gutiérrez & Rogoff, 2003; Holland, Lachicotte, Skinner, & Cain, 2001; Hutchins, 2000; Lave & Wenger, 1991; Lemke, 2001; Moje & Lewis, 2007; Rogoff, 2003; Saxe, 1991; Scribner, 1985a, b; Wertsch, 1985) and colleagues, research participants, and community allies who have integrated critical cultural studies and unrelentingly attended to hegemonic patterns as they have defined and pursued their research agendas (Cammarota & Fine, 2008; Heath, 1983; John-Steiner, 1999; Nasir & Hand, 2006; Nasir, Rosebery, Warren, & Lee, 2006; Varenne & McDermott, 1998). We are always responsible to establish our focus in ways that advance the field and identify its parameters, and each of us has the opportunity to begin our next task with a question—whether it is designing a study, analyzing data, drafting a manuscript, mentoring a student or more junior colleague, or contributing an act of service to our department or field. How can I/we attend to power as it is performed, expressed, or circulated?

References

Apple, M. (2004). *Ideology and curriculum* (3rd edn.). New York, NY; London, UK: RoutledgeFalmer.
Blanck, G. (1990). Vygotsky: The man and his cause. In Moll, L.C. (Ed.), *Vygotsky and education: Instructional implications and applications of sociohistorical psychology* (pp. 31–58). Cambridge, UK: Cambridge University Press.
Booker, A., Vossoughi, S., & Hooper, P. K. (2014). *Tensions and possibilities for political work in the learning sciences.* Paper presented at the bi-annual International Conference of the Learning Sciences, Boulder, CO.
Cammarota, J., & Fine, M. (2008). *Revolutionizing education: Youth participatory action research in motion.* New York, NY: Routledge.
Cole, M. (1996). *Cultural psychology: A once and future discipline.* Cambridge, MA: Belknap Press of Harvard University Press.
Darder, A., Baltodano, M., & Torres, R. D. (Eds.) (2003). *The critical pedagogy reader.* New York, NY: RoutledgeFalmer Press.

Dewey, J. (1916). *Democracy and education: An introduction to the philosophy of education.* New York, NY: Macmillan.

Engeström, Y. (1999). Activity theory and individual and social transformation. In Y. Engeström, R. Miettinen & R.-L. Punamaki (Eds.), *Perspectives on activity theory* (pp. 19–38). Cambridge, UK: Cambridge University Press.

Engeström, Y., Miettinen, R., & Punamäki-Gitai, R.-L. (Eds.). (1999). *Perspectives on activity theory.* New York, NY: Cambridge University Press.

González, N., Moll, L. C., & Amanti, C. (Eds.). (2005). *Funds of knowledge: Theorizing practices in households and classrooms.* Mahwah, NJ: Lawrence Erlbaum Associates.

Gutiérrez, K. D., & Rogoff, B. (2003). Cultural ways of learning: Individual traits or repertoires of practice. *Educational Researcher, 32*(5), 19–25.

Heath, S. B. (1983). *Ways with words: Language, life and work in communities and classrooms.* New York, NY: Cambridge University Press.

Holland, D., Lachicotte, W. Jr., Skinner, D., & Cain, C. (2001). *Identity and agency in cultural worlds.* Cambridge, MA: Harvard University Press.

Hutchins, E. (1995). *Cognition in the wild.* Cambridge, MA: MIT Press.

Hutchins, E. (2000). Distributed cognition. *International Encyclopedia of the Social and Behavioral Sciences.* Elsevier Science. Retrieved from http://hip.cntb.webfactional.com/hip-site/uploads/2014/07/Hutchins_DistributedCognition.pdf

John-Steiner, V. (1999). Sociocultural and feminist theory: Mutuality and relevance. In S. Chaiklin, M. Hedegaard & U. J. Jensen (Eds.), *Activity theory and social practice: Cultural-historical approaches* (pp. 66–78). Aarhus, DK; Oakville, CT: Aarhus University Press.

King, D. (2012). Toward a feminist theory of letting go. *Frontiers: A Journal of Women Studies, 33*(3), 53–70.

Ladson-Billings, G., & Tate, W. (1995). Toward a critical race theory of education. *Teachers College Record, 97*(1), 47–68.

Lave, J., & Wenger, E. (1991). *Situated learning: Legitimate peripheral participation.* Cambridge, UK: Cambridge University Press.

Lemke, J. L. (2001). Across the scales of time: Artifacts, activities, and meanings in ecosocial systems. *Mind, Culture, and Activity, 7*(4), 273–290.

Moje, E. B., & Lewis, C. (2007). Examining opportunities to learn literacy: The role of critical sociocultural literacy research. In C. Lewis, P. E. Enciso & E. B. Moje (Eds.), *Reframing sociocultural research on literacy: Identity, agency, and power* (1st edn.). Mahwah, NJ: Routledge.

Nasir, N., & Hand, V. (2006). Exploring sociocultural perspectives on race, culture, and learning. *Review of Educational Research, 76*(4), 449–475.

Nasir, N., Rosebery, A. S., Warren, B., & Lee, C. D. (2006). Learning as a cultural process: Achieving equity through diversity. In R. K. Sawyer (Ed.), *The Cambridge handbook of the learning sciences* (pp. 489–504). Cambridge, UK: Cambridge University Press.

National Research Council. (2000). *How people learn: Brain, mind, experience, and school: Expanded Edition.* Washington, DC: National Academies Press. doi:10.17226/9853. Retrieved from http://www.nap.edu/catalog/9853

Rogoff, B. (2003). *The cultural nature of human development.* New York, NY: Oxford University Press.

Sawyer, R. K. (Ed.). (2005). *The Cambridge handbook of the learning sciences.* Cambridge: Cambridge University Press.

Saxe, G. B. (1991). *Culture and cognitive development: Studies in mathematical understanding.* Hillsdale, NJ: Lawrence Erlbaum Associates.

Saxe, G. B. (2012). *Cultural development of mathematical ideas: Papua New Guinea studies*. Cambridge, UK: Cambridge University Press.

Scribner, S. (1985a). Knowledge at work. *Anthropology & Education Quarterly, 16*(3), 199–206.

Scribner, S. (1985b). Vygotsky's uses of history. In J. V. Wertsch (Ed.), *Culture, communication, and cognition: Vygotskian perspectives* (pp. 119–143). Cambridge, UK: Cambridge University Press.

Varenne, H., & McDermott, R. (1998). *Successful failure: The school America builds*. Boulder, CO: Westview Press.

Vygotsky, L. S. (1978). *Mind in society: The development of higher psychological processes*. Cambridge, MA: Harvard University Press.

Vygotsky, L. S. (1993). The fundamentals of defectology (abnormal psychology and learning disabilities). In R. W. Rieber & A. S. Carton (Eds.); J. E. Knox & C. B. Stevens (Trans.), *The collected works of L. S. Vygotsky. Volume 2: The fundamentals of defectology (abnormal psychology and learning disabilities)*. New York, NY: Plenum.

Wertsch, J. V. (1985). *Vygotsky and the social formation of mind*. Cambridge, MA: Harvard University Press.

INDEX

abstract theorizing 29–30
academic identity 20
activist praxis 29–30
activity systems: CHAT perspective 88; health care activity system 14–15, 18; history and 16–17; units of analysis and 14–15; use in critical and sociocultural theories 23
activity theory 7, 18, 22
adaptation 75, 147
Adler, Alfred W. 74
African holocaust 121
agency: concept of 8, 20, 164; mediation and 20, 21–2; more-than-human agency 131–2; power in 21–3
AIDS Coalition To Unleash Power (ACT UP) 94
Althusser, Louis 58
American Society for Disability Studies 83
anomalous children 72–3
anomalous human 72–4
Anzaldúa, Gloria 140
apprentice tailors 11
Aristotle 54
artifacts: cultural forms 19; discourses and 22; histories of 10, 17; mediation and 7, 8–9, 164; power and 9–10; school curriculum as historical artifact 17
AsianCrit 31
Asians 55
authoritarianism 141, 142, 149

"authoritative" language 9
authority 9, 149
axiology 36

banking education 141, 144–5, 148
Berry, Halle 56
Biklen, D. 83
biological difference 70, 74
biological discourse 54
Black Feminist Thought (Collins) 56
blackness 56–7
Boal, Augusto 140
Booker, Angela N. 24
Bororo people 124
Bourdieu, Pierre 21, 22
Bracero Program 34
Braga, Lucia Willadino 78–9
Brazil 78–81, 82, 85
Brown, A. 57
Brown, K. 57

Cain, C. 21
Cambridge Handbook of the Learning Sciences, The (Sawyer) 2
campus racism 88
Cartesian logics 120–2
Castro, A. 129
causal reasoning 125
Center for Activity Theory and Developmental Work Research 18
Change Lab 18, 19
chattel slavery 130

children: anomalous children 72–3; design experiment in Brazil 78–81, 82, 85; education of blind and deaf 77–8, 82, 85; gendered messages of commercials targeting 108; heterosexual matrix 96; Indigenous thought and 124
cisgender people 105
cognitive development 23
cognitive science 1
Cole, Michael 10, 13, 15, 16, 22, 78–9, 150, 151, 157
collective continuance 115, 118
college peer culture 23
Collins, Patricia Hill 56
colonialism 116, 118–20, 127
coloniality: issues in theories of learning 117; overview of historical developments of coloniality of human exceptionalism 120–3
colour-blindness 32, 34, 39
communication analysis 51
communities of practice 21
compensation 74
complexes 123–6
concept development 126
concepts 123–6
conquest of Americas 121
constraint: concept of 8, 20, 164; power in 21–3
constructivism 1
context 6, 11, 75–6, 164
contradiction 15
control 84
counter-narratives 35–6, 39–40
counter-storytelling 35–6, 39–40
critical disability studies (CDS): background 70–1, 82–3, 165–6; case for complementarity 87–8; design challenge for learning science 170; focus on commonalities 83–5; focus on differences 85–7; interdisciplinarity of 84, 86–7; Marxism as common source of ideas in 86; relating theory to practice 87; social formation 85–6
critical discourse analysis 51
critical legal studies (CLS) 29–31
critical literacy 152
critical pedagogy: centrality of cultural and pedagogical mediation 147–50; design challenge for learning science 171; education defined by 142; Freirean tradition and 140–5; human as social and historical being 146–7; micro-processes/practices of 143; Migrant Student Leadership Institute 156–8; relationship between everyday and scientific concepts 150–5; sociocultural theories and 145–55, 167; Vygotskian understandings of re-mediation 156
critical race theory (CRT): concept of 28–9, 164–5; CRT examination of science education vignette 43–4; design challenge for learning science 169–70; emergence and evolution of 29–32; generations of theory 31; impact of 37; interfaces of sociocultural perspectives and 37–44, 164–5; poststructural race theory and 54; research methodologies in 36–7; science education vignette 41–2; sociocultural examination of science education vignette 42–3; themes of 32–6; Vygotskian propositions 37–8, 40
critical social theory 82, 84
critical theory 23–4, 51, 142
critical thinking 153
cultural development 75
cultural forms 19
cultural historical activity theory (CHAT): background 70–1; case for complementarity 87–8; commonality of DS/CDS and 84–5; complementarity of DS/CDS and 85–8; concept of 39; interdisciplinarity of 84, 86–7; Marxism as common source of ideas in 86; relating theory to practice 87; social formation 85–6; sociocultural examination of science education vignette 43; units of analysis and 14–15
cultural historical theory 38, 71–2, 118–19
cultural history 16
cultural mediation 146
cultural modelling 151
cultural psychology 7, 40
Cultural Psychology (Cole) 146
culture 131–3, 150
curiosity 153–4
curriculum standards 9

Daniels, H. 118
Davis, L. 83
"decolonial attitude" 117
"decolonial dialogues" 117
defectology 72
"deficit model of cultural variations" 40
Derrida, Jacques 51
Descartes, René 120–2

dialectical thinking 142–3, 144
"disability": compensation of 74, 76; concept of 70–1; design experiment in Brazil 78–81; effects of feelings of inadequacy 74–6; examples of Vygotskian-inspired work with anomalous people 76–81; "medical model" of 82; problem of 74; as social formation 83, 85–6; Vygotsky's approach to the anomalous human 72–4
Disability Rights activism 82
disability studies (DS): background 70–1, 82–3, 165–6; case for complementarity 87–8; focus on commonalities 83–5; focus on differences 85–7; interdisciplinarity of 84, 86–7; Marxism as common source of ideas in 86; relating theory to practice 87; social formation 85–6
discourse 51–2
discourse theory 22
distributed cognition theory 7
double stimulation method 18, 19
'double world' 146
Du Bois, W.E.B. 140
"dysontogenesis" 75

education: banking education 141, 144–5, 148; of blind and deaf people in the Soviet Union 76–8; as defined by critical pedagogy 142; discourse and racemaking in learning settings 54–6; educational practice 149–50; interpellation and creation of racialized subjects of 58; politics of representation in 56–7; poststructural race theory in 54–8; queer approach to 104–9; vignette analysis of high school mathematics classroom 58–66
educational technology 1
Education for All Handicapped Children Act 78
Education for Critical Consciousness (Freire) 146
Eisenhart, M.A. 22
"elementary" psychological functions 8
elementary school classroom research context 103–4
encapsulation 151
Enciso, P. 17
Engeström, Yrjö 14–15, 23, 110, 151, 152, 154
Enlightenment 51

epistemic authority 120
epistemicides 120–1, 126, 131
epistemic racism 120, 126
epistemological curiosity 153–4
epistemology 36
Erickson, F. 150
erotic desire 97
ethnic identity 20
eugenics 73
everyday knowledge 150
everyday practices 150–5
exclusion 21, 84
"expansive learning" model 151
expansive transformation 15
expectations 10

"false consciousness" narratives 144
Fanon, Frantz 57, 140
feelings of inadequacy 74–6
field 22
Fifth Dimension Program, The 78–81, 151
figured worlds 22
"formal" language 9
form–function analysis 7, 18–20
Foucault, Michel 21, 22, 51, 54
Frankfurt School 51, 84, 142
Freire, Paulo 139, 146–50, 152–5
Freudo-Marxism 51
funds of knowledge approach 13–14, 151

Gay-Straight Alliance (GSA) 101–3
gender 21, 95–7, 108
gender dissonance 105
"gender line" activity 103–4, 105
gender norms 97–8, 105–6
gender variance 105–6
genetic method 8, 18–19, 164
German idealism 51
Germany 73
Giroux, H. 142
Glory (film) 56
Gramsci, Antonio 140
Greeno, J.G. 6
Griffin, P. 151
Grosfoguel, R. 120–2

Harris, Cheryl 130
health care activity system 14–15
Hegelian–Marxist philosophy 142
heterosexuality 104–5
heterosexual matrix 95–7, 109
"higher" psychological functions 8

historical/contextual analyses 32, 34–5, 36, 39
historical materialism 16, 146
historicity 15
history: artifacts and 10; concept of 8, 16–17; power and 17
Holland, D. 21, 22, 23
horizontal expertise 152
How People Learn (Committee on Developments in the Science of Learning) 2
human activity 146–7
human development 18, 23, 37–8, 39, 71, 110
human exceptionalism 117, 119–23, 126
human–human interactions 117–18
hybridity 151

identity: learning in everyday life and 10; queer theory 94–8; sociocultural theories 23, 53; use of form–function analysis to study development 20; variance 104–6; varied identities 104–6
identity formation 21, 53
identity-in-practice 97
illegibility 121
illogicality 121
inclusion 78
Indigenous African peoples 130
Indigenous peoples: collective continuance of 115–17; epistemicides 120–1; erasure of Indigenous presence 128–30; readings of Indigenous peoples in Vygotsky 123–6; settler-colonialism 127–8; structuration of chattel slavery 130
individual cognitive perspective 6–7
individual racism 33
individuals 53
Individuals with Disabilities Education Act (IDEA) 78
Individuals with Disabilities Educational Improvement Act (IDEIA) 78
inequity 116
inferior subjects 120, 121, 125
ingenuity 153–4
institutional racism 33
integration 147
interest convergence 35

John-Steiner, V.P. 148
Jovanović, G. 116

Keller, Helen 75, 77–8

Kirshner, Ben 101, 102
knowledge 11, 122
knowledge construction 148
Knowles, R.T. 129

Lachicotte, W., Jr. 21
Ladson-Billings, G. 29
language 9, 21, 51–2, 53, 147
language acquisition 78
LatCrit 31
Latour, B. 131
Lave, J. 10, 12
learning environments: discourse and racemaking in learning settings 54–6; high school mathematics classroom vignettes 64–6; institutional racism in 33; learning in everyday life 10–12; model learning environments 151; oppressive features of 143–4; role of teacher in 148–9; science education vignette 41–4; use of texts in 151 *see also* schools
learning in everyday life: concept of 7, 10–11, 164; power in everyday learning 12
learning sciences: background and development of 1; issues of power and oppression and 2; power and sociocultural theories of learning 6–24; publications representing 2; queer theory in 93–110; sociocultural theories 3
learning spaces 1
Lee, Spike 56–7
Lego commercials 108
Levy-Bruhl, Lucien 124
liberalism 32, 33–4, 36, 39
Life in Schools (McLaren) 143
linguistic racism 55
linguistic reasoning 125
local literacies 151
Luria, Alexander 71, 78–81, 146, 147
Lyotard, Jean-François 51

Macedo, Donaldo 149
Malcolm X 56
Maldonado-Torres, N. 117, 120
Marxism 84, 86, 142, 147
Marx, Karl 84–5, 86, 142, 146
master and apprentice hierarchy 12
mathematics ability: Asians 55; high school mathematics classroom vignettes 58–66
Matusov, E. 118–19
McLaren, Peter 143
mediated action 23

mediated thought 126
mediation: agency and 20, 21–2; artifacts and 7, 8–9, 164; concept of 7, 8–9; heterosexual matrix 96; power and 9–10
mediational means: constraint and 20; discourse theory and 22; history as embedded in 17, 39; identity formulation 96; sociocultural analysis of 42; study of 131; as unit of analysis 13, 23; use of 9; Vygotsky's research on 38, 40, 75–6, 166
Meehan, T.M. 148
Meekosha, H. 84, 85
meritocracy 32, 34, 39
Meshcheryakov, Alexander 77–8
"MetaCognitive Dimension" (MCD) 79
microgenesis 16, 38
Mignolo, W. 117
Migrant Student Leadership Institute (MSLI) 156–8
mind 150
Mitchell, W.J.T. 96
more-than-human agency 131–2
Morrison, Toni 154–5
multi-voicedness 15

narratives 37, 107–8, 143
Nasir, N. 20, 23
Native Americans 129–30
nature 131–3
nature of knowledge studies 1
neoliberalism 119
neutrality 32, 34, 39
Nietzsche, Friedrich W. 51

objectivity 32, 34, 39
object-oriented activity 23
Okazaki, S. 55
ontogenesis 16
ontogeny 38, 71
ontology 36
oppression 141

parrots 124
participation 20, 23
participatory action research (PAR) 19–20
Pedagogy of Freedom (Freire) 150
Pedagogy of the Oppressed (Freire) 141
personally mediated racism, 33
phylogenesis 38, 71
phylogeny 16
Piaget, Jean 1
pole vaulting example 20

positivism 142
"posthumanism" 126
poststructural discourse analysis 51
poststructural race theory (PRT): concept of 54, 165; critical race theory and 54; discourse and racemaking in learning settings 54–6; in education 54–8; interpellation and creation of racialized subjects of education 58; race, regulation, and the politics of representation 56–7
poststructural theory: introduction to 50–2; sociocultural theories and 52–4; vignette analysis of high school mathematics classroom 58–66
power: contexts of 168–9; in everyday learning 12; history and 17; mediation and 9–10; in poststructural theory 53–4; power imbalance 40; re-mediating learning sciences' relationship to study of 171–2; sociocultural research methodologies 19–20, 53–4; units of analysis and 15–16
practice 22
praxis 146
presentism 34
primary disability 74, 75
primitive reasoning 125
primitive thought 117, 123–6
progress narratives 107–8
prolepsis 139
psychological development 72
punishment/rewards system 119
"purity of blood" 121

qualitative research 36–7
"queer" 94
QueerCrit 31
queer desires 105
Queer Endeavor, A 102
Queer Nation 94
queerness 95, 104, 106
queer theory: activist stance 108–9; designing for contradiction and resistance 107–8; design principles 104–9; elementary school classroom research context 103–4; frameworks 94–8; identity 94–8; intersectional perspectives 109; in learning sciences 93–110; perspective on identity 94, 97–8; queering design practices 98–100; research contexts 100–4; sociocultural theories and 95–6, 166–7; undergraduate

teacher education course research context 100–3

race: concept in poststructural race theory 54; constraints and 21; discourse and racemaking in learning settings 54–6; historical/contextual analyses 36; politics of representation and 56–7; racial subjects and 58; regulation and 56–7
race discourse 56–8
race interpellation 58
racial discourses 57
racial formation 54
racial formation theory 55
racial hierarchies 31, 32, 34
racial hierarchy 34
racial identity 54
racial imaginary 121
racial induction 58
racial justice 33–4
racial subject making 58
racial subjects 58
racism: campus racism 88; elimination of 32, 36, 40; epistemic racism 120, 126; institutional racism 33; linguistic racism 55; as ordinary 32–3, 39; personally mediated racism, 33; systematic and systemic 57
reframing 151
regulation 56–7
representation 52, 56–7, 131–2
research methodologies 36–7
Richardson, T.A. 117
rights discourse 30

SARAH Hospital 79
Saxe, G.B. 18–19, 20, 23
school-based reading/writing 152–3
school curriculum 17, 129, 143
school knowledge 142
schools 22, 33, 141, 151 *see also* learning environments
scientific concepts 150–5
Scribner, S. 150
Scribner, Sylvia 3
secondary disability 74, 83
settings 75–6, 78, 100–3
settler-colonialism: background 127–8; conceptions of nature and culture and 131–2; design challenge for learning science 171; erasure of Indigenous presence 128–30; issues in theories of learning 117–18; legitimacy of 129; in sociocultural theories 127–33; sociocultural theories and 167; structuration of chattel slavery 130
settler-colonial time-based ontologies 128–9
settlers 127–8
sexism 120
sexual identity 95–6
sexuality 95–7
Shear, S.B. 129
Shuttleworth, R. 84, 85
signs 38, 40, 71
situated learning theory 7, 10–12, 53
situated practice 78
Skinner, D. 21
sloganism 141
social formation 83, 85–6
social interactional processes 53
"Social Justice Academy" (SJA) 103, 105
sociocritical literacy 151
sociocultural concepts: agency 8, 20–3; constraint 8, 20–3; genetic method 8, 18–19; history 8, 16–17; learning in everyday life 7, 10–12; mediation 7, 8–10; units of analysis 8, 12–16
sociocultural theories: centrality of cultural and pedagogical mediation 147–50; cognitive approaches and 6–7; critical disability studies and 166; critical pedagogy and 145–55, 167; critical theories and 23–4; design challenge 169; eroding foundational premises of coloniality embedded in Cartesian logics 122; ethic of trans-ontologies in 115–34; human as social and historical being 146–7; interfaces of critical race theory and 37–44, 164–5; key sociocultural concepts 7–23, 164; Migrant Student Leadership Institute 156–8; neoliberalism and 119; queer theory and 95–6, 166–7; relationship between everyday and scientific concepts 150–5; settler-colonialism and 127–33, 167; sociocultural research methodologies 19–20; toward critical sociocultural theories of learning 162–72
Soden, G.J. 129
Sokolyansky, I.A. 76–7
Soviet Union 72–3, 76–8, 82, 85, 86
special education 78
standards 119, 129
stories 37
street slang 9

subject–object relations 131
Sue, S. 55
Sullivan, Anne 75
syncretic learning 152

Tate, W. 29
teacher–student binary 145
technology 1
tenBroek, Jacobus 82
testing 119
textbooks 57, 151
timescales 8, 16, 164
time–space relations 128, 130
tools 38, 40, 71
Torres, Carlos 140
transgender people 105
Trans*Literacies Project 103–4
trans-ontologies: colonialism in thought of Vygotsky 118–19; directions and questions for cultivating decolonial ethics towards 133–4; ethic of 115–34; overview of historical developments of coloniality of human exceptionalism 120–2; readings of Indigenous peoples in Vygotsky 123–6
TribalCrit 31

undergraduate teacher education course research context 100–3
United States 78, 82
units of analysis: concept of 8, 12–15; in poststructural theory 51–2, 53; power and 15–16; types of 13–15, 164; use in critical and sociocultural theories 23
University of Colorado Boulder 100
unmediated thought 126

vertical expertise 152
vignette analysis of high school mathematics classroom: background 59; cross-cutting theoretical issues 64–6; vignette #1 59–60; vignette #1 analysis 60–2; vignette #2 63; vignette #2 analysis 63–4
violence 57, 120–1, 126
vision 8–9
voice 30
von den Steinen, Karl 124
"Vygotskian academia" 118
Vygotsky, Lev S.: approach to disability 70, 72–4, 165–6; centrality of cultural and pedagogical mediation 147–8; colonialism in thought of 118–20; cultural historical theory 71–2; education of blind and deaf people in the Soviet Union 76–8; on effects of feelings of inadequacy 74–6; evaluations criteria and the historical in 116; examples of Vygotskian-inspired work with anomalous people 78–81; historical materialism 16; human development 18, 23, 37–8; influence of 2; learning in everyday life 10; Marxism and 147; mediation 8–9, 21, 40; primitive thought 117; readings of Indigenous peoples in 123–6; subject–object relations 131; units of analysis 12–13; Vygotskian understandings of re-mediation 156

Washington, Denzel 56–7
Wenger, E. 10, 12
Wertsch, J.V. 8, 9, 13, 20, 23
White, Leslie 146
whiteness 35, 56, 57

Helping you to choose the right eBooks for your Library

Add Routledge titles to your library's digital collection today. Taylor and Francis ebooks contains over 50,000 titles in the Humanities, Social Sciences, Behavioural Sciences, Built Environment and Law.

Choose from a range of subject packages or create your own!

Benefits for you
- Free MARC records
- COUNTER-compliant usage statistics
- Flexible purchase and pricing options
- All titles DRM-free.

Benefits for your user
- Off-site, anytime access via Athens or referring URL
- Print or copy pages or chapters
- Full content search
- Bookmark, highlight and annotate text
- Access to thousands of pages of quality research at the click of a button.

REQUEST YOUR **FREE** INSTITUTIONAL TRIAL TODAY

Free Trials Available
We offer free trials to qualifying academic, corporate and government customers.

eCollections – Choose from over 30 subject eCollections, including:

Archaeology	Language Learning
Architecture	Law
Asian Studies	Literature
Business & Management	Media & Communication
Classical Studies	Middle East Studies
Construction	Music
Creative & Media Arts	Philosophy
Criminology & Criminal Justice	Planning
Economics	Politics
Education	Psychology & Mental Health
Energy	Religion
Engineering	Security
English Language & Linguistics	Social Work
Environment & Sustainability	Sociology
Geography	Sport
Health Studies	Theatre & Performance
History	Tourism, Hospitality & Events

For more information, pricing enquiries or to order a free trial, please contact your local sales team:
www.tandfebooks.com/page/sales

 | The home of Routledge books

www.tandfebooks.com